Reinhold Niebuhr and Paul Ramsey

Reinhold Niebuhr and Paul Ramsey

Idealist and Pragmatic Christians on Politics, Philosophy, Religion, and War

Kevin Carnahan

LEXINGTON BOOKS
A division of
ROWMAN & LITTLEFIELD PUBLISHERS, INC.
Lanham • Boulder • New York • Toronto • Plymouth, UK

Published by Lexington Books
A division of Rowman & Littlefield Publishers, Inc.
A wholly owned subsidiary of The Rowman & Littlefield Publishing Group, Inc.
4501 Forbes Boulevard, Suite 200, Lanham, Maryland 20706
http://www.lexingtonbooks.com

Estover Road, Plymouth PL6 7PY, United Kingdom

British Library Cataloguing in Publication Information Available

Library of Congress Cataloging-in-Publication Data

Carnahan, Kevin, 1976-
Reinhold Niebuhr and Paul Ramsey : idealist and pragmatic Christians on politics, philosophy, religion, and war / Kevin Carnahan.
p. cm.
Includes bibliographical references and index.
ISBN 978-0-7391-4475-6 (cloth : alk. paper)
1. Niebuhr, Reinhold, 1892-1971. 2. Ramsey, Paul. 3. Theology—United States—History—20th century. 4. Pragmatism—History--20th century. 5. Idealism, American—History—20th century. 6. War—Religious aspects—Christianity. I. Title.

BX4827.N5C27 2010
230'.044092273—dc22 201002796

The paper used in this publication meets the minimum requirements of American National Standard for Information Sciences—Permanence of Paper for Printed Library Materials, ANSI/NISO Z39.48-1992.

Printed in the United States of America

For Jennifer, Kathleen, and Lucy
loves of my life.

Contents

Part III: War

Preface

In the first decade of the new millennium, as America contemplated the war in Iraq, I contemplated the kinds of arguments being deployed about this war. What struck me was the parallel between the arguments over Iraq and another set of arguments I had been reading. As a student of moral theology, I had been analyzing the arguments of Paul Ramsey and Reinhold Niebuhr, especially as they diverged over the morality of the Vietnam conflict. I heard echoes of this argument around me almost a half a century after Ramsey and Niebuhr battled it out on the pages of popular political and theological journals.

The parallelism between the arguments at these two points in American history was partially predictable. Some of the participants in arguments about the Iraq war were students of Ramsey and Niebuhr. Still, something about the shape of the arguments suggested to me that there was something more going on than could be explained by simply tracing out lines of immediate intellectual parentage. To find answers, I went back to Niebuhr's and Ramsey's works to find the currents that they themselves were following.

I began by working back from Niebuhr's and Ramsey's arguments on Vietnam to their broader moral/theological conceptions of war, then to their moral theological worldviews. Still, it seemed to me that there was some further level at which the two great scholars diverged. What I found, through a long process of digging, was that Niebuhr and Ramsey fit into a broader argument in American intellectual life. Jamesean pragmatism and absolute idealism represented overlapping but also contrasting worldviews in relation to which Niebuhr and Ramsey were trained. These worldviews influenced Niebuhr's and Ramsey's views of morality, political society, and war. In part, the echoes I heard in the contemporary debate about Iraq go back to arguments between these two schools of thought.

In this book the order of presentation is the opposite of the order of discovery. I begin with a schematic analysis of pragmatism and absolute idealism with special attention to the facets of these positions that influenced Niebuhr and Ramsey. I then move toward the more particular ways in which the influences of these positions worked out in relation to Ramsey's and Niebuhr's moral theologies, conceptions of political society, and finally their understandings of war. The end result is narrowly crafted to focus on locating Ramsey and Niebuhr in their particular intellectual and theological milieu.

With this narrow focus, my analysis here ends with the Vietnam conflict, on which I comment briefly.[1] The task of linking these two figures to contemporary events is an important one. Ramsey's followers have continued in many ways to develop the views of political society and war that he articulated. Niebuhrian analysis has waxed and waned throughout the decades. By the end of the last millennium, it had been almost extinguished by versions of liberalism more pacifistic and optimistic than Niebuhr favored. Christian realism has, however, seen a new resurgence after September 11th, and Niebuhr's fingerprints can be seen on many elements in Barack Obama's political philosophy, not the least his foreign policy and views on war. At present, I am only able to point toward some of the ways in which the arguments I treat here are still ongoing. At some point in the future I may return to tracing out in more detail how it is that the works of these two scholars link up with the present. Until then, I shall have to leave it to my reader to draw conclusions.

I am indebted to countless people who have helped me to develop as a scholar and produce the current work. I am always dependent upon my close friends who ground me as a person, and remind me of my origins. For this, I thank especially Dan Shurtz, Robert Zajkowski, and Nick Wyant. My family too is a constant source of support. I would be lost without Katy and Robert, my siblings, and rudderless without the influence of my mother and father. More immediately for this project, I am indebted to The United Methodist Church for supporting my graduate work with a Dempster Graduate Fellowship, and to the Southern Methodist University Graduate Program in Religious Studies for supporting me in many ways, including awarding me the Schubert Ogden Fellowship for Academic Excellence in Theology. I owe a great deal to my colleagues in graduate school and in my early teaching career, who were constant conversation partners through the process: David Watson, Gary McDonald, Peter Jones, J. Aaron Simmons, Daryl Jefferies and especially Oleg Makariev. I also owe a great deal to the many scholars who, through review of some version of this manuscript or through the impartation of intellectual virtue, have allowed me to develop and refine the present project. Jouette Bassler, William Babcock, Rebekah Miles, and William Abraham were vital influences in making me the scholar that I am. Charles Curran, Joseph Allen, and Richard B. Miller not only taught me about scholastic excellence, but also provided extremely helpful criticism of this project. Last, and most important, was the influence of Robin Lovin, who has been a wonderful mentor in all aspects of my academic life.

Finally, I am most grateful for Jennifer, Kathleen, and Lucy; women to whom I am particularly bound by the duty and affection of love. It is to these women that this work is dedicated.

Notes

1. For a more developed treatment of Ramsey and Niebuhr's work during Vietnam see the last chapters of my dissertation, "Sin, guilt, justice and war: Paul Ramsey and Reinhold Niebuhr on the moral framework for just war thought." (Ph.D. Dissertation, Southern Methodist University, 2007).

Introduction

In the summer of 1962 Paul Ramsey finally secured the arrangements. That fall Reinhold Niebuhr would teach part time for a semester at Princeton where Ramsey was on faculty. Ramsey had been trying to get Niebuhr to Princeton for some time, and he had hoped that Niebuhr would be able to spend a whole year. Health issues and other complications had delayed Niebuhr's visit and limited his stay. Regardless, Ramsey was pleased with the fruits of his efforts. For the semester he and Niebuhr lived two doors from one another.[1]

We have no record of the conversations that took place between Ramsey and Niebuhr that semester, but it would have been well worth it to have been a fly on the wall. In 1962 Niebuhr was not far beyond the zenith of his scholarship. Ramsey was in the midst of some of the most fruitful years of his own work. They may have discussed the emerging conflict in Vietnam. They may have argued about Christian views on anthropology or love. Almost any conversation would have been worthy of note. In the later half of the twentieth century Niebuhr and Ramsey were two of the most influential figures in Protestant moral theology. After the Second World War both articulated rich visions of Christian moral responsibility in a changing world order.

Their friendship was grounded in appreciation of each other's thought. There was a great deal in common between them. Ramsey had been converted from pacifism early in his career while reading Niebuhr's work on war. Though Ramsey's views changed as he matured, there were few departures from his continued admiration for Niebuhr's thought. In 1967, while condemning much of the Church for its mode of political activism, Ramsey made an exception for Niebuhr as a theologian who at one time possessed the rare political theological "competence" to make explicitly political demands.[2] In his later works, Ramsey became a staunch defender of Niebuhr's theology against the critiques leveled by John Howard Yoder and others.[3] This respect was mutual. When editors came to Niebuhr in the mid nineteen-fifties to collect essays for a book on his work and legacy, Niebuhr suggested Ramsey would be the perfect author for a response on his social ethics.[4] A decade later while preparing a volume of responses to Joseph Fletcher's *Situation Ethics*, Ramsey returned the favor by asking Niebuhr to submit an essay. Niebuhr begged off the project due to health problems, but wrote that he had confidence in Ramsey's own ability to argue the case against situation ethics. "Weakness alone," Niebuhr writes, "forbids me to go into detail on all the knotty problems you discuss wisely."[5]

Their similarities and their mutual respect, however, did not prevent serious disagreements between them. Their widely noted divergence on the morality of the Vietnam War was only the most publicly accessible of these disagreements. Niebuhr's venom against the manifestation of American hubris in Southeast Asia clashed with Ramsey's unflagging confidence that there could be no viable moral argument against the war. It was in the midst of this conflict that Ramsey accused his friend of irresponsibility in facing the uncertainties of global politics. Though he would later retract this charge, Ramsey's rhetoric speaks to the severity with which their views clashed at this time.

Given their apparent similarities and fondness for one another, how should we understand the disagreements between these two pivotal figures in American moral theology? No doubt, to some extent their disagreements are due to important divergent tendencies in their theologies. Niebuhr's understanding of Christian love emphasized the imperfections of human historical activity in ways that were partially in tension with Ramsey's conception of love, which stressed the absolute moral duties of faithful relationships. Differences in their doctrines of sin, providence, and eschatology can be further tied to divergences in their conceptions of society and the role of the Christian within society. Their positions in Vietnam were also influenced by their different approaches to war. By the 1960s Niebuhr was focused on the dangers of idolatrous pride in

American foreign policy. Ramsey was caught up in the project of articulating a morally positive view of justifiable war as a faithful act of love.

There is a great deal of work to be done in unpacking these particular theological differences. But is this all there is to say on the matter? Are these differences merely manifestations of the idiosyncrasies of these two creative theologians, or is there something more going on here? There is a pattern to be discerned in their disagreements; a pattern which suggests an underlying structure that informs the points at which they conflict. Niebuhr's theology is constructed in a way that alerts the Christian to various modes of uncritical extremism, while Ramsey's theology is constructed so as to highlight the existence of enduring moral structures in human life. The consistency of these patterns in Ramsey's and Niebuhr's works points to something more than the shape of Ramsey's and Niebuhr's individual moral intuitions alone. These were deeply ingrained schemes of thought; schemes related to wider social movements in the culture that surrounded both Niebuhr and Ramsey.

The work of these two theologians bridged a century of massive change in American moral theology. With roots that extend back to generations of pre-World War American theology, Ramsey and Niebuhr participated in reshaping American dialogue in the political and theological turmoil of the post war era. Thus, their lives occupy a key position in the broader drama of American moral theology. Locating them in this drama allows one to understand part of how American theology came to be what it is today. It also aids in showing why Niebuhr and Ramsey came to disagree so vehemently on important theological and political points.

This book argues that Niebuhr's and Ramsey's moral theologies are reflective of deeply ingrained traditions of thought in American life, traditions which continue to influence contemporary dialogue. As I shall argue, Niebuhr's and Ramsey's arguments are reflective of an ongoing debate between two schools of American philosophy: pragmatism and absolute idealism.

American Roots

Niebuhr and Ramsey were preceded by another set of intellectual giants whose relationship parallels Niebuhr's and Ramsey's own. At the turn from the nineteenth to the twentieth century two renowned American philosophers defined many of the terms of scholarly debate in the United

States. They were friends and intellectual sparring partners. William James represented the school of pragmatism while his companion and opponent Josiah Royce took up the standard of neo-Hegelian absolute idealism. Until the middle of the twentieth century the conflict between these schools and these scholars dominated arguments about epistemology, metaphysics, sociology, theology and morality in America. In the field of morality, with which this text is most interested, pragmatism focused on the dangers of fanaticism. It advocated attention to lived experience and insisted upon the importance of maintaining space for a public dialogue on moral issues. Idealism, in contrast, emphasized the dangers of atomistic moral relativism. It stressed the need for respect for order, continuity with communal tradition, and reverence for structures of authority in social life. During their experiences in graduate school Niebuhr and Ramsey were immersed in the arguments between these traditions. Niebuhr was trained in the pragmatic tradition while Ramsey was tutored in absolute idealism. On opposite sides, they were groomed by mentor scholars to continue the debate.

Neither Ramsey's nor Niebuhr's positions are entirely intelligible apart from their development and location in terms of this ongoing debate between the pragmatic and idealistic positions. Idealism and pragmatism constitute part of the context out of which Niebuhr and Ramsey would develop their more robustly Christian theologies later in their careers. The tensions between Niebuhr's and Ramsey's theologies can be correlated with the distinctive moral dangers to which they were exposed in their early training. Many of Niebuhr's and Ramsey's theological maneuvers are reflective of strategies developed by idealists and pragmatists for dealing with the moral dangers these schools of thought recognized best.

While several scholars have noted the influence of pragmatism on Niebuhr, the enduring influence of the shape of the debate between pragmatists and idealists is rarely noted in contemporary scholarship. Most theologians working today do not draw directly from these traditions, nor did Niebuhr or Ramsey in their mature works. If these schools are so important in American moral theology, why are they not more visible? Given the apparent difference between contemporary debates and the debates of the pragmatists and idealists, it is helpful to say something about how contemporary moral theological discourse developed without full recognition of its debts to this earlier period.

A Bomb on the Playground of the Theologians

World War II was the occasion for a series of shifts in American and global culture. The rise of Nazism led many European intellectuals to emigrate. Traditional centers of philosophy and theology were upended during this period and the relatively youthful intellectual scene in the United States benefited in the process. The most significant European export in theology was not a scholar, however, but rather a set of ideas represented under the title "neo-orthodoxy." Exactly how to characterize this movement is still a debated question, but there is no doubt about its impact. Nor is there any question about whose thought lay behind the beginnings of this movement. Arriving in English translation from the late 1920s through the middle of the century, the works of Karl Barth appeared to turn the world of theology upside down—or perhaps set it upright for the first time in modernity. Here, it seemed, was a new starting place for theology, one which threw the whole history of human thought into question.

The first step in Barth's early moral theology was to deny the claims of all humanly constructed systems of morality. This was a reaction against tendencies in Liberal Protestant theology, which sought to discern the movement of God in the synthesis of historical human traditions. Barth concluded that it was this fixation on human schemes of thought that led the German theological establishment to its misguided support of the German State in the First World War. By the Second World War, Barth's rejection of values grounded in the German culture provided the life raft on which the Confessing Church survived through Nazi persecution. Christian loyalty was to the Word of God and not to any nation, tribe, or philosophical system of thought. The Christian did not interpret what God was doing in the world; the Christian awaited God's interpretation of the world.

This was at the time, and remains in contemporary theology, an earth-shaking position. In the context of Nazi Germany, Karl Barth had freed Christian theology from the shackles of a depraved human culture. This act became a model of theological excellence throughout the protestant world. The revelation and activity of the Trinitarian God had displaced human culture at the center of theology. For many who followed

Barth, fidelity to the Christian God and the Christian tradition became the most significant, if not the only, criterion for good theology.

The upshot of this movement for the shape of theological dialogue was significant. Philosophy and social science could aid theological investigation, but no philosophical position could be treated as essential or foundational to Christian theology or ethics. Many theologians trained in philosophical traditions ceased referring to their own philosophical backgrounds. As arguments against "culture Christianity" grew, content from philosophical sources was often set aside for explicitly theological argument. Topics of philosophical debate appeared to fade into the background. Christian theology was reclaiming its own language, its own topics of debate, and its own forms of argument. When treating issues such as truth, sociology, politics, and morality the theologian first had to address the Christian grounding of her or his position.

The terms of American theological argument thus had to change. Pragmatism and idealism could no longer provide the categories of theological debate. In neo-orthodox theological circles the influence of these philosophical schools appeared to fade away; often denounced into oblivion by those who represented more "faithful" Christian positions. Niebuhr and Ramsey became masters of this new rhetorical strategy. In arguing with Paul Lehmann, Ramsey could claim that Lehmann's reliance on the thought of William James raised "the crucial question about just how formative the Christian biblical context or the faith and ethics of the Reformation" had been in Lehmann's theology.[6] Niebuhr often focused his own critique on the faithlessness of absolute idealist tendencies in Liberal Protestantism. "Having made reason and history the means of redemption, [Liberal Christianity] had no real place for the Biblical doctrine of redemption. And having interpreted history in Hegelian terms, it had no real place for revelation—that is for the invasion of the historical by an absolute word of God."[7]

The Endurance of the American Traditions

The strategy of this rhetoric was to portray one's opponent as a secular philosopher in theological clothing. Thus did explicit appeals to pragmatism and idealism fade into the background of American theological education and dialogue. Unfortunately, for all its effectiveness, this framework for theological argument often failed to capture the complexity of the real situation. Too often participants caricatured each other's positions. Theologians underestimated the diversity of expressions that grew from Christian theological premises. They also often overlooked the extent to which Christian perspectives overlapped with other views of the world.

Niebuhr and Ramsey themselves are useful examples of the complexity of the actual situation. They were certainly not, in their mature works, philosophers parading as theologians. They had been spurred, in part by Barth, to draw for their foundations upon the language, reasons, and traditions of the Christian religion. Their mature positions were Barthian only in highly qualified senses, but this is only problematic if one confuses Barthian *per se* with Christian. The Christian tradition is rich and deep, and Niebuhr and Ramsey became articulate representatives of various veins within this tradition.

But, despite the shifts at the roots of their thoughts, it was not the case that their encounters with the philosophies of idealism and pragmatism were rendered insignificant. The lingering shadow of these philosophical schools is at least to be seen in exactly what each theologian selected for criticism on the grounds of faithfulness. It is no accident that Ramsey, who was trained in idealistic philosophy, picks on a fellow theologian for his reliance on pragmatism while Niebuhr, who was trained in pragmatism, chooses to chastise the creeping influence of Hegelian idealism in theology.

The continuing influence of these schools of thought, however, goes deeper than the selection of Ramsey's and Niebuhr's preferred polemic targets. Niebuhr and Ramsey had been sensitized by these schools in ways that would be reflected in their later positive moral theological systems. The problems to which idealism and pragmatism had respectively sensitized Niebuhr and Ramsey were real problems. The resources pragmatism and idealism provided for dealing with these problems were often profound. The tension between the idealists and pragmatists was reflective of a perennial tension in modern human culture. Over time, Niebuhr and Ramsey found Christian languages that were well suited to addressing the issues they had been sensitized to in their early philosophical encounters. But, changing the terms of the debate did not lead to entirely new questions, even if it did lead to a reformulation of the questions, and occasionally opened new avenues for addressing them.

In this more complex world, claims of faithfulness and unfaithfulness to the Christian tradition were not as definitive as their advocates often assumed. In America, theologians worked to be faithful to the Christian tradition and true to the reality of the social tensions they perceived. They drew upon the resources of the Christian tradition to articulate anew many of the debates that preceded the apparent Barthian revolution in theology. Arguments between pragmatists and idealists were transformed into arguments within the Christian tradition. These arguments were not the same as they were before the realignment of Christian theology in the middle of the century, but neither were they completely different.

In their arguments about moral theology, society, and war, Niebuhr and Ramsey were indebted to American traditions whose arguments long preceded them. Understanding these American traditions and their influences allows one to gain a greater grasp of Niebuhr's and Ramsey's thought. To the extent that American theology today still reflects these influences, exploring these traditions also sheds light on conflicts that have continued after Niebuhr and Ramsey passed out of the story themselves.

This Study

This book is a critical analysis of the part Ramsey and Niebuhr play in this story of American moral theology. It relates the mature thought of these two theologians to the traditions of pragmatism and absolute idealism, and explores how Niebuhr and Ramsey re-grounded central issues from the pragmatist/idealist debates in Christian language. The purpose of this work is not, however, simply descriptive. As an American moral theologian, I am also interested in continuing the dialogue within contemporary theology between those concerned with the moral dangers highlighted by these different traditions. Thus this work also offers a set of mutual critiques of each position from the perspective of the other. Perhaps because I myself lean more toward pragmatism, I do not aim at any point to propose a synthesis of the two positions, but I do find that ongoing engagement between the two is fruitful for the refinement of each.

I have divided my treatment into three parts reflecting three different areas in which pragmatism and idealism influenced Ramsey's and Niebuhr's works. The first part explores the dangers of fanaticism and atomistic relativism which are highlighted by the traditions to which Ramsey and Niebuhr were exposed in their graduate work, and relates how Niebuhr and Ramsey framed the core themes of love and natural law in their later theologies to combat these moral dangers. Chapter 1 explains how Ramsey and Niebuhr came into contact with pragmatism and idealism, and suggests some of the most obvious ways in which their later works draw upon the insights of these schools. It also explicates some of the criticisms Ramsey and Niebuhr leveled at the traditions to which they were respectively exposed. Chapters 2 and 3 show how it is that Niebuhr's Augustinianism and his development of the idea of Christ's relevant but impossible love provide a foundation for the virtues necessary to avoid moral fanaticism, while Ramsey's development of the ideas of natural law and covenant love hedge against the dangers of atomistic moral relativism. Chapter 4 produces a dialogue between these positions that sheds light on some of their relative strengths and weaknesses. While Niebuhr is appropriately oriented against moral fanaticism, at times his scheme says too little about the need for moral structure in the ambiguous world of history. While Ramsey rightly opposes moral relativism, his emphasis on the need for moral order at times oversteps in positing a clear line between putatively orderly and secure deontic judgments and supposedly disorderly and insecure prudential judgments.

The second part of the book focuses on some of the ways in which Niebuhr's and Ramsey's political, theological conceptions of society diverge. Chapter 5 investigates Niebuhr's and Ramsey's divergent views of social institutions and authorities in relation to their conceptions of sin and providence. Niebuhr develops a doctrine of sin as idolatry and focuses on the judgment of God in history as the central concept in his doctrine of providence. These doctrines keep his moral theology oriented against any idolatrous fanaticism that would allow absolute loyalty to any historical institution or authority. Ramsey develops a doctrine of sin as treachery and understands providence primarily in terms of God's immanent work in maintaining and transforming the orders of creation. This allows Ramsey to focus on the dangers of atomistic relativism which might challenge the stability and progress of moral order in history. While Niebuhr's position is at times unwarrantedly pessimistic concerning the possibility of moral activity on the part of social units, Ramsey's position is often insufficiently critical concerning given social authorities and institutions.

Chapter 6 explores Ramsey's and Niebuhr's perspectives on democratic public dialogue and the role of the Christian within this dialogue.

The first section in the chapter focuses on the centrality of the concept of pluralism in Niebuhr's understanding of democracy, and the centrality of concepts of unifying ethos and common social principle in Ramsey's understanding of democracy. The second section of the chapter shows how Ramsey and Niebuhr deploy different conceptions of Christian responsibility in public dialogue in ways that correlate with their conceptions of society. While Niebuhr conceives of the Christian as a humble prophet, interpreting and calling out instances of idolatrous fanaticism in political life while avoiding any fanatic claim to infallible knowledge, Ramsey sees the Christian as Christian functioning to provide stability and order to public discourse by means of proclamation only on issues of common social principle. In the end, I argue, Niebuhr's position is stronger than Ramsey's inasmuch as Ramsey's is built on a problematic idealistic anthropology and sociology.

The third part of the book explores the divergent moral, theological conceptions of war that contributed to Niebuhr's and Ramsey's disagreements over Vietnam. Influenced by one of William James' last essays, Niebuhr's work reveals his sensitization to the dangers of fanaticism on the part of the war-party and the peace-party. Reacting against idolatrous militarism and pacifism in his mature works, Niebuhr conceives of war primarily as a manifestation of the judgment of God which falls upon all as sinners in history. Thus, Niebuhr stresses that while war may at times be the best option available, there is no valid claim to perfect righteousness in a time of war. The humble prophet in a time of war ought to call out the exaggerated positions proposed by those in the war-party or the peace-party. War ought to evoke a disposition of penitent responsibility which allows for realistic analysis of and reaction to developments during the conflict.

Ramsey's moral conception of war is in part reflective of the idealistic tradition's approach to war as a necessary and positive political act within history. Working to defend the place of war in what he takes to be the natural structure of international relations, Ramsey proposes that war is properly undertaken as a delimited act of covenant love within history. In an anarchic international order, states will have recourse to military means as they act to defend and spread justice as seen from their own particular perspectives. In order to avoid the mistake of setting the social practice of war outside the boundaries of moral analysis, it is necessary to articulate a clear moral obligation to wage war and a clear set of limitations that guide action within wars. A recovery of the just war idea is central to this project.

In the end Ramsey's conception of war produces a strong statement concerning the need for moral order within war, and as such offers a necessary antidote to amoralist realism or utilitarianism that is often pervasive in war ethics. At the same time Ramsey's position is insufficiently critical concerning the ends of war, and says too little about the importance of and necessary conditions for realistic prudential analysis in times of war. The Niebuhrian conception of war as God's judgment at times overstates the moral ambiguity of war, and occasionally wrongly suggests that one necessarily incurs guilt in any use of force. Still, Niebuhr's approach serves to highlight the virtues necessary to a realistic analysis of war.

In each of the above areas, the moral dangers to which pragmatism and absolute idealism sensitized Niebuhr and Ramsey were driving forces in their later recovery and development of theological categories. Whether they were aware of it or not, their exchanges in the fall of 1962 were part of a long running dialogue in American history. They each practiced theology in ways that changed the categories of this dialogue, but their positions continued to reflect strains of thought that had long been the subject of debate in America. To the extent that they passed on these concerns to their own students and followers this debate continues today. By learning about Ramsey's and Niebuhr's context contemporary theologians may learn about their own.

Notes

1. Ramsey to Ursula Niebuhr, August 3rd 1962, Ramsey Papers, Box 20, Duke University Library.

2. Paul Ramsey, *Who Speaks for the Church?* (Nashville, Tenn.: Abingdon Press, 1967), 49.

3. See Ramsey's comments on Niebuhr in *Speak Up For Just War or Pacifism* (University Park, Pa.: Pennsylvania State University Press, 1988), and *Reinhold Niebuhr Today*, ed. R.J. Neuhaus (Grand Rapids, Mich.: Wm. B. Eerdmans, 1989).

4. See Robert W. Bretall to Paul Ramsey - Ramsey Papers, Box 14, Duke University Library. Ramsey would agree to submit an essay, but not on Niebuhr's social ethics. See Paul Ramsey, "Love and Law" in *Reinhold Niebuhr: His Religious, Social, and Political*

Thought, ed. C.W. Kegley, and R.W. Bretall (New York: The Macmillan Company, 1956), 79-124.

5. Ramsey to Niebuhr, May 18th 1966, Ramsey Papers, Box 20, Niebuhr to Ramsey, June 18th [1966], Ramsey Papers, Box 20, Duke University Library.

6. Paul Ramsey, *Deeds and Rules in Christian Ethics* (New York: Charles Scribner's Sons, 1967), 67.

7. Reinhold Niebuhr, *Essays in Applied Christianity*, ed. D. B. Roberts (New York: Meridian Books, 1959), 124.

Part I
From Philosophical Ethics to Moral Theology

Chapter 1
Pragmatism and Idealism

Niebuhr and Ramsey both attended graduate school at Yale, albeit several decades apart from one another. While at this institution, they each fell in with mentors who would introduce them to the works of the pragmatists and the absolute idealists. This chapter will locate these two theologians in relation to these philosophical schools. It will also discuss the two primary moral dangers to which pragmatism and idealism respectively sensitize their practitioners. Pragmatism took aim at *moral fanaticism* which endangered the ongoing process of social criticism necessary to a genuinely public search for the common good. Absolute idealism focused on the danger of an *atomistic moral relativism* that abandoned the immanent social, moral structure against which actions can be conceived as meaningfully moral and immoral. It is also important here to get a picture of some of the ways in which Niebuhr and Ramsey were, even from the beginning, also critics of each of these positions. While they were open to the insights of these schools, Niebuhr and Ramsey were never simply identified with either of their perspectives.

Christian Pragmatism

Niebuhr was not long at Yale studying for his B.D. when he came under the influence of D.C. Macintosh, a young and charismatic philosopher of religion. Working largely in the Jamesean pragmatic tradition, Macintosh was laboring to produce an alternative to idealist proposals in religious epistemology available at the time.[1] His epistemology eschewed metaphysical speculation in favor of a pragmatic and empiricist approach to religious value.

Niebuhr was influenced by Macintosh, especially by his empiricism and pragmatism. This influence shows most explicitly in the B.D. and M.A. theses that Niebuhr produced when under Macintosh's tutelage, but the influence ripples through all of Niebuhr's work.[2] Perhaps the most prominent signs of this influence can be seen in Niebuhr's apologetic writings.[3] Here, however, I am interested in the moral problem to which Niebuhr's encounter with pragmatism sensitized him: moral fanaticism.

Pragmatism and Moral Fanaticism

Pragmatism has philosophical roots which extend at least as far back as the Enlightenment, but the immediate sources for this school of thought are to be located in the unique development of the American democratic tradition.[4] Preceding the pragmatists, the transcendentalists had sought to defend conceptions of the worth and self-reliance of individuals necessary to underwrite participation in the process of democratic discourse. The pragmatists were the successors to the transcendentalists, and, as successors are bound to do, they carried on many of the values of their predecessors while contributing their own insights in the process. The American Civil War in many ways provided the historical occasion for the shift between the two schools. Witnessing the destructiveness of opposing ideologies that refused to participate in compromise, the early pragmatists were chastened from the optimistic heights of transcendentalist notions of confident self-reliance, but they maintained course in articulating and defending the tradition of democracy. If a clash of ideologies could bring about such terror, a reinvigoration of the practices of democracy might be the only way of avoiding such terror. Democracies allow social conflicts to be arbitrated through continual debate.[5] At the same time, the pragmatists also learned from the burgeoning field of evolutionary science. In a shifting world where even established species must adapt to survive, those who close their own positions to new experience and criticism run the dangers of embracing suicidal delusion.[6] Drawing on these sources, pragmatism came to focus on the necessity of maintaining a sense of the partiality and incompleteness of all perspectives of the good while stressing the necessity of active participation in the search for the good. In a pluralistic world, people and groups begin from often conflicting presupposed standards. In this climate pragmatism aimed at preventing any one particular ideology, group, or person from establishing a monopoly upon claims to truth and value. As Louis Menand writes, the essence of pragmatism is found in "the belief that ideas should never become ideologies—either justifying the status quo, or dictating some transcendent imperative for renouncing it."[7]

For our discussion here, it is helpful to highlight the shape of the moral danger against which pragmatism was primarily oriented. Moral fanaticism is an ideal type denoting a position that exhibits several problematic tendencies. First, the morally fanatic position holds itself closed to criticism. Grounding its claims in some source said to be beyond critique, it finds little reason to participate in a public process of discernment. Second, the morally fanatic position holds a reductive view of the sources of identity and morality, and correlatively, a reductive account of the good. Diversity in experience and perspective are prematurely homogenized by the fanatic so as to fit with the dominant themes of the morally fanatic position. Goods sacrificed in the realization of the goals of the morally fanatic position are either radically devalued or denied their status as goods at all. These characteristics of the morally fanatic position often lead to a moral perfectionism wherein the position claims to be able to realize all true goods simultaneously through the realization of its particular project, thus justifying any apparent costs in service to this goal.

Fanatic positions may further be divided into paternalistic and sectarian varieties. Paternalistic fanaticism seeks to impose its reductive conception of the good on the world. Sectarian fanaticism withdraws from wider social engagement so as to maintain its reductive picture of the good within a sacrosanct community.

In contrast to moral fanaticism, pragmatism sought to provide the context for an ongoing dialogue between individuals and groups concerning the definition of the good. This dialogue was to be grounded in a non-reductive accounting of experiences of the good. Both paternalistic fanaticism and sectarian fanaticism are denied as all are called to participate in a common exchange of accounts of experiences which may transcend or challenge particular ideologies. William James at one point draws upon the metaphor of a hotel with many residents to illumine this task.

> [Pragmatism] lies in the midst of our theories, like a corridor in a hotel. Innumerable chambers open out of it. In one you may find a man writing an atheistic volume; in the next someone on his knees praying for faith and strength; in a third a chemist investigating a body's properties. In a fourth a system of idealistic metaphysics is being excogitated; in a fifth the impossibility of metaphysics is being shown. But they all own the corridor, and all must pass through it if they want a practicable way of getting into or out of their respective rooms. No particular results then, so far, but only an attitude of orientation, is what pragmatic method means. *The attitude of looking away from first things, principles 'categories,' supposed necessities; and of looking towards last things fruits, consequences, facts.*[8]

While it is possible, in the wake of contemporary arguments, to read back into such statements a reductive form of consequentialism, such a reading misses the point of James' project. The pragmatist places stress upon particular experienced features of the world rather than a general theoretical account so as to maintain a space within which proposed norms and institutions can be fruitfully challenged and assessed. Speculative accounts of life at times oversimplify the complexities of reality so as to fit reality within the proposed system. Problems that might lead to challenges to the system are obscured or denied altogether leading to reductive conceptions of the good and identity.[9] Reacting to these reductive harmonizing tendencies, pragmatism sought to stress the reality of particular experiences and goods, even if some of these goods had to be sacrificed in the realization of a better balance of goods.

Pragmatism also stressed the need for the virtues of criticalness, humility, and responsibility in the search for the common good. In relation to speculative accounts of reality, pragmatism supported critical participation; allowing one to take part in such accounts while warning one against falling into a moral fanaticism that reduced her or his identity and value to being irretrievably grounded in any one particular account alone.[10] Remembering that each person has only a partial view of reality, pragmatism endorsed the virtue of humility.[11] One must remember her or his own finitude and frailty even while arguing for the particular conceptions that one finds most suiting to life. Thus, no person is justified in claiming sole ownership of the "hall" or confusing her or his own "room" with the whole of the hotel. At the same time, the pragmatists recognized that each individual and each particular position has something to contribute to and a stake in the search for truth and goodness. As James writes: "neither the whole of truth nor the whole of good is revealed to any single observer, although each observer gains a partial superiority of insight from the peculiar position in which he stands. Even prisons and sick-rooms have their special revelations."[12] Thus pragmatism called for responsible participation in this search. In the common space between their rooms, all are enjoined to participate.

These concerns would find their way into Reinhold Niebuhr's own thought. Niebuhr's early work combined the influence of pragmatism with a Marxist appreciation of the importance of power relations.[13] This mixture, which eventually gave way to his later more explicitly Augustinian perspective, provided a vantage point from which Niebuhr found ample reasons for combating moral fanaticism. Narrow nationalistic conceptions of the good had driven the imperialism of the last century and buttressed the simplistic judgments of the victors at the end of the First World War. Reductive conceptions of the good of the race underwrote a holocaust. At the same time Marxists asserted a reductive conception of science, history, and the good that in the end was used to justify Stalin's gulags. The century could be read as a repetitive lesson that a reductive absolute good could become the justification for the destruction of any other good which stood in the path of those who sought to realize their morally fanatic goal. Projects for realizing the perfect economic or political system, nation, or race again and again ended in atrocities.

Niebuhr's encounter with pragmatism made him sensitive to this type of moral danger. His perspective on institutions, tradition, reason, and political authority were all shaped in part by his focus on the danger of allowing any one finite source or comprehensive account of reality to attain an unassailable position in the moral life. All moral sources in history, Niebuhr often reminds us, are ambiguous and must be held open to criticism. No speculative account can be sufficient to absolve us of the responsibility of checking against the relative experiences of actual life.[14]

The Particulars of Niebuhr's Pragmatism

It is helpful at this point to explore some of the ways pragmatism's influence appears in Niebuhr's thought. His mature views are shaped in the context of his own theology and cannot accurately be presented simply as an outcome of the influence of pragmatism. Still, his encounter with pragmatism did sensitize him to the danger of moral fanaticism and suggested to him some of the tools appropriate for countering this danger. I will focus on Niebuhr's conception of the shape of morality as seen from a human perspective, his anti-ideological tendencies, his critical stance toward human authorities and specialists, and his particularist tendencies when approaching the analysis of social institutions.

As Niebuhr approaches specific moral conflicts he begins from the assumption that no group in any particular argument has a stranglehold on the conception of the right or the good. Rather, moral conflicts appear first as instances in which groups with differing conceptions of the good vie for dominance in defining what will constitute the good in practice. In such a conflict the moralist must resist the temptation to claim a god's eye view in adjudicating between the positions. For the human, the world appears first as a world constructed not of essential moral ideas, but as a world full of tensions and competing moral claims. Moral duties are, for Niebuhr, not derived from the perceived essences of particular relationships or activities, but are discovered in the process of life as the conditions of arrangements which minimize the conflicts between goods and create the possibility for cooperation as it is relatively available in the world. Niebuhr is wary of the establishment of sacrosanct goods which are to be maintained without question just as he is attentive to the danger of any position which appears to deny the reality of substantive experienced goods that do not fit within its scheme. In many conflicts, Niebuhr suggests, there will be no clear access to what is good or right, and as such the best solution will be found in a formal situation in which the power between different groups is balanced in ways that prevent any one group from gaining absolute dominance.[15] Only in finding a way to restrain the fanatic tendencies of all groups will there be a chance for establishing relative justice.

Niebuhr's wish to maintain openness to criticism in moral claims also leads him to be suspicious of accounts of morality which draw moral norms from purportedly universally rational or self evident metaphysical categories. All reason and all metaphysics, Niebuhr reminds his reader, are the products of historical processes. It is dangerous to treat these kinds of accounts as if they come to humanity fully formed and simply require application. History is filled with cases in which the reason or worldview of one group justified a system which ultimately functioned not to serve the increase of justice but to unnecessarily and unjustly repress the goods of some other group. To avoid uncritical participation in such injustice Niebuhr suggests a program of "Christian pragmatism." This pragmatism consists in "the application of Christian freedom and a sense of responsibility to the complex issues of economics and politics, with the firm resolve that inherited dogmas and generalizations will not be accepted, no matter how revered or venerable, if they do not contribute to the establishment of justice in a given situation."[16]

Similar reasoning leads Niebuhr to challenge overstated claims concerning the moral deference proper in relation to specialists, experts and political authorities. The claim to special position always tempts one to overextend her or his claims to power and knowledge, absolutizing the claims of the self above other selves and the claims of the class of specialists above other members of the society.

> The conception that what society needs, and if intelligent enough, will be able to secure, is 'trained and experienced specialists' to perform the 'expert functions' of government, betrays an additional class prejudice, the prejudice of the intellectual, who is so much the rationalist, that he imagines the evils of government can be eliminated by the expert knowledge of the specialist. Any kind of government must of course avail itself of the specialized knowledge of experts. But the idea that such expert knowledge can ever guarantee the impartiality and justice of a state is to overestimate the impartiality of reason in general and the reason of experts in particular. Politics are given their general direction by pressure of interest of the groups which control them; the expert is quite capable of giving any previously determined tendency both rational justification and efficient detailed application. . . . there is no educational process which can place any class in possession of all the facts, or cause it to appreciate all the feelings which actuate another class.[17]

While his views become more tempered as his theology develops, he never abandons his stress upon the tension which must be sustained between the necessity of specialists and authorities and the criticism of these figures necessary to pursue the common good.[18]

Niebuhr's debt to pragmatism also affects his approach to social institutions. Particular social structures that at some point in history are determinative of familial, cultural, or national life can easily become absolutized, inflexible, and function as the locus for a reductive conception of the good. This is especially true when the structure of social institutions is linked to a determinative metaphysical proposal. For these reasons, while Niebuhr does not doubt that there are enduring, morally substantial structures in human social history, he is resists beginning social analysis with an essentialist theory of social institutions. Commenting on the problem any historical study of social phenomena faces, Niebuhr notes that the "endless variety" of social structures in history defy our expectations. As such, Niebuhr finds, we must be careful in what we claim about our perceptions.

> The inquiry, which seeks to distinguish the permanent from the novel and historically contingent factors of community, must confine itself to historically and empirically established patterns and forces. It must eschew metaphysical speculations which seek to discern, in the wide drama of history, ontological essences which merely wait upon history for the actualization of potency into reality. History is a realm in which human freedom and natural necessity are curiously intermingled. Man's freedom constantly creates the most curious and unexpected and unpredictable emergences and emergencies in history. All efforts to discern patters of recurrence, after the manner of Spengler and Toynbee, or patterns of development in the fashion of Hegel, Spencer, or Comte, must do violence to the infinite variety in the strange configurations of history.[19]

In an ever changing world, all perspectives must be open to critique. There are no secure shortcuts in the process of public debate and discernment.

Niebuhr's Critique of Pragmatism

In these many ways one can find in Niebuhr the traces of his encounter with pragmatism. Still, pragmatism would not be the spring from which Niebuhr began theology. Niebuhr would, in time, move beyond James and much of the pragmatic tradition in favor of a recovery of more distinctively Christian frameworks for thought. Before elaborating these frameworks, it is important here to suggest some of the problems that led Niebuhr to in part modify and in part reject the pragmatist project.

There are many points at which Niebuhr distinguished himself from the pragmatists in his later life. Niebuhr found the pragmatists to be overly optimistic about the possibilities for reforming humanity through means such as education and overly confident in the positive progressive evolution of the human race. Pragmatism also, he suggests, makes too little of the need for attention to the use of power which is often the only means of providing an actual sociological space for the kind of discussion pragmatism envisions.

Niebuhr was also uneasy with certain relativist tendencies in pragmatic epistemology and morality. At times, James collapsed the truth of an idea too completely into the usefulness of an idea.[20] This threatened to relativize all truth claims in a way unacceptable to Niebuhr and others in the Christian Realist movement.[21] The early pragmatists were right to stress the partiality of particular views of the truth, but wrong in failing to emphasize that truth also transcends every particular view. Niebuhr also recognized this tendency toward relativism in pragmatic ethics. In 1957, four years before Ramsey would begin to publish his own major tracts against the contextualists, Niebuhr criticized Barth's theology for its "extreme pragmatism, which disavows all moral principles."[22] "Looking at every event afresh," Niebuhr writes, leaves one "ignorant about the instructive, though inexact, analogies of history" which are central to moral analysis.[23] Though one should always hold particular claims open to criticism, this does not mean that she or he ought to reject all claims to enduring moral truth. Humanity, as Niebuhr writes, can go wrong by "obscuring what is permanent in human nature."[24] It is incumbent on a moralist to take seriously those moral norms gathered through past social and individual experience, even as she or he holds them up to criticism.

For our purposes perhaps the most important criticism that Niebuhr makes of pragmatism is found in his reaction to the thinness of the pragmatic tradition. Epistemically this thinness could be found in the temptation of naked empiricism to which pragmatists occasionally fell. There is a danger for the pragmatist who focuses upon the space afforded by common experience that she or he might come to think of experience is an "innocent" category. She or he may come to believe that empirical investigation provides a source of data which exists independent of the influence of the tradition from which the perceiver arises. This, Niebuhr suggests, is a mistake to which Americans are particularly prone.

> The illusion that it is possible to have an empirical inquiry without a framework of guiding presuppositions is so widespread, particularly in America, that it is regarded as outrageous to criticize a culture from the standpoint of 'dogmatic,' that is, Christian, presuppositions. . . . Actually, no empirical observation is possible without a conceptual framework.[25]

No one, Niebuhr reminds us, begins an investigation as a *tabula rasa*, rather all begin from particular intellectual, cultural, and ultimately religious standpoints.

Niebuhr also found that the thinness of the pragmatist tradition carried certain moral limitations. A meaningful moral life, Niebuhr argues, must be caught up in a narrative that allowed for the final completion of all the partial goods realizable within historical reality. Pragmatism offered no such narrative. Niebuhr here breaks with James, and with Macintosh, by explicitly locating his own mature position within the Christian tradition and Christian narrative. As Robin Lovin notes, while "Macintosh moved cautiously from experience to the reality of God, Niebuhr moved boldly from the reality of God to experience."[26] Niebuhr's theology would always be a theology enlightened by the pragmatism he had encountered, but it would always first be Christian theology.[27] It is to the elaboration of this theology that we shall turn in the next chapters. But before we turn towards Niebuhr's theology we must take up the task of shedding some initial light upon the other half of our study.

Back to Idealism and On to Theism

In contrast to Niebuhr, Paul Ramsey spent most of the first decade of his own scholarship immersed in the works of the absolute idealists. While taking PhD courses at Yale in the early 1940s Ramsey found himself caught up in the work being done by C.W. Hendel, the head of the philosophy department at Yale. In 1941 and 1942 Ramsey took two of Hendel's courses: The Philosophy of History, and Social and Political Philosophy. Ramsey's collected papers contain six pages of cramped handwritten notes on Hendel's essay on political obligation from the book *Contemporary Idealism in America*. The essay was one of the required readings for Social and Political Philosophy.[28] T.H. Green, one of the British idealists, was, according to Ramsey's class notes, Hendel's favored political philosopher.[29] In Hendel's courses Ramsey was immersed in the works of J.J. Rousseau, G.W.F. Hegel, Green, and the absolute idealist tradition of thought generally. It was also in these courses that Ramsey first came into contact with the natural law tradition. Hendel's lectures covered natural law from the Roman development of *jus gentium* to modern developments in Bodin, Grotius, and T.H. Green. Notably, however, in Hendel's treatment, religious figures like Thomas Aquinas and Martin Luther seem to have played a relatively small role. Ramsey soon gained Hendel's respect for his hard work, and began a long collegial relationship with this philosophical mentor.[30]

The copious notes that Ramsey kept from these courses speak to the impact they had on him. But one need not rely only on these to see the influence of idealism on Ramsey's early thought. In his dissertation at Yale, Ramsey began a project to which he would allude in his early writings with the watchword "back to idealism and on to theism."[31] Ramsey's dissertation, which he developed in conversation with Hendel,[32] is a defense of the absolute idealism of Josiah Royce and Bernard Bosanquet against some of the criticisms leveled by figures in the pragmatist and "neo-protestant" traditions.[33] Ramsey titled the work "The Nature of Man in the Philosophy of Josiah Royce and Bernard Bosanquet", suggesting a contrast with Niebuhr's recently released *The Nature and Destiny of Man*. He specifically names William James, D.C. Macintosh, and Reinhold Niebuhr among idealism's mis-interpreters.[34] Time has come, Ramsey suggests, for a critical recovery of idealism's insights for contemporary moral theology. We need not go into all of the particulars of Ramsey's argument. What is most important for our purposes is the role of idealism in sensitizing Ramsey to the danger of atomistic moral relativism, and arming him with certain tools to combat this danger.

Absolute Idealism and Moral Relativism

In his dissertation, Ramsey comes at one point to the heart of what he understands to be the moral argument between pragmatism and idealism. Both, he finds, charge the other with moral quietism in principle. The idealist, says the pragmatist, in believing that all actuality is part of the perfect Absolute, has no need for moral discernment in practice. The pragmatist, says the idealist, in thinking her or himself independent of objective moral structures, renders moral decision impossible.[35] Thus the two argue into the night with no resolution in view.

While recognizing that both sides misconstrue each other's positions, Ramsey's response to this dilemma suggests that the most promising route in resolving the debate is found by focusing on the ways in which the idealist position allows one to make sense of moral decisions.[36] The concern of the idealist, Ramsey argues, is primarily to maintain that there are morally important decisions to make. Central here is the idealist claim there exists an immanent moral structure to which members of society ought to conform, one which is accessible to human minds in the process of rational moral discernment as deployed the context of institutions and practices of the present society.

Some background is helpful at this point in illuminating the strain of thought on which Ramsey is drawing. Unlike pragmatism, absolute idealism does not see the greatest moral dangers of history in terms of moral fanaticism. Rather, it is organized around a rejection of atomistic moral relativism.[37] This form of idealism developed as a reaction to certain trends in enlightenment thought and the perceived upshot of these trends in the terrors of the French Revolution. The enlightenment, on the idealistic reading, tended to objectify reality. Humans came to be seen as objects driven not by rational will, but by their passions. Reason came to be conceived as the calculative function of the mind. Reason was deployed to attain the goals set by these passions. Alienated from their cultural and relational foundations by these enlightenment trends, individuals came to see all things including society, nature and fellow persons as means properly used in the pursuit of fulfilling personal desires. The structure of morality was thus abandoned in favor of purported individual interest.

G.W.F. Hegel reacted to these trends in enlightenment thought by synthesizing two other attempts to overcome the errors of the earlier enlightenment. Immanuel Kant had properly rejected individualistic passions in favor of reason, but had erred in conceiving reason in terms of individualistic theoretical and practical consistency. The Romantics had properly proposed a more holistic conception of the individual as embedded in nature and community, but had failed to stress the dangers of relying on evanescent passions in guiding human actions. Hegel's system, which became the ground for the later development of myriad diverse versions of absolute idealism, joined the Kantian and Romantic programs by positing the ultimately rational character of the holistic system of nature and society out of which the individual arises. In this system, the structure of nature, society, and the individual are seen as an outgrowth of the progressive self realization of the Absolute, a governing mind that self-reflectively expresses itself thorough the vehicle of finite reality. In this way absolute idealism sought to replace the enlightenments atomistic conception of social relations with a picture of the finite individual as a rationally autonomous self that arises and can be fulfilled only in the context of a framework of given structured social institutions and practices.[38] Within this idealistic framework, it is a rejection of this structure, especially in favor of some mode of atomistic individualism or dream of structureless ideal society, that provides the most significant challenge to morality.[39] Such a rejection collapses the given structure of social reality and as such denies the world's, and the self's, very essence.[40] As Ramsey jotted in his graduate class notes, for Hegel the self must be a "conformist first."[41]

Ramsey's most in-depth exposure to this tradition took place while exegeting the works of Josiah Royce and Bernard Bosanquet for his dissertation. It is helpful to elaborate upon the position represented by Bernard Bosanquet, on whom Ramsey was focusing in his own above rejection of moral relativism. Relevant here is Bosanquet's understanding of the self and its will, and of the "dominant ideas" and general will of human societies. The self, according to Bosanquet, who was as much influenced by Plato as Hegel, consists in a "'mental system' or 'set of ideas' which is more than the physical individual and reflects one's relations with others."[42] The will of the self is correlatively to be understood as "a great mass of associated ideas guiding attention and action."[43] Ideas reflecting one's relation with others arise only from an actual process of human interaction, and as such, for Bosanquet, there can be no proper human self or will apart from society.

If there can be no real self apart from the society, there can also be no moral will outside of the conceptual structure provided by life in the society. According to Bosanquet, individuals living within the practices of a particular culture gain access to a common set of "dominant ideas" around which their lives are arranged. These ideas exist, often in a muddled and only partially conscious form, in the minds of the community and are enacted (with varying degrees of accuracy) in the everyday practices of community members. These ideas define the moral duties of the individual in her or his station. They "express and determine the relations of individuals to one another and, consequently, provide the foundation for a coordination and division of labor as well as concerted action."[44] Indeed, the comprehensive set of these ideas are immediately identical with the general will of the society, and ultimately identical with the will of the Absolute. They designate the structure of the common good at which the society aims.

This is not to say, Bosanquet maintains, that there are no mechanisms for change within the society.[45] The Absolute is constantly thinking itself out in history, and as such one can expect there will be adjustments within the structure of finite society as the situation of the culture changes and as the ideas of the Absolute come to more refined actuality. Bosanquet suggests that the common ideals of those within the society may serve to prompt reforms. But, as Bosanquet emphasizes, lest these ideals tempt one to reject the moral structure of the society, they ought not to be construed as transcendent measures that stand over against the dominant ideas of the society.[46] The ideals of the society must be conceived as calling members of the society to manifest more excellently the conceptually framed essence of those stations in which they are located. Just as the "principle of health" calls the sick person to regain physical excellence that is her or his true essence even while ill, social ideals call society to conform all the more fully to those essential moral/conceptual structures known through and manifested in the society's present practice and existence. These ideas which arise from and in turn guide the practice of the community are the only sources for morally meaningful life.

Needless to say, an individual who is disabused of these dominant ideas is, within Bosanquet's scheme, at a loss. Since the self consists in ideas that arise from and cohere with the dominant ideas of the society, the thought of a self independent of the society makes no sense. Without adherence to guiding ideas that arise from the practices of society, the populace of the society would at best collapse into a crowd of uncoordinated and unfulfilled atomistic organisms devoid of moral motivation and driven by their short term passions. Without belief in the present reality of the moral structure and the location of the self within this structure, the difference between morality and immorality is denied, and the world is handed over into anarchy and the war of all against all. For, Bosanquet writes, "take away the general will and nothing but force is left."[47] Such is the gravity of the danger of atomistic moral relativism as proposed by this absolute idealist, and such is the moral danger to which Ramsey was sensitized in his early work.

As with moral fanaticism for Niebuhr, idealism's focus on atomistic moral relativism was more than an abstract concern for Ramsey. In his life he would see social changes that would often raise the specter of chaos. In the midst of the sexual and social revolutions of the nineteen-sixties and seventies it would often seem that anarchy was breathing down the neck of modern civilization. Rapidly advancing technologies would bring apparently new moral dilemmas to the fore in the areas of war and medical ethics. At the same time, the movements of situationism and contextualism would arise in moral theology, challenging the existence of any enduring norm except the requirements of love or God's will in the moment of decision. Such movements sought to transform the society not through participation in its given structure, but rather by eradicating the structures of the past and engineering a novel and socially structureless future. In such a context, it was easy to lose track of the norms and institutions that provided a framework for moral reasoning and limits to the excesses of human passion.

Thankfully, in addition to diagnosing the danger of moral relativism, the absolute idealists had also suggested a set of focal points, attention to which might aid in avoiding this danger. The Absolute rolls itself out in history. Thus, the collected wisdom of history as embodied in social institutions and cultural norms provides access to the essential order of reality. Ongoing active participation in the reasoning processes arising from extant social practices allows one to further participate in the process of the Absolute's thought. All creation is caught up within what the Absolute has done in establishing order and what the Absolute is doing in transforming this order. As such, to protect the meaningfulness of the moral life one must focus attention upon the structures provided by tradition, history, contextualized reason, and the extant order of society while rejecting atomistic conceptions of individualism, the use of disruptive transcendent ideals, and the overestimation of the beneficial uses of calculative reasoning in recasting reality. Only thus can one avoid the dangers of atomistic moral relativism.

The Essence of Ramsey's Idealism

Ramsey's mature position, like Niebuhr's, must be filled out in the context of his richer theological project. Still, it is important to note here some of those ways in which Ramsey's approach has been influenced by idealism. I will focus on Ramsey's conception of the subject of morality, the relevance of social institutions, the significance of historical norms, the value of individuals, and the danger of atomistic individualism.

Holding the center against moral relativism remains a fundamental concern throughout Ramsey's work. In early articles Ramsey rails against the "pragmatists" who have drained society of substantial moral conceptions of justice.[48] By 1960 Ramsey more explicitly writes of the need for an account of the "morphology of man" in order to do Christian ethics.[49] "Christ," Ramsey later asserts, "does not reign over a structureless world or over men who are bereft of any sense of natural justice."[50]

Ethics for Ramsey is conceived primarily as the practice of describing the enduring structure of moral reality to which practice should conform. The particular vocations, social institutions, acts, and relationships in which humans take part have certain essential shapes. The moralist works to highlight and define the terms that refer to enduring essential forms in moral reality. These terms and their detailed explications provide guidance within the ever changing world of history. The gravest danger for Ramsey is that society might lose respect for these forms, or lose the language that allows it to speak of this moral structure.

This essentialist approach can be seen in Ramsey's view of social institutions and practices. Notable is his analysis of politics. Reasoning within the context of the practice of politics, Ramsey believes it is possible to gain access to a relatively clear conception of what politics ought to be within the confines of history.

> The use of power, and possibly the use of force, is of the *esse* of politics. By this I mean it belongs to the very *act of being* politics. You never have politics without the use of power, possibly armed force. At the same time the use of power, possibly the use of force, is inseparable from the *bene esse* of politics. By this I mean that it is inseparable from politics' *proper* act of being politics, inseparable from the well being of politics, inseparable from the human pursuit of the national or international good by political means.[51]

Ramsey's analysis of actual political activity depends upon this account of what politics ought to be. Politics is not simply what a person does when seeking to wield officially sanctioned power. There is a kind of reason inherent in the act of politics. It is a particular kind of act entailing particular norms to which all participants should conform.

This essentialist approach also impacts Ramsey's perspective on the significance of particular preferentially oriented relationships, and the role of specialists and authorities in history. As we have seen, for Bosanquet, the Absolute always becomes self-aware in the context of particular practices within history. To heighten this awareness, the Absolute differentiates and specializes individuals into particular stations so as to better serve the whole.[52] Together, while not individually fully aware of the whole, each in pursuing its own specified duty contributes to the knowledge and good of the whole and thus to the realization of the Absolute.

While Ramsey qualifies this position in his critique of idealism, and he traces his own treatment of vocation to Luther rather than Bosanquet, it seems clear that Bosanquet's conceptualization of one's "duties and station" left some impression on Ramsey's thought.[53] In an article written shortly after his dissertation, Ramsey suggests that the appropriate human reaction to sin "is not a response that would require all-inclusiveness, but only the response appropriate to his 'vocation' as it is determined by the Will of God."[54] Vocational relationships, which in Ramsey's later works are rolled into the concept of covenantal relationships, become for Ramsey one of the frameworks through which Christian love must be channeled in history. Further, Ramsey retains great respect for the importance of specialized forms of activity, and often stresses the dangers of confusing the different spheres of specialization for those functioning in roles such as moralist, doctor, and magistrate.

Ramsey's perspective on tradition, historically proven norms and language, and the extant order within any moment of history also reveals the influence of his early encounter with idealism.[55] As Ramsey writes in his dissertation, for the absolute idealists, all progress must be conceived as consistent with the acts of the Absolute in the past. In bringing novel possibilities to fruition, the Absolute does not remake the whole order, it looks about within the present order "to find some gap or corner that needs to be filled in."[56] Without the guidance of the past, the individual is left without standards for action and without the bonds which provide for human community.

Ramsey's later works reveal his own great appreciation for the moral significance of history and extant order. At one point, Ramsey suggests that the Protestant model for social reform should function analogously to the system of precedent in jurisprudence. Here, under normal circumstances, the judge is guided by the "deposits of history," but also is allowed to work in the vague meaning between deposited precedents to find the best way to resolve the particular case, and thus improve the system of justice as a whole.

> In general . . . it is *through the interstitial spaces* in what the law allows the judge to do in his official capacity, and by illuminating the imponderable human relations and indeterminate freedoms that still remain after the steady attention to the prism of the case, that a profound religious apprehension of human existence may serve to transform natural justice and raise the good law to a higher power.[57]

Later, Ramsey would find amenable a similar statement in the work of Max Kohnstam.

> Christians need to learn, he [Kohnstam] said, in dealing with international relations, the lessons we have already learned about domestic society, namely that 'love passes not directly from man to man, but through structures.' There are no solutions in international relations but to look *inside the existing structures for cracks where a change must take place.*[58]

Finally, idealism sensitized Ramsey to the value of individuals and the dangers of atomistic individualism. From their Kantian roots, the absolute idealists had inherited a strong sense of the dangers involved in treating the individual only as a means that could be used in service to some transcendent goal. Since individuals are, the idealists claimed, distinctive facets of and vehicles for the Absolute, they are each inherently valued.[59] To treat particular individuals as exchangeable units constitutes a rejection of the uniqueness of each individual's place in the Absolute and thus denies the real moral value of the individual. But, this perspective on the value of the individual is always, for the absolute idealist, grounded in an account of the identity of all individuals as vehicles for the Absolute, caught up in the structure of the Absolute's thought. Thus, atomistic conceptions of individualism are rejected as corrosive to the moral fiber of the self and the society. The individual always constitutes an "identity in difference" as her or his valued distinctiveness is expressed within the structure provided by the Absolute.

Although he shifts his emphasis between the poles of individual distinctiveness and moral continuity among individuals depending on the problem with which he is working,[60] Ramsey is influenced by both of these insights in idealistic philosophy. Ramsey's appreciation of the valuable distinctiveness of individuals often appears in his treatments of the ethics of war, and in his arguments with the situationists. However, it is portrayed most clearly in his writings on medical ethics.

> Only a being who is a sacredness in the social order, can withstand complete domination by 'society' for the sake of engineering civilizational goals—withstand, in the sense that the engineering of civilizational goals cannot be accomplished without denying the sacredness of the human being.[61]

Ramsey was also sensitized by idealism to the dangers of atomistic individualism. This influence can be seen in an exchange with Stanley Hauerwas. After the publication of *The Patient as Person*, Hauerwas claimed that Ramsey had taken a Kantian turn toward "individualism." Ramsey, in a letter to Hauerwas, denies the charge stating: "It really is strange to have that charge lodged, since I think that liberalism in all its forms is precisely that kind of fragmentation and is the deadly disease of modern societies."[62] The disease to which Ramsey refers is the moral relativism to which idealism had sensitized him. The "atomistic individualism of secular thought in the modern period," Ramsey writes, functions as an "acid that eats away at moral relations, and at the very idea that there are moral bonds between man and man or between one moment and another."[63]

Ramsey's Critique of Idealism

In all of the above ways, Ramsey was influenced by his early encounter with absolute idealism. Yet, his early project went beyond a recovery of idealism; it was also a criticism of this position. Ultimately, Ramsey argues in his dissertation that the greatest insights of idealism lead to a modification of idealism's own claims. In its best moments, idealism points toward structured self-Other relationships in which the self is inextricably enmeshed. But, idealism obscures these insights at times by embracing the image of the self as "the motion of a part-whole or microcosmic-macrocosmic identity."[64] The concept of the *identity* of the self, the society, and the Absolute, Ramsey tells us, betrays the insights of idealism because the emphasis on self-Other *identity* prevents the idealist from effectively implementing her or his insights into genuine self-Other *relationships*.

This mistaken claim to self-Other identity makes problematic the idealistic account of moral responsibility, progress, individuality, and a number of other concepts. It also leads idealism into a form of idolatry.[65] The self in such a system too easily claims to identify her or his own will with the will of God, and too easily limits her or his own concern to that of the local society. But no self, and indeed no historical society, ought to make such absolute claims. "No merely human community," Ramsey writes, "however universal, can command the whole devotion of man. Unless God Himself be a member thereof, man cannot be wholeheartedly devoted to any community."[66]

The correction to absolute idealism, Ramsey argues, is found in an idealistically enlightened theism. Keeping the best from the idealistic tradition, but breaking idealism's idolatry, the Christian theologian can benefit from this great tradition of philosophy. As Ramsey writes, the correction of idealism "requires only that the identity between the finite individual and the Infinite be removed. Man's nature is fundamentally as idealism has pictured it . . . but the 'infinite' which is really an ideal possibility of his attainment and which is obligatory upon him is only a relative 'infinite,' and it is still subject to *the* Infinite who stands over against him as an Other."[67] Ultimately, Ramsey would eventually conclude, the Christian tradition itself could appropriate and better articulate the insights of idealism using the idea of covenant relations.

Comparisons and Contrasts

One might expect tensions to emerge between scholars who are informed by the differing emphases of these two schools of thought. Yet, it is important to keep this tension in perspective. It is all too easy to suggest simple contrasts. Pragmatism and idealism do not offer contradictory programs. Such would only be the case if pragmatism were oriented toward the production of moral relativism or absolute idealism toward the production of moral fanaticism. But such is not the case. Indeed, the moral dangers of fanaticism and relativism, as developed here, do not stand in antithetical relationship to one another. They function more like different guiding metaphors for making sense of the particular moral pitfalls faced by one and one's society. It is often possible to describe immoral acts in terms of either danger, and the descriptions and remedies proposed by those wielding these divergent conceptions of immorality at times overlap in significant ways.[68] Those influenced by pragmatism, Niebuhr included, have caricatured idealism as synonymous with moral fanaticism. Those influenced by absolute idealism, Ramsey included, have caricatured pragmatists as relativists. While there may be some kernel of truth found in each of these caricatures, a recognition of the possibility of overlap between the two positions ought lead one to be cautious in suggesting simple accounts of their relations.

Beyond this qualification, it is also important to note how Niebuhr and Ramsey are critiquing and modifying the positions from which they emerge. Niebuhr transforms pragmatism in the light of Christian realist claims. The irreducibly pluralistic picture of the world suggested by some pragmatists is rejected in favor of a realist conception of truth and morality. The naked empiricist tendencies of pragmatism are supplanted with a view of the world developed through a recovery of traditional Christian claims. Thus, Niebuhr embraces a specifically Christian moral realism, grounded in the symbols of a particular historical community, even while stressing the extent to which the scheme of moral truth remains hidden from humanity.[69] Pragmatism leaves its mark on Niebuhr's moral sensibilities, and sensitized him especially to the dangers of moral fanaticism, but this does not determine Niebuhr's view of the world.

Ramsey, on the other hand begins with the analysis of an idealistic system that emphasizes the danger of moral relativism, and stresses the accessible structure of moral reality. But, Ramsey's dissertation is his argument that the best elements in this school of thought lead toward theism. He effectively increases the pluralism in idealism by severing the identity of the individual, society, and the Absolute. The individual is always within a set of stable relationships but exists with a limited knowledge of these relationships, and must be able to transcend the claims of any particular relationship in reaction to God as the ultimate Other. The individual may follow God's plan, but will not do so perfectly since the individual and divine wills are not identical. Each person remains with a view of the universal and not a universal view.

With these trends laid out it seems clear that Ramsey and Niebuhr were, in important ways, traveling from two different directions toward a common point. This common point will appear differently to them as their perspectives are shaped by the emphases they have inherited, but their two perspectives will not be easily set in simple contradiction to one another. Inasmuch as these early influences are long lasting in Niebuhr's and Ramsey's thoughts, the two will have differences of perspective. They will be important differences, but they will not be significant enough to prevent a beneficial mutual critique between the two positions Niebuhr and Ramsey represent.

With this basic relationship between the two established, it is also important to say that knowledge of the traditions from which the two theologians draw also suggests a list of likely strengths and weakness in their approaches. One might expect Niebuhr's approach to be best suited to dealing with problems in which reductive approaches to authority, identity, and relative values mislead moral discernment. On the other side, one might expect that Ramsey's moral theology will be tailored toward a careful analysis of the structure of moral acts and relationships in ways that are resistant to relativizing tendencies in ethics. In the end, each position may be open to criticism from the perspective of the other in the areas where their emphases leave them vulnerable.

Before any conclusions are reached with regard to these tendencies, it is necessary to establish a great deal more about the theology, methodology, and practice of these two men. I have here only suggested the beginnings of the dialectical processes which culminate in the theologies put forth by Ramsey and Niebuhr. Ramsey's and Niebuhr's positions are not properly understood apart from their early intellectual context. But neither are their insights reducible to an analysis of this context. Ramsey and Niebuhr continued on to recover strains of the Christian tradition in the process of their own theological developments. The end result would be two differing, but overlapping moral theologies.

Notes

1. See D.C. Macintosh, "The Threat of Captivity: Second Thoughts about Idealism" in *The Pilgrimage of Faith in the World of Modern Thought* (Calcutta: The University of Calcutta, 1931), 127-55.

2. For an account of the impact of pragmatism on his B.D. and M.A. theses, see Richard Fox, *Reinhold Niebuhr: A Biography* (Ithaca, N.Y.: Cornell University Press, 1996), 30-36.

3. See Robin Lovin, *Reinhold Niebuhr and Christian Realism* (New York: Cambridge University Press, 1995), 41-71, 79-89.

4. Jeffrey Stout, *Democracy and Tradition* (Princeton, N.J.: Princeton University Press, 2004), 19-41.

5. Louis Menand begins his history of American pragmatism with an account of the horrors of the Civil War. Especially poignant is his recounting of the way in which Oliver Wendell Holmes was converted from a "crusading" mentality in approaching moral rightness to a position grounded in the protection of continuous dialogue. See *The Metaphysical Club* (New York: Farrar, Straus, and Giroux, 2001), 52-67.

6. See Bruce Kuklick *A History of Philosophy in America, 1720-2000* (Oxford: Clarendon Press, 2001), 129-33

7. Menand, *The Metaphysical Club*, xii.

8. William James, *Pragmatism* (Buffalo, N.Y.: Prometheus Books, 1991), 27. James credits this metaphor to "the young Italian pragmatist Papini."

9. See Hilary Putnam on "alienated" views of truth, *Reason Truth and History* (New York: Cambridge University Press, 1981); and *The Many Faces of Realism* (La Salle, Ill.: Open Court, 1987).

10. This is a characteristic of pragmatism at its best. It is not always consistently applied. See Jeffrey Stout on John Dewey's concept of "militant atheism." *Democracy and Tradition*, 31-41.

11. Bruce Kuklick traces the term "pragmatism" to a passage in Kant's *Critique of Pure Reason* in which the great philosopher is reflecting on the fragility of hypothetical imperatives. "If in our thoughts," Kant writes, "we imagine the happiness of our whole life at stake, our triumphant judgment disappears, we tremble lest our belief has gone too far. Thus pragmatic belief has degrees of strength varying in proportion to the magnitude of the diverse interest involved." *A History of Philosophy in America*, 133.

12. "On a Certain Blindness in Human Beings," in *Essays on Faith and Morals*, ed. Ralph Perry (New York: Meridian Books, 1962), 284. Both the need for humility and the need for responsible participation can be seen in the "Law of Errors" which was drawn up by early pragmatists. According to this "law" all observers are subject to error in their observations. But by analyzing the overlap in the recorded observations of multiple careful observers it is possible to establish a useful account of the object of observation. See Menand, *The Metaphysical Club*, 177-200.

13. The emphasis on power sets Marxism apart from pragmatism. Still, pragmatist and Marxist schemes do overlap with one another, especially in their anti-Hegelian moods. Niebuhr's encounter with Marxism has been stressed in several other accounts of his thought. See, for instance, Ronald Stone, *Professor Reinhold Niebuhr: A mentor to the twentieth century* (Louisville, Ky.: Westminster/John Knox Press, 1992), 84-111; and Kenneth Thompson, "The Political Philosophy of Reinhold Niebuhr," in *Reinhold Niebuhr: His religious, social, and political thought*, ed. C.W. Kegley and R.W. Bretall, 158-62.

14. Niebuhr does, in an early work, offer an endorsement of a kind of moral fanaticism in motivating social change. See *Moral Man and Immoral Society: A study in ethics and politics* (Louisville, Ky.: Westminster John Knox Press, 2001), 276-77. His later works do not abandon his appreciation for the kind of passion which is stirred up by moral fanaticism. Still, as Robin Lovin has argued, Niebuhr's mature position seeks to relate this passion with a sense of responsibility for what can realistically be achieved within history. See Lovin, *Reinhold Niebuhr and Christian Realism*, 97-105.

15. See Niebuhr's treatment of capitalism and communism in *Children of Light and Children of Darkness: A vindication of democracy and a critique of its traditional defence* (New York: Charles Scribner's Sons, 1944), 117-18.

16. Reinhold Niebuhr, *Faith and Politics*, ed. Ronald Stone (New York: George Braziller, 1968), 55; See also Niebuhr on natural law in *Faith and History: A comparison of Christian and modern views of history* (New York: Charles Scribner's Sons, 1949), 180-81.

17. Niebuhr, *Moral Man and Immoral Society*, 214-15.

18. As Robin Lovin notes, it might be said that Niebuhr introduces what would later be called the 'hermeneutics of suspicion' into theological ethics. *Reinhold Niebuhr and Christian Realism*, 7.

19. Reinhold Niebuhr, *The Structure of Nations and Empires: A study of the recurring patterns and problems of the political order in relation to the unique problems of the nuclear age*. (New York: Charles Scribner's Sons, 1959), 7.

20. James, *Pragmatism*, 28.

21. See Macintosh's comments in *The Pilgrimage of Faith*, 176-77. Also see Lovin, *Reinhold Niebuhr and Christian Realism*, 46-54.

22. See Niebuhr, *Essays in Applied Christianity* (New York: Meridian Books, 1959), 186. Nor does Niebuhr's position on the subject waver. In a letter to Paul Ramsey, late in Niebuhr's life, Niebuhr would write concerning the contextualist ethics of Paul Lehmann that "his pragmatic emphasis is so great that I doubt whether he has studied the whole problem of ethical standards sufficiently." Reinhold Niebuhr to Paul Ramsey, 18 June 1966, Box 20, Paul Ramsey Papers, Duke University Library.

23. Niebuhr, "Why is Barth Silent on Hungary," in *Essays in Applied Christianity*, 187.

24. Niebuhr, *Faith and History*, 174. He is most emphatic on this point in his analysis of sexual ethics. See Niebuhr on Bertrand Russell and sexual ethics in *Faith and History*, 181; also Reinhold Niebuhr, "Kinsey and the Moral Problem of Man's Sexual Life," in *An Analysis of the Kinsey Reports on Sexual Behavior in the Human Male and Female* (New York: Dutton, 1954). Both citations are noted by Ramsey in his own analysis of Niebuhr's position. See "Reinhold Niebuhr: Christian Love and Natural Law," in *Nine Modern Moralists* (Englewood Cliffs, N.J.: Prentice-Hall, Inc., 1962), 121, 262 *nn.* 30, 31.

25. Reinhold Niebuhr, "Intellectual Autobiography" in *Reinhold Niebuhr: His religious, social, and political thought*, ed. C.W. Kegley and R.W. Bretall, 13-14.

26. Lovin, *Reinhold Niebuhr and Christian Realism*, 64.

27. "He never gave up liberalism or pragmatism," writes Ronald Stone, "but the mature Niebuhr based his theology on the Christian tradition." See Ronald Stone, *Prophetic Realism: Beyond Militarism and Pacifism in an Age of Terror* (New York: T&T Clark, 2005), 123.

28. Charles W. Hendel, "The Meaning of Obligation" in *Contemporary Idealism in America*, ed. Clifford Barret (New York: The Macmillan Company, 1932). See Ramsey's notes on Social and Political Philosophy in Box 43, The Paul Ramsey Papers, Duke University Library.

29. Hendel held that Green was the greatest English philosopher since Locke. T.H. Green, *Lectures on the Principles of Political Obligation* (London: Longmans, 1941) was one of the central texts for Hendel's courses. See Ramsey's notes and collected handouts from these courses in Box 43, The Paul Ramsey Papers, Duke University Library.

30. In correspondence to Ramsey, Hendel writes in 1941, after their first class together, that he is determined to treat Ramsey "as a colleague." See also C.W. Hendel to

Paul Ramsey, 4 July 1943, and C.W. Hendel to Paul Ramsey, 19 June 1941, in Box 11, The Paul Ramsey Papers, Duke University Library.

31. See Ramsey, "The Nature of Man in the Philosophy of Josiah Royce and Bernard Bosanquet." (Unpublished Ph.D. Dissertation, Yale University, 1943.), 424; "The Idealistic View of Moral Evil: Josiah Royce and Bernard Bosanquet," *Philosophy and Phenomenological Research* 6, no. 4 (June, 1946), 589.

32. Ramsey corresponded with Hendel several times on the topic. At one point early on in the formulation of the dissertation Hendel even seems to have suggested that Ramsey might have done well to focus on T.H. Green as his exemplar of idealism. See C.W. Hendel to Paul Ramsey, 19 June 1941, both in Box 11, The Paul Ramsey Papers, Duke University Library.

33. Ramsey, "The Nature of Man," 173, 239. How closely Ramsey was following Hendel here is not clear. One point in Hendel's graduate lectures concerned the "Revolt against Idealism in Pragmatism." Unfortunately, Ramsey did not record any of the further content under this point. See Ramsey's class notes on The Philosophy of History, The Paul Ramsey Papers, Box 43.

34. Ramsey's argument is not, for the most part, that the substance of Niebuhrian theology and social theory is flawed. It is rather that idealism, when given a sympathetic and sensitive reading, can be seen as consistent with an anthropology that functions similarly to Niebuhr's own. The "new" theories of the critics of idealism, according to Ramsey, are not so new, nor so superior as their proponents suppose.

35. Ramsey, "The Nature of Man," 174. "The absolutist finds the position of a man, confronted moment after moment, as James envisages, with the task of deciding autonomously which way the battle for a good universe is to go, a situation of such intolerable seriousness as 'logically' to make action either one way or another as utter impossibility."

36. Ramsey's position is overly dismissive of the differences between the two positions. He assumes that at the end of the day their disagreements are more a matter "of psychology than of logic." "The Nature of Man," 174.

37. The following account is dependent upon Charles Taylor, *Hegel and Modern Society* (New York: Cambridge University Press, 1979).

38. On Hegel's modern/pre-modern view of society, see Charles Taylor, *Hegel and Modern Society*, 81.

39. As Alasdair MacIntyre writes, for the Hegelian "what gives sanction to our moral choices is in part the fact that the criteria which govern our choices are not chosen. Therefore, if *I* make up my mind for myself, if *I* set myself my goals, I can at best provide a counterfeit of morality. Where, then, do I find criteria? In the established social practice of a well-ordered community." *A Short History of Ethics: A history of moral philosophy from the Homeric age to the twentieth century* (Notre Dame: University of Notre Dame Press, 1997), 208. For an argument that puts a Hegelian inspired opposition to atomistic relativism in relation with a more positive statement of the value of individuality see Charles Taylor, *The Ethics of Authenticity* (Cambridge, Mass.: Harvard University Press, 1991).

40. Even atomistic individualist movements pose no final threat to the Absolute. These movements are, in fact, instances of moral failing which are used by the providential "cunning of reason" to clear the path for further rational development in new and improved social frameworks in later civilizations.

41. See Ramsey's class notes on Social and Political Philosophy, The Ramsey Papers, Box 43.

42. William Sweet, *Idealism and Rights: The social ontology of human rights in the political thought of Bernard Bosanquet* (New York: University Press of America, 1997), 129. On Bosanquet's use of Plato see William Sweet, "Was Bosanquet a Hegelian?" in *The Bulletin of the Hegel Society in Great Britain* 31 (1995), 39-60.

43. Bernard Bosanquet, "The Reality of the General Will" in *The British Idealists*, ed. David Boucher (New York: Cambridge University Press, 1997), 138.

44. William Sweet, *Idealism and Rights*, 137.

45. It should be noted that the British Idealists in general, and Bosanquet in particular, were involved in social reforms, especially as concerned the right to education and advocacy on behalf of the poor. See David Boucher, introduction to *The British Idealists*, ix-x.

46. "The word 'Ideal' or 'Ideals' is one for which I have always felt a certain distaste. It seems to suggest a *prima facie* contrast with reality; and reality, the real reality, is to me what especially fires the heart and imagination." Bernard Bosanquet, *Social and International Ideals: Being studies in patriotism* (London: Macmillan and Company, 1917), 97. Elsewhere, Bosanquet criticizes transcendent Christian eschatological ideals inasmuch as these can distract from the moral duties that arise from and bind one to her or his station within history. See Bernard Bosanquet, *Science and Philosophy, and Other Essays* (Freeport, N.Y.: Books for Libraries Press, 1927), 333-34, 339-45.

47. Bosanquet, *Social and International Ideals*, 313.

48. Ramsey, "A Social Policy for Liberal Religion," *Religion in Life* 13, no. 4 (Autumn, 1944), 495.

49. Paul Ramsey, "Faith Effective Through In-Principled Love," *Christianity and Crisis* 20 (May 30, 1960), 76-78.

50. Ramsey, *Nine Modern Moralists*, 5.

51. Paul Ramsey, *The Just War: Force and political responsibility* (Lanham, Md.: Rowman and Littlefield, 2002), 5. When David Little suggests that Ramsey was offering a "persuasive definition" of politics, as opposed to a descriptive definition, Ramsey accepts this characterization with a qualification. The concept of "persuasive definition" carries an anti-realist/emotivist connotation. "A normative view of politics," like his, Ramsey notes, "means to say something about the real nature of political society, and claims in that sense to report or convey some truth about the matter." Paul Ramsey, "Some Rejoinders," *Journal of Religious Ethics* 4 (Fall 1976), 205; See also David Little, "The Structure of Justification in the Political Ethics of Paul Ramsey" in *Love and Society: essays in the ethics of Paul Ramsey*, ed. James T. Johnson and David H. Smith (Missoula, Mont.: Scholars Press, 1974), 144-45.

52. Ramsey, "The Nature of Man," 122.

53. D. Stephen Long suggests that Ramsey's picture of providence bears great similarity on this point to the idealistic view of the Absolute rolling itself out. "The universe is," for both of these theories, Long writes, "a rational place where the Absolute works itself out (for Hegel the cunning of reason, for Ramsey providential ordering) through the particular loyalties, stations, and orders of finite individuals." *Tragedy, Tradition, Transformism: The ethics of Paul Ramsey* (Boulder, Colo.: Westview Press, 1993), 29.

54. Ramsey, "The Idealistic View of Moral Evil," 587.

55. See Ramsey, "The Nature of Man," 347.

56. Ramsey, "The Nature of Man," 18.

57. Ramsey, *Nine Modern Moralists*, 231. Italics mine. It is important to note here that Emil Brunner, on whom Ramsey is drawing, has suggested the spatial metaphor

himself. Brunner writes that "because no man, as a member of an institution, is *only* a member of an institution, but always and only a person, there is room for love even in the most impersonal of institutions, not in the actual activity of the institution itself, but 'between the lines.'" *Justice and the Social Order*, trans. Mary Hottinger (New York: Harper and Brothers, 1945), 129.

58. Ramsey, *The Just War*, 498. Italics mine

59. As Ramsey notes, for Royce, the individual "is not merely *this*, but *such a this* that its place can be taken by no other." Ramsey, "The Nature of Man," 9.

60. In his early work with social rights, Ramsey tends to stress the need for *continuity* in the midst of difference, thus emphasizing that rights only inhere in individuals to the extent that they serve the common good. See "A Social Policy for Liberal Religion," 495-507. In his later work on medical ethics Ramsey stresses the *difference* of the patient from the doctor even while the two can be "joint adventurers in a common cause." See Paul Ramsey, *The Patient as Person: explorations in medical ethics* (New Haven, Conn.: Yale University Press, 2002), 6. The difference in stress is possibly due to the difference in the kinds of covenants involved. The society/individual covenant relates to voluntariness differently from covenants between individuals. Still, one should not rule out the possibility that this shift represents an adjustment of Ramsey's moral practice given the particular subject matter of medical ethics. For a reading of Ramsey which argues that he did, in fact, take a substantial turn toward protecting the individual in his later work, see Charles Curran, *Politics, Medicine, and Christian Ethics: A dialogue with Paul Ramsey*. (Philadelphia: Fortress Press, 1973).

61. Ramsey, *The Patient as Person*, xlvi.

62. A substantial portion of this letter is printed in the D. Stephen Long, appendix to *Tragedy, Tradition, and Transformism*, 205.

63. Paul Ramsey, *Deeds and Rules in Christian Ethics*, 44.

64. Paul Ramsey, summary to "The Nature of Man."

65. Ramsey concludes that "idealistic treatment of the judgment of God is rendered inadequate because in the background is an identification of the self judged with the Self that gives the judgment." "The Nature of Man," 296. See also Paul Ramsey, *Basic Christian Ethics* (Louisville, Ky.: Westminster/John Knox Press, 1993), 303. This conclusion was related to a point that Ramsey had recorded in his notes from Hendel's course, The Philosophy of History. "Augustine: history is *not* simply a *human* subject; there is indeed no subject that concerns man alone. Human history alone is unintelligible: problems vanish as soon as we find the real frame of reference—the *divine plan*. There is a teleological order in which every event must be explained in terms of the *end* and *direction* and movement of the whole . . . 19th c.: Hegel even follows this same general view, with the exception that for Augustine the *end* was transcendent, for Hegel immanent in the historical development itself." See Box 43, The Paul Ramsey Papers, Duke University Library.

66. Ramsey, "The Nature of Man," 323. Ramsey concludes that this applies to "attachment even to the Christian community."

67. "The Idealistic View of Moral Evil," 584. This article is a revision of a chapter from Ramsey's dissertation. The article is specifically tailored to fit with the problem of evil and responsibility in idealism, but in his dissertation Ramsey deploys parallel suggestions for dealing with each of the problems idealism faces with regard to the identity of self and Absolute. Interestingly, Ramsey hints later on that he has not abandoned an ideological anthropology. In 1962 while relating Alexander Miller's materialistic understanding of Christianity, Ramsey notes that it is a hard position for him to relate "for it

happens that I hold another philosophical view of human nature." See *Nine Modern Moralists*, 61.

68. The problems of twentieth century Communism might be described by the pragmatist as an outcome of the success of a reductive epistemic and moral position leading to authoritarianism. The idealist, on the other hand, may describe these problems as the upshot of a movement that rejects the given diversity of social moral structures in favor of the realization of the extrinsic goal of "absolute freedom." For the pragmatic argument, see Cornel West, *The Ethical Dimensions of Marxist Thought* (New York: Monthly Review Press, 1991). For the idealistic argument see Charles Taylor, *Hegel and Modern Society*, 100-125.

69. On Niebuhr's moral realism, see Lovin, *Reinhold Niebuhr and Christian Realism*, 11-18; 72-118.

Chapter 2
From Pragmatism to Relevant, Impossible Love

There is a great deal of development in Niebuhr's thought in the years between his graduate work and the eventual elaboration of his mature theology. In this time he was influenced by Marxism, Liberal Protestantism and pacifism, and Barthian neo-orthodoxy. It is striking, however, the extent to which Niebuhr's mature theology on the far side of these influences reflects the concerns that he had encountered when studying James and the pragmatists. The pragmatists had attempted to construct a system that protected against either paternalistic or sectarian fanaticism, and thus underwrote a genuinely public search for the good. No one ideology could claim ownership of the good, and all were enjoined to participate responsibly in the public search for the good. Niebuhr, in time would produce a system that functions similarly. Like James', Niebuhr's mature position serves to draw inhabitants of differing reductive ideological standpoints out from ghettoized existence to participate in a humble, critical and responsible search for the common good. But Niebuhr's system would not be a secular philosophy, it would approach the problems pragmatism had recognized in a distinctively theological context.

Niebuhr's early encounter and continuing interaction with pragmatism has been treated in previous scholarship more thoroughly than Ramsey's interaction with idealism.[1] Some studies, following the Barthian rhetoric that Niebuhr himself deployed against idealism, have gone so far as to suggest that Niebuhr was simply a pragmatic philosopher in theologians clothing.[2] I shall not retread the territory of previous studies by focusing on stages of development as I will when treating Ramsey's evolution. Rather, in this chapter I will focus upon the way in which the shape of Niebuhr's mature theology served as a functional parallel for pragmatic philosophy in combating fanaticism. In the process, I will highlight the thoroughness of the theological grounding of Niebuhr's work, especially in the light of his early encounter with the work of Karl Barth.

The theology of his day was, Niebuhr found, ripe for anti-fanatic criticism. The social gospel movement, represented in the works of Walter Rauschenbusch, was grounded in the belief that involvement in patterns of generally pacifistic social activism offered an opportunity for the reestablishment of, and participation in, the Kingdom of God on earth. In the model of paternalistic fanaticism, this movement identified its own project with participation in the revealed project of God in Christ. Seeking to become like Christ, the members of the social gospel movement attempted to recast the world into the Kingdom of God, and thus overstepped in claiming ownership of the good. This school was partially corrected by Barthian neo-orthodoxy which stressed the uniqueness of God's act in Christ, and provided Niebuhr with the seminal idea of the impossible possibility of Christ's action in the world. But Niebuhr eventually found that Barth betrayed his deepest insights by embracing another form of fanaticism in which the believer was tempted to identify her or his community with God beyond history. Thus the believer was prone to deny the significance of the search for the historical good, and identify her or his critical stance as standing outside responsibility for the vicissitudes of history.[3]

Neither position, from the perspective of Niebuhr's mature theology, represents a viable statement of the substance of Christian faith. Both bear the marks of theological and moral fanaticism wherein the good of society and the identity of Christians within the society are reductively conceived. But pragmatism itself, as a secular philosophy, offered no answers to these forms of fanaticism. Drawing upon the most profound elements of Barthian and Liberal theologies, Niebuhr reconstructed a balanced Augustinian conception of the limitations and possibilities available in history between the incarnation and the eschaton. This recovery checked both the immanent fanaticism of the social gospel Christology and the otherworldly fanaticism of Barthian Christology. In Niebuhr's mature theology, God in Christ saves the world through an act in which the transcendent and perfect God empties God's self into the limitations and imperfections of sin-stained history. God's revelation in this act was both impossible to apply directly to history, thus countering social gospel fanaticism, and relevant to every historical decision, thus countering Barthian fanaticism. In the end, Niebuhr concluded, a proper understanding of God's act in Christ was the antidote to both paternalistic and sectarian forms of fanaticism. It is this divine act which finally stands over against every claim to ownership of the perfect good. It is this same divine act that delegitimates every effort to wall oneself or one's community off from the public search for the relative good available in history.

The upshot of this reconstructed Augustinianism is a scheme for Christian moral thought that can be profitably compared and contrasted with Ramsey's own. In Niebuhr's thought the divine love revealed by and in Christ is not conceived as the grounding for a system of actual duties within history. It is conceived as the distinctive act of God in Christ, offering ultimate redemption, but not immediate perfection of persons and acts within history. As such, love is not a simple possibility within history. Perfect love is a relevant impossibility. It is the ground for the humble, critical and responsible moments of historical morality, but is simply applicable to no particular historical decision. Pragmatism's virtues were thus recast in a Christian moral theology.

For those who are not Niebuhr scholars, it is worthwhile to note what is novel in the reading of Niebuhr's theology presented here. First is the centrality of Barthian insights in Niebuhr's mature theology. Niebuhr himself publicly parted from Barth's theology later in his own career, and obscured the extent to which several of his own foundational theological ideas were indebted to Barth. This chapter emphasizes two of these foundations: (1) The originally Barthian conception of the impossible possibility of Christ, and (2) the Barthian claim that all Christian anthropology must be grounded in an account of Christ's nature and activity. Both, I find, were ideas that Niebuhr never left behind. Second, the account of love that I develop here diverges from well known alternatives. There is a tradition of interpretation (including Ramsey's own) that reads Niebuhr's account of love as focusing too exclusively on self-sacrifice to the detriment of other-orientation.[4] I provide a reading on which other-orientation (indeed the radical requirement of other-fulfillment) is central to Niebuhr's conception of love. This leads to a third novelty in this treatment. If one finds that self-sacrifice (a dispositional quality) is definitive of love, it follows that if love is impossible, it will be subjectively impossible. This is to say that the problem of loving will be purely a failure of motivation and will. When the requirement of other-fulfillment is given equal billing, it becomes clearer why Niebuhr's account of the impossibility of love has both objective and subjective dimensions. The relation between these two facets of impossibility is key to grasping Niebuhr's treatment of war, where both the objective and the subjective facets are clearly in play. All historical action is marked by both objective and subjective limitations which prohibit perfection. The fact of pervasive and necessary imperfection of human action within history leads to the final novelty of this treatment of Niebuhr. If Christology is, as I argue here, a central element in Niebuhr's theology, how can Niebuhr make sense of the perfection of Christ if Christ was a person in history? Here, I find that Niebuhr was a more subtle theologian than many have given him credit for. In Niebuhr's writing, one can find a distinction between the historical and trans-historical dimensions of Christ which points toward a solution to the conundrum of necessary objective historical imperfection. All of this theological content underwrites Niebuhr's project to show that Christian theology has within itself the resources to combat the moral phenomena that the pragmatists found so troubling, and it was in developing and deploying such a scheme that Niebuhr moved from a young student of philosophy to one of the most significant moral theologians of the twentieth century.

I will begin the chapter by touching upon the vein of Augustinian thought that was one of the primary sources in Niebuhr's work in framing a Christian reaction to moral fanaticism. Following this short excursus, I will continue on into Niebuhr's work in recovering this Augustinian tradition by exploring the development of Niebuhr's Christology and his correlated conception of the ultimate norm of love in relation to his reading of Barth and Rauschenbusch. With this background, I will then undertake an explication of the function of Niebuhr's conception of perfect love in combating moral fanaticism. By thus laying out the core of Niebuhr's theology, it will be possible to see how Niebuhr understood the Christian tradition to provide an adequate response to the moral dangers pragmatism had highlighted in the contemporary world.

The Augustinian Tradition

Considered descriptively, Christian tradition has an ambiguous history regarding moral fanaticism. Figures as integral to the tradition as Eusebius of Caesarea and Bernard of Clairvaux gave religious sanction to morally fanatic proposals which identified God's ultimate plan with the religio-political projects of the Constantinian Empire and Western Christendom respectively.[5] In the sixteenth century, Anabaptist movements would spawn both militant and sectarian pacifist churches that sought, by force or by withdrawal from society, to participate in the Kingdom of God.[6] Even the Christian scriptures are not free from tales which reveal morally fanatic trends.[7] Yet, there is within Christian tradition also to be found a vein of thought opposed to moral fanaticism; a vein grounded in some of the original symbols of the faith. One of the most eloquent expressions of this tradition is to be found in the works of St. Augustine.

Caught up in a Eusebian brand of moral fanaticism in his middle age, Augustine rejected this tradition in later life. In his mature writings Augustine challenges both the paternalistic forms of moral fanaticism, and those rebellious varieties of moral fanaticism which reject participation in the common good in favor of sectarian or ascetic withdrawal from society.[8] His response to each is found in a theological characterization of the possibilities and limitations of history.

Where Eusebius had seen the Roman Empire as the bearer of a new Christian age within history, Augustine rejects such a claim as theologically flawed. Human acts within history ought not to be confused with God's saving acts, especially as represented by the definitive act of God in Christ. Sacred history could know of no new age between the coming of Christ and God's final historical act in bringing the eschaton. All of the creation has been skewed by sin and depends upon the grace of God's act in Christ for ultimate salvation. In the *saeculum*, the interim between the incarnation of Christ and Christ's return, human society knows of no true justice, or peace. The work of creation and redemption necessary for the establishment of such perfection is properly left to God.

Nor did Augustine stop his criticism of reductive perfectionism at the level of the society. Even the peace of the soul is caught up in the imperfection of the age before the eschaton. This peace is subjectively stymied inasmuch as the self is never, in history, entirely victorious over its own vicious tendencies.[9] But even if one were able to attain subjective rectitude in history peace would still elude her or him. By sin, history has been skewed such that the human is subject to pains and unnatural contortions of the self, even in the midst of well intentioned actions. Augustine thus derides those philosophers who "have wished with amazing folly, to be happy here on earth and to achieve bliss by their own efforts." The tragedies of history and the "exigencies of human society" make human flourishing within history impossible.[10] No human life in history proceeds without the loss of some genuine human good. The sacrifices of these goods are always, for Augustine, perceived as a punitive reminder of the sin which each person bears. The participant in history, if wise, "cries out to God, 'Deliver me from my necessities.'"[11]

The brokenness of history is not, however, an excuse for withdrawal from responsibility for those goods realizable within history. Recognizing that one is stymied in the search for perfection does not necessitate an abandonment of all approximations thereof. Though perfect peace exists only in the eschatological kingdom, the wish for peace continues to draw individuals and societies within history to establish the relative peace of Babylon which sustains the world within history. Thus, there are possibilities for relative justice and relative peace within history that are worthy of and indeed demand the contributions of the Christian believer. One ought not shirk the duties incumbent upon her or him to seek the relative good of the society and defend the flawed justice available in the period before the eschaton. Rather, the Christian, with proper disposition in service to the greater good, accepts even those distasteful duties to society in which some human goods are necessarily sacrificed, and works to improve the relative justice approximated within the society.[12]

Thus, for Augustine, human sin renders impossible any culmination of human *telos* within history. Only the act of God's grace in Christ is sufficient to bring about the possibility of culmination, and this culmination lies beyond the *saeculum*. Yet, for the relative betterment of the "peace of Babylon" the Christian does seek to participate in and realize the common good available within the *saeculum*; raising the level of those overlapping goods which all in the society seek. It was this tradition which Niebuhr was to recover in his own elaboration of a Christian theology and ethics.

The Recovery of Christology

Augustine's theology piqued Niebuhr's interest as early as 1926, though Niebuhr would later recall that the substantial impact of Augustine's work came rather later in his own development.[13] Regardless, the impact is clear. Niebuhr's mature moral theology homes in upon the balance of historical limitation and historical responsibility reflected in Augustine's work. It was a balance Niebuhr found absent in other theologies of his own era.

Niebuhr, Barth, and Rauschenbusch

The early twentieth century was, in the United States, a time of heady optimism. Technological advances opened what seemed a world of infinite possibilities for social progress. But, this was also a time of social turmoil. Rapid movement of capital in society aggravated growing divisions between social classes. This unique mixture of optimism and unrest gave impetus to both militant and pacifistic utopian programs to recast society. In theology, the more generally pacifistic tendencies found expression in the social gospel movement, represented by Walter Rauschenbusch.

Theology in this period, Niebuhr would later write, had imbibed too much of the draft of modernity and Hegelianism, and thereby bought into the conception of salvation through human social progress. Augustinian doctrines of sin and Christology had been effaced and replaced with a scheme in which the "sin" of human ignorance and institutional corruption was gradually cured through God's immanent reform of social structures.[14] Rauschenbusch could speak of the importance of Christ in terms of Jesus' role as the imparter of a unique form of God consciousness passed on to early believers, and recovered by means of modern biblical criticism. Thanks to the advances of modern society, Rauschenbusch was convinced that the ultimate goal of Jesus, the establishment of a Kingdom of God on earth, was finally within reach.[15]

This position was not, for Niebuhr, without its insights. Much of Niebuhr's young theology reflected Liberal tendencies manifested in Rauschenbusch's work.[16] Even in Niebuhr's mature theology, he was able to recognize and credit Rauschenbusch with the "genuine achievement" of recovering the spirit in which the prophetic call to social righteousness rang from the Christian scriptures.[17] The God of the prophetic tradition called for genuine attention and reaction to public issues.

But, Niebuhr was eventually to reject this position on both theological and moral grounds. Theologically, the social gospel movement did not adequately express the uniqueness of God's act in Christ. "The cross of Christ," Niebuhr writes, "is a scandal in the field of ethics, and the social gospel obscured the pinnacle of the truth of the cross." In the social gospel movement, Christ's act of perfect love was cut down to a historically human act, one that could be replicated by others enlightened by Christ's own God consciousness.[18] This theological error led in practice to an unacceptable form of moral fanaticism. Without recognition of the uniqueness of Christ's act, the social gospel too easily sanctified its own social project and identified it with God's ultimate will in history. As Niebuhr writes, "when modern Christians sought to interpret [Christ] merely as man, as moral example . . . they succeeded only in reducing Christian faith to the general moral sentimentality of the age or even in aggravating that sentimentality."[19]

These criticisms of Liberal theology were not entirely novel. Niebuhr owed much of his perspective on the social gospel to another theologian of the era. Karl Barth's reputation preceded him in America, and American theologians were eager to read the upstart German theologian when his first books were translated into English in the late 1920s and early 30s. It was in this climate that Niebuhr himself first read Barth in 1928. The encounter with Barth was, by all accounts, earth shaking. Like Augustine after the sack of Rome, Barth rose to prominence in a society that, though previously identifying its cause with God's own,[20] had been soundly defeated in a brutal war. Like Augustine, Barth reacted to the crisis not with soothing words, but with a reminder of God's goodness and his own society's failure in light of that goodness.[21] Barth, as Niebuhr related at the time, was to be read as an "apostle of the absolute," reminding history of its severe limitations.

Central to Barth's recovery of Christian doctrine was his focus upon Christology. "Just what," Niebuhr asks after reading Barth, "is the significance of Christ and how does he become the center and basis of our religion? Simply that he resolves the conflict between God and man, between man's finitude and his infinite hopes."[22] It is Jesus, Niebuhr tells us, who reveals through his morality the inadequacy of history's highest morality. Christ incarnate is, in a phrase that Niebuhr will use many times in his later theology, the impossible possibility. He quotes here directly from Barth:

> God stands in contrast to man as the impossible in contrast to the possible, as death in contrast to life, as eternity in contrast to time. The solution to the riddle, the answer to the question, the satisfaction of our need is the absolutely new event whereby the impossible becomes of itself possible, death becomes life, eternity time and God man.[23]

The core of this Barthian Christology will become central in Niebuhr's own mature moral theology. The surest protection against paternalistic, theological fanaticism is to be found in the perfection of Christ. It is the sight of this perfection, Niebuhr suggests, which allows the Barthians to assume critical distance from every historical movement.[24] Neither the status quo nor any reform movement lives up to the ultimate revelation of God's action in Christ. No systematic account of the goods of history escapes the critical eye of one who has seen the goodness of the Cross with the eye of faith. Notably, what Niebuhr finds so attractive in Barth's position is a Christian parallel of what Louis Menand has located as the essence of pragmatism itself.[25] In reading Barth's theology, Niebuhr discovered that the transcendence of Christ opens a potential space between progressive and conservative versions of fanaticism.

Still, in many ways Niebuhr was disappointed by what he perceived to be Barth's development of this doctrine.[26] Niebuhr was concerned about what he perceived to be certain tendencies toward dualism in Barthian theology.[27] For Barth, the eternal and infinite God was often defined over against history and finitude. God was perfect goodness over against historical failure. God was perfect power over against finite impotence. This, Niebuhr believed, led to problematic tendencies in Barthianism. On the one hand, God's ultimate goodness was construed as standing over against history in such a way that the relative values and moral distinctions of history could be razed to the ground.[28] On the other hand, God's ultimate power was construed in a way that threatened to make all the moral efforts of finite humanity meaningless. As Niebuhr recalls, Barth once suggested that the first step in Christian ethics ought to be found in accepting, in the light of God's already present victory over history, that "the care of the church and the care of the world is not our care."[29]

Niebuhr feared that in Barthian Christology, Christ comes to stand over against the imperfections in which sinful finite history is enmeshed, but because Christ is conceived as a manifestation of a God who is absolutely Other, Christ does not enter fully enough into history to participate in and through this participation redeem these imperfections.[30] This was, to Niebuhr, an unacceptable formulation of Christology. The upshot, he believed, is an otherworldly moral fanaticism in which the believer abandons responsible participation in the search for the relative good within history.[31] Seeking to identify her or himself with the transcendent position of God outside of history, the believer feels free to "hurl irresponsible anathemas at both sides [of historical conflicts] from the religious security and sense of religious superiority of his own position."[32] Barth had, on Niebuhr's reading, corrected the excesses of the social gospel, but had erred in his own formulation of theology and morality in ways that demanded correction. The impossible possibility of Christ would have to be reconceived.

No matter how unqualified Niebuhr's occasional rejections of their positions, Barth and Rauschenbusch were Niebuhr's traveling companions. One had grasped the importance of historical values and the need for a prophetic vocation for the Christian within history, but failed to see that the ultimate perfection of history was properly left to the unique action of God revealed in Christ. The other had recovered the uniqueness of Christ's act, but had in the process obscured the relative goods that Christ had come to redeem. Neither offered an adequate solution to the problem of moral fanaticism. To solve this Christological and moral problem and restore the Augustinian balance of relativity and responsibility in the *saeculum* Niebuhr would have to redraw the terms of analysis. The love of God revealed in the unique act of Christ as God's only begotten son would have to be a relevant impossibility in history, revealing God's power through God's act of powerlessness, realizing God's perfection through participation in the frustrations of history. It is this perfect love, Niebuhr tells us, that is the ultimate norm of human nature even if no merely historical human can realize it.

Christ's Love as the Ultimate Norm for Human Existence

Humanity is, for Niebuhr, a normative term. To be human is to be a kind of creature, created by God with a particular essential nature.[33] This nature provides the ultimate measure, standard, or law of human existence. It defines a particular *telos* at which the human is properly aimed, a particular state of activity in which the human should ideally take part. Life in accord with this nature will be a life fulfilled, a life in which the *telos* of the person, the meaning and perfection of life, is actualized.

This suggests that Niebuhr's approach to morality is to be understood as falling within the tradition of natural law broadly construed. Such is certainly true. But it is important to qualify this statement inasmuch as Niebuhr was critical of most statements of natural law ethics. Humanity has, Niebuhr believes, in the course of its collective existence, come to articulate some enduring norms that properly guide human action.[34] But rationalist, naturalist, and traditionalist approaches to providing a comprehensive and determinate account of the content of the natural law have tended toward moral fanaticism; overstating their claims to certainty, and to providing inflexible accounts of definitive shape of social structures and appropriate human desires.[35] Repeatedly these approaches have claimed that the structures they propose are identical with the essential structures for humanity and human society. Again and again history has belied these claims when these purportedly eternal structures give way to new structures in processes that allow for new and more fulfilling possibilities in human life.

The problem with these natural law theories, Niebuhr posits, is to be found in their lack of appreciation for the full height and depth of human nature, and their ignorance concerning the true limitations of history. Natural law theories have the tendency of conceiving of history as self-sufficiently meaningful. They seek to articulate systems that allow for a realization of human essence in history. The problem is that history does not allow for such a realization. The human being is not simply to be identified with reason as reason exists in any particular culture in history, nor with given natural impulses. At the core of the human being is a spirit which yearns for something more than can be provided in history by either reason or natural impulses. The human as a spiritual being always has a sense of her or his true moral essence that transcends any system that can be produced or embodied in history. History is a realm of perpetual frustration and conflicting goods. Morality within history does not concern a full realization of one's nature through adherence to one system of order, it consists in an effort to find approximations of goodness available under the particular circumstances of history in which one finds her or himself.[36] Here Niebuhr's mature account overlaps with the pragmatism he had encountered in his early studies.

Niebuhr's claims on these points, however, are not drawn simply from experience, they are theologically grounded. The human urge to find a source of meaning beyond the bounds of limited history is, he believes, an experience that is close to universal. But, it is the revelation of God that makes this a substantial human experience. Without God's answer to the human need for something more, one could hardly formulate the question properly. "Christian faith affirms," Niebuhr tells us, "that the same Christ who discloses the sovereignty of God over history is also the perfect norm of human nature."[37] The essential nature and governing principle of human life is first revealed in Christ.

For Niebuhr, the teachings of Jesus and the activity of God manifest in Christ's actions, especially on the cross, reveal the ultimate law of human life as perfect love.[38] This law is first definitively revealed in the teachings of Jesus. Here God's loving action is exposed as an action which is oriented toward the fulfillment of every creature in need. It is the comprehensiveness of this orientation that is central to perfect love. God's love refuses to compromise in orienting itself toward the good of any one person or group at the expense of another on any grounds. Thus Jesus analogizes God's love using the natural phenomena of sunlight and rain.[39] As these natural resources fall indiscriminately on all in the world, so God's love does not discriminate in providing goods to particular persons in God's creation for any reason.

But, Jesus does not simply teach about this love. As Christ, Jesus actualizes this love. In Christ's act on the cross, God "reconciles the whole of the world to Godself," allowing for the ultimate salvation of every person.[40] Christ's act is not an act oriented preferentially toward the salvation of this or that person or community, but toward the provision of the ultimate good of salvation for every neighbor in need. This is the ultimate act of indiscriminate love, which defines, for Niebuhr, the true form of loving action. Undertaking preferential or prudential actions, which consist in selecting persons out for the reception of goods while leaving others in need, cannot be ultimately fulfilling for the human. Such acts cannot constitute acts of perfect love. As long as any neighbor suffers, the human cannot validly claim a realization of her or his own *telos*. Christ's death on the cross, his self giving, oriented toward the fulfillment of the need of every neighbor in need, Niebuhr tells us, is the "goodness" of Christ and the "symbol of the fulfillment of human selfhood."[41]

The Impossibility of Love

It does not take a great deal of observation to find that the law of love as conceived by Niebuhr is not only fragile, but is in actuality broken on the shoal of history.[42] Within history, Niebuhr contends, "the final possibilities of social virtue cannot be realized."[43] Like Augustine, Niebuhr conceives of history as a realm in which the frustration of human *telos* is a foregone conclusion. Such are the wages of sin. Also following Augustine, Niebuhr finds that human fulfillment is stymied both subjectively and objectively.

Subjectively, the person's telos is stymied by sin inasmuch as she or he finds her or himself unable to orient her or himself toward the good of the neighbor. Ever so subtly, and often self-deceptively, the self seeks escape from the fragility of its own situation and sinfully overreaches her or his own position as she or he grasps for self fulfillment. We shall have the opportunity to explore this doctrine in more depth in a later chapter. Here, it is only necessary to note that such sinful self-orientation is, in a famous Niebuhrian paradox, inevitable but not necessary.[44] To state this more positively, one might say that Niebuhr holds that sin is universally pervasive even while each person is her or himself responsible for his or her own failure to orient the self properly. No human, save Jesus alone, is able to traverse historical existence without a falling to the inevitability of a sinful will, and every person chooses this sinfulness in her or his own freedom.[45]

The role of historical existence in objectively frustrating human fulfillment is, perhaps, more straightforward. The subjective failure of humanity leads to a modification of the context in which humanity finds itself. The particular sins of the self contribute to the corruption of historical institutions, the emergence of particular sins in one's neighbors,[46] and the need for a system of imperfect, only relatively just order to protect history from the corrosion of sin itself. Due to the contributions of sin, conflicts arise in historical order in which there is no option allowing for the self to orient her or himself toward the good of all involved. Humanity's sinful actions set God's original providential plan askew, and require the implementation of a new order maintained within the boundaries of God's judgment.[47]

In history skewed by sin, the human is faced with a set of irresolvable dilemmas in the effort to realize her or his *telos*. In the attempt to actualize the self's orientation toward the need of the neighbor, it will be necessary to take part in the prudent calculation required to determine to which neighbor goods are due. It is not love, by Niebuhr's Christocentric definition, to choose sides in a conflict. But to fail to choose sides also breaks the bonds of love. For "as soon as life and interest of others than the agent are involved in an action or policy, the sacrifice of those interests ceases to be 'self-sacrifice.' It may become an unjust betrayal of their interests."[48] At every turn the human, trapped in a world skewed by her or his sin, finds that the flourishing life of original justice is gone. As Niebuhr writes, the *finis* of human life within history always comes before the realization of human *telos*, and thus "frustrates the possibility of achieving *telos*."[49] All life in history, as a consequence of sin, suffers the fate of ending short of achieving its own fulfillment and goodness. History is a realm of only imperfect persons and projects and complete goodness within history is an impossibility. The human, having abandoned faithful life, is driven into a wilderness maintained by God's judgment. Such, for Niebuhr, is the message of the Prophets, and such is the judgment of the cross. The pragmatic view of a moral world filled with a plurality of real, conflicting goods thus finds a theological parallel within an account of sin-stained history.

The Cross as a Sign of Defeat and Salvation

An answer to the fanaticisms of Rauschenbusch and Barth is to be found in the account of divine *kenosis* and suffering involved in God's actual participation within this frustrated and sinful history. In Christ, God's perfection accepts the pain of historical imperfection, and by this act takes up history and perfects it. Such is Niebuhr's mature conception of Barth's impossible possibility.

According to Niebuhr, those who see the cross as a symbol of historical success,

> do not understand that the perfect love of Christ comes into the world, but that it does not maintain itself there; that the cross therefore stands at the edge of history and not squarely in history; that it reveals what history ought to be but not what history is or can be; and that Christian faith has quite rightly seen in this cross a revelation of the nature of the

> divine and eternal as well as of the ultimate historical possibility and impossibility.[50]

God, in God's definitively loving act, empties Godself into the form of a man within the boundaries of history. Entering into a world set ajar by the sins of others, God accepts the suffering of sin-stained historical existence. "He involves Himself in the guilt and suffering of free men who have, in their freedom, come in conflict with the structural character of reality."[51] Here, Christ cannot reach his own perfection. He cannot enact the virtue of love perfectly in history.[52] Jesus dies in the effort to fulfill all human need, and even the perfection of this act is frustrated by the limitations of sin-stained history. There remains a deluge of human need. Such is the depth of the suffering Jesus accepts that it reaches even to the frustration of his own historical *telos*. "He was," Niebuhr writes, "'true man.' He walked on earth, subject to the necessities of human life, *and did not escape either death or the tragedy of martyrdom*."[53] According to Christian tradition, God does not annul the suffering associated with this frustration, God accepts its pain. Christ's sacrifice on a cross at the hands of the Roman Empire is thus the ultimate sign of the frustration of love within history. Within history, not even a perfect inner desire overcomes the limitations brought about by sin. On the cross, Jesus' life is rent asunder as is the perfect love that he symbolizes. "It is God," Niebuhr writes, "Who suffers for man's iniquity. . . . the contradictions of history are not resolved in history."[54]

Were Jesus simply human, the crucifixion would have been but the disappointing end of a massive tragedy. Yet, it is the good news of the story that this is not the last word. The character of pure love *is* found in Jesus' life and exemplified in the act on the cross as this act is understood in relation to its relevance for salvation beyond history. Christ's death on the cross exemplifies the fulfillment of selfhood because in Christ's sacrifice God is *trans-historically* reconciling the world to Godself.[55] This is only possible because of the multiple dimensions present in Christ's act. In its historical dimension alone, love is frustrated. But, Christ's act when viewed in both its historical and trans-historical dimensions can be seen to actualize the virtue of love by acting as the means by which God provides for the ultimate redemption and fulfillment of the whole of the creation. In God's act of *kenosis*, God's perfection is manifested in God's ability to empty Godself even into the imperfect world of sin, taking onto Godself this imperfection and, without annulling it, providing for its ultimate perfection. God in this act trans-historically actualizes the *telos* of creation through a participation in the historical frustration of this *telos*.

Considered solely within the bounds of history, Jesus remains an example of perfect love defeated, a flare which must burn out in history. But, the "drama of Christ's life was seen by faith to be more than a drama in history, and therefore Jesus was more than a revered historical martyr."[56] Faith which sees beyond history is able to discern Jesus as the transcendent and perfectly loving Christ, the act of God who empties Godself so as to take on the suffering of imperfection while enacting ultimate perfection.[57] God's act in Christ is the impossible possibility.

The Relativized Meaningfulness of History

According to this Christology, God and God's ultimate action *is* to be contrasted with every historical action, institution, and social movement. All of these human endeavors suffer the wages of the sins in which they themselves participate, and as such no historically realizable cause should be identified with God's ultimate will for the creation. Thus theological, paternalistic fanaticism is rejected. Those who claim to participate in God's victorious and undistorted reign over history fail to appreciate the actuality of the sinful brokenness of history and as such deny the height of God's goodness as embodied in the suffering endured in God's historical action in Christ. They stand with Peter, whose messianic expectations led him to anticipate historical victory rather than crucifixion.[58] Those who claim the ability to participate in God's ongoing saving acts or institutions within history commit idolatry and question the sufficiency of God's action in Christ.[59] Only God's action in Christ, by virtue of its divinely unique historical/trans-historical character, is able to participate in perfection, and this act alone is sufficient to redeem history in the eschaton.

> To assert that the Jesus of history is the Christ, and that 'God was in Christ reconciling the world unto Himself,' is an affirmation of faith which insists that the variance between man and God cannot be finally overcome by the virtue of man. All human virtue remains ambiguous to the end. It can be overcome only by a 'suffering' God who takes the sins of the world upon Himself.[60]

But, unlike Barth's early Christology, which Niebuhr reads as maintaining too great a distance between Christ and history, Niebuhr's Christology does not abandon the relative goods of history as insignificant. God's act in Christ entered into history and took upon God the suffering associated with historical imperfection while perfecting the partially realized potentiality of Christ's historical act. God did not annul the imperfection of the historical act, nor was the quality of the historical act irrelevant to God's use of the act. Thus, God reveals that, rather than rejecting imperfect historical goods, the divine plan for salvation includes the redemption of these goods.

> Sin and death are . . . threats to the meaning of our existence. But they do not cancel out the fragmentary meaning of our existence, the provisional joys and the incomplete realizations in life. The Christian hope is, in other words, not something which adds another meaning to life above the meaninglessness of our existence. It springs from a faith in Christ Who has triumphed over sin and death and Who cleanses and completes our life.[61]

Jesus is God come *into history* so as to redeem history rather than reject it for a new non-historical mystical creation. No other human act can achieve the height of God's act. But the recognition of such should not lead any human to the futile effort to protect her or his "purity" by abandoning the partial realizations of virtue and the good available within the imperfection of history. It is this imperfection that God is willing to suffer in Christ and these partial realizations that God ultimately perfects through Christ's action. The Christian life is one in which the self should, with humility before God, feel responsible for enacting the greatest heights of moral action and order possible within the imperfection of history.

Criticalness, Responsibility, and Humility

Since the natural law of humanity in its freedom is the ultimate norm of human existence, and since this law is identical with the perfect love revealed in Christ, Niebuhr's view of Christ as the impossible possibility is at the heart of Niebuhr's moral theology.[62] Here the virtues found in pragmatism are recast on Christian theological grounds. Requirements for criticism of every historic action and institution, humility in recognition of one's finitude, sin, and the ultimate gift given by God, and responsibility which requires the preservation of those goods available within the relativities of sinful history all follow from Niebuhr's analysis of the action of God in Christ. Like Augustine before him, Niebuhr makes strong claims concerning the limitations brought by sin and the indelible imperfection of the self and the society within history. Also like Augustine, Niebuhr links these with a stress upon the uniqueness of the saving act of Christ which both enters into and stands over against historical imperfection. This allows Niebuhr to produce an account of the *saeculum* between Christ's act and the eschaton wherein the projects undertaken and goods achieved and defended by humanity are meaningful, but not ultimate. No project within history bears the significance or security of divine action, and no historical struggle ought to be treated as tantamount to the ultimate struggle between good and evil. But neither are the relative goods of history reduced to insignificance. Thus Niebuhr's distinctive recovery of the Augustinian tradition reveals that Christianity includes within itself the resources to combat moral fanaticism.

In elaborating the ethical implications of this position so that they might be profitably contrasted with Ramsey's project, it is most important to note how the language of love functions in this moral theology. The concept of divine love revealed by and in Christ is not the first principle in a system of actual duties within history. The ideal of love is a relevant impossibility. It is the ground for the humble, critical and responsible moments of historical morality, but simply applicable to no particular historical decision.

Christ's Love and Conviction of Sin

The relevance of love is first found in its impossibility. As a measure beyond possible realization within history, love stands as a "principle of indiscriminate criticism," over against all standards and institutions within the sinful world.[63] The first movement in Christian ethics is always, for Niebuhr, a movement of criticism—locating the whole of the creation in the context of God's judgment and God's offer of salvation. Thus love as an indiscriminate measure functions to convict those within history of sin.

Jesus' loving act provides humanity with an inchoate glimpse of the kingdom of heaven as a "community of brotherly love." This community consists in a community of persons enacting the virtue of love. In such a community freedom, equality, and justice exist in uncompromised forms, inseparable from love itself. In such a community the needs of one's neighbors do not conflict and these needs can be and are, in accordance with God's ultimate providential plan, fulfilled by the many finite contributions of each of its inhabitants who act out of their faith in God's plan.

The original justice embodied by such a community is not possible within history, and the fact of its absence stands as a reminder of God's judgment in history, convicting historical humanity of its own sins and its own sinfulness. The Christian God is a God of love and justice; the order of judgment God has established in history does not come without meaning. The tragedies of this history serve to chasten the creation in its pride and to remind it of its proper place before God.

In practical terms, this measure of love has three primary effects. First, it serves as a hermeneutical guide for reading the story of history. No reading is adequate that exempts the self from sin. God is just and the human tragedies of history do not come without warrant. The injustice humanity faces in history is partially the consequence of its own injustice. Second, the indiscriminate measure of love reminds the Christian to be humble due to her or his continuing sinfulness. Being chastened for past sins is no guarantee of current righteousness, and knowing of her or his sinfulness she or he will maintain an openness to the criticism and contributions of others that may point out continuing waywardness.[64] Finally, the indiscriminate measure of love reminds of the idolatry and ultimate futility of perfectionist projects within history. The order of God's judgment is established because of the sinful overreaching of humanity. The frustrations one faces in every effort to realize her or his own telos stand as constant reminders that the power to achieve or participate in perfection comes only through God and God's act in Christ, and is not available to any historical project, be it conservative or progressive.

The Responsibility of Love

Love functioning as an indiscriminate form of criticism, as we have seen, does not lead Niebuhr to collapse moral distinctions within history.[65] Though it convicts one of past sins, alerts one to continuing sinfulness, and reminds one of the imperfection of all historical human efforts, it does not render all possibilities within history as intrinsically immoral. Indeed, central to Niebuhr's Christology is the idea that God works through history so as to maintain the meaningfulness of the partial virtues and goods that can be maintained there. Like Augustine's perfect peace, Niebuhr's perfect love is nowhere present within history, yet history cannot exist entirely apart from it.[66] As such, the imperfection of one's project and the sinful tendencies of the self and the self's society provide no excuse for withdrawing from responsibility for the realization of that approximation of love available before the eschaton. The limited self-transcendence of humanity in general and the view of Christ available to the Christian in particular facilitate the rise of the self in its freedom above its current state and enable the self to work to recreate itself, its actions, and its society in light of God's action.

Nor is the Christian left without a morally substantive ideal, even if this ideal must remain transcendent from any simple application. In the inchoate vision of the community of brotherly love and in the perfect actions of Christ as seen from the perspective of faith, one gains knowledge about what history is called to be. This knowledge is relevant to every historical decision. At times, Niebuhr speaks of love's function as a "principle of discriminate criticism."[67] This cannot indicate a source which provides for the direct application of love to the world. Such is impossible. But love does require a comparative analysis of the available alternatives within history in light of the transcendent ideal.[68] Drawing on the insights provided by the Christian narrative and the facts one perceives in the world, the Christian must seek out the best approximation of the transcendent ideal in terms of action, and enact that approximation.[69]

There is great room for disagreement in judgments about these approximations because God has not revealed the measure of an approximation of love, and beginning from one's particular reading of the Christian narrative does not provide final security in perceiving the facts of historical morality or the facts of the world. Persons will disagree on the extent to which one society with relatively more freedom and another with relatively greater equality approximate the kingdom. Even regulative principles such as freedom and equality are themselves proximate measures which have been constructed in the process of measuring the good within history. They spring not from revelation, but from the messy process of discernment as undertaken within human society through history.[70] In some cases there will be broad agreement as to the measures and the conclusions of these relative judgments, and thus justified belief in their adequacy. But each remains, especially in its application, open to criticism.

Conclusion

Niebuhr in his mature theology recovers a strain of the Christian tradition that contains within itself the means for combating moral fanaticism. By recovering an Augustinian emphasis on the distinctive activity of Christ in history, Niebuhr produces a doctrine of the *saeculum* wherein historically bound projects and goods are both meaningful and necessarily imperfect. Niebuhr has produced a distinctively Christian account of the humility, responsibility, and criticalness that enable a profitable search for the relative common good. James had argued that each person's perspective contained "special revelations" that made her or his contributions to public discussion valuable. Niebuhr finds that the revelation of Christ's perfect love is *relevant* in that that it allows the Christian a transcendent critical ground from which to contribute to the historical search for the good. James had claimed that "neither the whole of truth nor the whole of good is revealed to any single observer."[71] Niebuhr reminds the Christian that it is the perfection of the love that is revealed that makes it *impossible* to apply it directly within history. In the midst of a broken aeon, the Christian too must participate in the search for truth and goodness in the midst of messy practice. Like James, Niebuhr has provided for responsible participation in a public space between the comprehensive accounts of historical morality fostered by various institutions and schools of thought. Unlike James, Niebuhr has drawn this account from within the Christian tradition, and grounded it on no less firm a foundation than Christology.

God in Christ is the author and only possible guarantor of perfection, and such perfection exists only beyond history. It is delusional to pretend that any merely human project within history is sufficiently powerful, knowledgeable, or virtuous to participate directly in God's activity or that any human group could attain such purity as to justify withdrawal from the tragedy of common life in the world. It is impudent to claim ownership of that action which belongs to God. It is God's perfect act in history that reveals humanity's own imperfections and permanently humbles the one who beholds it.

In the end, it is the Christian's identity as Christian, falling under the demands and judgment of God, that provides for the relative excellence of her or his heightened participation in the common discourse of the society. This identity provides one with a sense of serious responsibility to the common good available in history, but it also serves to restrain morally fanatic tendencies that would lead one to uncritically embrace any particular social ideology. It is only as a Christian, with this religious reservation against every historical dogma and ideology, that she or he participates in social dialogue as a humble and self-admittedly fallible advocate for the relative goods of democracy, communism, minority rights, majority rule, or any other historical measure she or he finds to be the best approximation of love at that point in history. In the interim between the incarnation and the eschaton, the Christian is the one ideally prepared to work with others in fear and trembling as they together seek to provide the relative goods necessary to the peace available in history.

Notes

1. See, for instance, Martin Halliwell, *The Constant Dialogue* (New York: Rowman and Littlefield, 2005), 29-78.

2. See Stanley Hauerwas, *With the Grain of the Universe: The Church's witness and natural theology* (Grand Rapids, Mich.: Brazos Press, 2001).

3. There are, in contemporary scholarship, widely differing interpretations of Barth and Barthian theology and social thought. See for instance George Hunsinger, *How to Read Karl Barth: The shape of his theology* (New York: Oxford University Press, 1993), and Stanley Hauerwas, *With the Grain of the Universe*, 141-241. Many of these interpretations seek to undercut the Niebuhrian, and more generally mid-century Anglo (as opposed to continental) interpretation of the Barthian position. I have no particular interest in defending the accuracy of Niebuhr's exegesis of Barth. I am interested in Niebuhr's theological development. Regardless of the correctness of the conception of Barth he produces, it is this conception in relation to which he develops his own theological position. As such, my treatment of Barth here ought to be taken as a rehearsal of Niebuhr's reading rather than as an argument in favor of reading Barth in this way. The same caveat applies, mutatis mutandis, to the treatment of Rauschenbusch in this chapter.

4. See Ramsey, "Love and Law" in *Reinhold Niebuhr: His Religious, Social, and Political Thought*, ed. C.W. Kegley, and R.W. Bretall (New York: The Macmillan Company, 1956), 79-124. Ramsey is followed by others. See, for instance, Joseph Allen, *Love and Conflict: A Covenantal Model of Christian Ethics* (New York: University Press of America, 1995), 96.

5. On Eusebius, see R. A. Markus, *Saeculum: History and society in the theology of St. Augustine* (New York: Cambridge University Press, 1988), 49-50. On Bernard, see his

letter in Arthur F. Holms, ed., *War and Christian Ethics: Classic and contemporary readings on the morality of war* (Grand Rapids, Mich.: Baker Academic, 2005), 88-91.

6. See Lisa Sowle Cahill, *Love Your Enemies: Discipleship, pacifism, and just war theory* (Minneapolis, Fortress Press, 1994), 160-75.

7. See Michael Walzer, "The Idea of Holy War in Ancient Israel," *Journal of Religious Ethics*, 20 (Fall, 1992), 215-28.

8. Concerning his mature opposition to the aggressive form of moral fanaticism, see R. A. Markus, *Saeculum*. On his opposition to the charge that Christianity itself constitutes a sectarian version of moral fanaticism, see David Hollenbach's treatment of Augustine in *The Common Good and Christian Ethics* (New York: Cambridge University Press, 2002), 120-36.

9. Augustine, *Concerning the City of God Against the Pagans*, trans. Henry Bettenson (New York: Penguin Books, 1972), 893.

10. Augustine, *City of God*, 852-64.

11. Augustine, *City of God*, 861.

12. Augustine, *City of God*, 859-61, 881-84; 890-91.

13. See Charles C. Brown, *Niebuhr and His Age: Reinhold Niebuhr's prophetic role and legacy* (Harrisburg, Pa.: Trinity Press International, 2002), 32, and Reinhold Niebuhr, "Intellectual Autobiography," in *Reinhold Niebuhr: his religious, social, and political thought*, ed. C.W. Kegley and R.W. Bretall 9.

14. Reinhold Niebuhr, *Essays in Applied Christianity*, ed. D. B. Robertson (New York: Meridian Books, 1959), 124-25.

15. "For the first time in religious history we have the possibility of so directing religious energy by scientific knowledge that a comprehensive and continuous reconstruction of social life in the name of God is within the bounds of human possibility. . . . Christ is immanent in humanity and is slowly disciplining the nations and lifting them to share in his spirit. By great process of self-purification the alien infusions in Christianity have been eliminated, and Christianity itself is being converted to Christ." Walter Rauschenbusch, *Christianity and the Social Crisis* (New York: The Macmillan Company, 1916) 209-10.

16. See Reinhold Niebuhr, "Ten Years that Shook My World" *The Christian Century* 56, no. 17 (April 26, 1939), 542-46.

17. Reinhold Niebuhr, "Walter Rauschenbusch in Historical Perspective," in *Faith and Politics*, ed. Ronald Stone (New York: George Braziller, 1968), 38.

18. As Rauschenbusch writes, Christ's "aim and effort would be to make himself not unique, but to become 'the first born among many brethren.'" See Walter Rauschenbusch, *A Theology for the Social Gospel* (Louisville, Ky.: Westminster/John Knox Press, 1997), 265.

19. Reinhold Niebuhr, "Christ vs. Socrates," *The Saturday Review* 37, no. 51 (December 18, 1954), 38.

20. See Arlie Hoover, *The Gospel of Nationalism: German patriotic preaching from Napoleon to Versailles* (Stuttgart: F. Steiner Wiesbaden, 1986).

21. See Eberhard Busch, *Karl Barth: His life from letters and autobiographical texts*, trans. John Bowden (Grand Rapids, Mich.: William B. Eerdmans Publishing Co., 1976), 81.

22. Reinhold Niebuhr, *Essays in Applied Christianity*, 142.

23. Niebuhr, *Essays in Applied Christianity*, 142-43. See Karl Barth, *The Word of God and the Word of Man*, trans. Douglas Horton (Chicago: Pilgrim Press, 1928), 197.

24. Reinhold Niebuhr, *Essays in Applied Christianity*, 148.

25. Menand, *The Metaphysical Club*, xii.

26. Niebuhr also disagreed with Barth on several related issues. I do not wish to understate the significance of these other disagreements, but am focused narrowly here upon their intersecting Christologies.

27. Reinhold Niebuhr, *Essays in Applied Christianity*, 160, also 148; and Reinhold Niebuhr, "The Quality of Our Lives," in *The Christian Century* 77, no. 19 (May 11, 1960), 570. When Niebuhr writes of his distaste for "metaphysical" interpretations of Christology, he is in large part reacting to interpretations (like that which he claims to find in Barth's writings) that begin by stating the problem dualistically in terms of the possibility of relating the human/finite and the divine/infinite. See Reinhold Niebuhr, *The Nature and Destiny of Man* (New York: Charles Scribner's Sons, 1964), 2:70-74.

28. As Barth writes: "Before God everything is impure and therefore nothing is especially impure." *The Epistle to the Romans*, trans. E. C. Hoskyns (New York: Oxford University Press, 1933), 517.

29. Quoted in Reinhold Niebuhr, *Essays in Applied Christianity*, 169.

30. While it is not clear to what extent he was aware of it, Niebuhr has here fixed upon a set of issues that parallel a controversy between traditional Lutherans and the Calvinists. The Calvinists claimed *finitum non capax infinitum* (the finite cannot contain the infinite) while the Lutherans had claimed the opposite (*finitum capax infinitum*). The Lutheran view stressed the reality of God's saving *kenosis* in the incarnation while the Calvinists stressed the continuity of God's majesty in the incarnation. The subtlety of distinctions involved between the two positions have not prevented Lutherans from suggesting that the Calvinist position is Nestorian while Calvinists charge the Lutherans with Monophysitism. Dietrich Bonhoeffer too had recognized Barth's Calvinist tendencies in this debate and lodged a more subtle critique of Barth's Christology on grounds related to but different from Niebuhr's own. See Eberhard Bethge, "The Challenge of Dietrich Bonhoeffer's Life and Theology," in *World Come of Age*, ed. Ronald Gregor Smith (Philadelphia, Pa.: Fortress Press, 1967), 36.

31. As Niebuhr writes: "If only a God-man, who transcends the conditions of finiteness absolutely, can define and delineate the norm of human existence, the contrition which contemplation of such a norm may prompt is quickly transmuted into complacency." Niebuhr, *The Nature and Destiny of Man*, 2:74. Such is, Niebuhr concludes, one likely upshot of Barthianism. See *Essays in Applied Christianity*, 148, 149.

32. Niebuhr, "The Quality of Our Lives," 571.

33. See Niebuhr, *The Nature and Destiny of Man*, 1:270.

34. See Niebuhr, *Faith and History*, 189. See also Reinhold Niebuhr, *Essays in Applied Christianity*, 187.

35. See Niebuhr, *The Nature and Destiny of Man*, 1:26-53.

36. See Niebuhr, "Reply to Interpretation and Criticism," in *Reinhold Niebuhr: His Religious, Social, and Political Thought*, ed. C.W. Kegley, and R.W. Bretall (New York: The Macmillan Company, 1956), 435-36.

37. Niebuhr, *The Nature and Destiny of Man*, 2:68. See also Reinhold Niebuhr, *Love and Justice: selections from the shorter writings of Reinhold Niebuhr*, ed. D. B. Robertson (Philadelphia, Pa.: The Westminster Press, 1957), 282. Niebuhr could also speak of morality as following from the structure of human nature. See Niebuhr, *Faith and History*, 174. Ultimately, these two starting points are not separable. Proper human function is

always interpreted by Niebuhr in light of the revelation of God's action in and beyond history.

38. As we will see below this applies to the acts of Christ considered in their trans-historical dimension.

39. Reinhold Niebuhr, *An Interpretation of Christian Ethics* (New York: Meridian Books, 1956), 46. See Mt. 5:45.

40. See Niebuhr, *The Structure of Nations and Empires*, 136. This claim, drawn from 2 Corinthians 5:19, constitutes what Niebuhr refers to as the "essential kerygma" of scripture and the "central message of the gospel." Notably, Niebuhr seems to identify this kerygma with Barth's early Christology. See Reinhold Niebuhr, *Essays in Applied Christianity*, 126-27, 133, and 142.

41. Niebuhr, *The Structure of Nations and Empires*, 136.

42. Here I am using fragile in a technical sense. Martha Nussbaum explains how Aristotle participates in reclaiming the fragility of goodness in the wake of Plato's effort to hedge off goodness from the threats of luck. Plato tries in his moral philosophy to reduce the good life to a set of internal dispositions oriented toward the abstract good. The good life is thus untrammeled by attachment to particular goods in the world. Aristotle's *eudaimonia*, by contrast, is partially constituted by the realization of particular goods outside the control of the agent. *Eudaimonia* is vulnerable to external circumstance. Without appropriate wealth, the human could not exercise Aristotle's virtue of generosity, and thus could not participate in the practice of *eudaimonia*. One cannot participate in the virtuous relation of friendship when one's friend has been killed. Niebuhr's conception of love is fragile in similar ways. See *The Fragility of Goodness: Luck and Ethics in Greek tragedy and philosophy* (New York: Cambridge University Press, 2001).

43. Niebuhr, *The Structure of Nations and Empires*, 135.

44. Niebuhr, *The Nature and Destiny of Man*, 1:255-59; see also Niebuhr, *Faith and History*, 33. Ramsey provides a clarifying exegesis of Niebuhr's concept of inevitability in his own early work. He claims that Niebuhr intends to say that humans, while free, face the 'overwhelming probability' of sinning. See Ramsey, "The Nature of Man," 286; and "The Idealistic View of Moral Evil," 585. There is no necessity that a coin flipped a thousand times will ever land tails up, but there is an 'overwhelming probability' that it will do so. In an analogous (but much more complex way) there is no necessity that a human with freedom to do otherwise will sin, but there is an 'overwhelming probability' that she or he will do so, and thus merit her or his place within the order of history governed by God's judgment.

45. Niebuhr writes that in Christ, the "guiltless one would expiate the guilt of the guilty; and that would be the only way of ending the chain of evil in history." *Faith and History*, 142.

46. Reinhold Niebuhr, "Must We Do Nothing?" in *From Christ to the World: Introductory Readings in Christian Ethics*. ed. W. Boulton, T. Kennedy, and A. Verhey (Grand Rapids, Mich.: W.B. Eerdmans Publishing Company, 1994), 423.

47. Niebuhr writes about the order imposed by God's judgment in the context of the Second World War: "We cannot contemplate our political life decently without a proper and grateful understanding of the 'grace' of God. For the grace of God is on the one hand the providential working in history by which God makes the wrath of man to praise him, and transmutes good out of evil. In the immediate situation, that means that he persuades sinful men to consider the miseries and necessities of their fellow men by throwing them into like miseries and necessities." Reinhold Niebuhr, *Love and Justice*, 294-95.

48. Niebuhr, *The Nature and Destiny of Man*, 2:88.

49. Niebuhr, *The Nature and Destiny of Man*, 2:293.

50. Reinhold Niebuhr, *Love and Justice*, 276.

51. Niebuhr, *The Nature and Destiny of Man*, 2:71

52. Jesus considered within the boundaries of history appears as an ascetic martyr, and thus is subject to all the limitations of historical asceticism. See Niebuhr, *An Interpretation of Christian Ethics*, 168.

53. Niebuhr, "Christ vs. Socrates," 38. Italics mine.

54. Niebuhr, *The Nature and Destiny of Man*, 2:46

55. Niebuhr, *The Nature and Destiny of Man*, 2:71. "The significance of the affirmation that God is revealed in Christ, and more particularly in his Cross, is that the love (agape) of God is conceived in terms which make the involvement in history a consequence of precisely the divine transcendence over the structure of history." See also Niebuhr, "Christ: The Hope of the World," *The Messenger* 19, no. 15 (August 10, 1954), 9; Langdon Gilkey, *On Niebuhr: A theological study* (Chicago: University of Chicago Press, 2001), 183.

56. Niebuhr, "Christ vs. Socrates," 8. See also *The Nature and Destiny of Man*: 2:75.

57. Niebuhr writes that "the perfection of Christ can be discerned only 'by faith.' The effort to reduce that perfection to a simple historical fact, which can be measured in terms of historical norms and standards, is to reduce paradox to absurdity." *The Nature and Destiny of Man*, 2:75.

58. Mark 8:27-37. See Niebuhr, *Essays in Applied Christianity*, 170.

59. In one article, Niebuhr notes that there are acts within the relativity of history that are "excellent examples of the working of Christ's spirit in the affairs of man." But he adds that they "become absurd when it is implied that the triumph of Christ depends upon them." See *Essays in Applied Christianity*, 327.

60. Niebuhr, "Christ vs. Socrates," 37.

61. Reinhold Niebuhr, "Christ and the Meaning of our Existence," *Episcopal Churchnews*, 119, no. 24 (Nov. 28, 1954), 8. See also *The Nature and Destiny of Man*, 2:46; *The Structure of Nations and Empires*, 118.

62. Niebuhr writes that "To regard [Christ] as this key which resolves mystery into meaning is to look at the whole drama of human existence without either obscuring the tragic factors in man's persistent egotism or in seeking vain methods of eliminating that egotism by mystical techniques of self-annulment or dangerous political strategies of suppressing self-interest . . ." See Niebuhr, "Christ vs. Socrates," 38.

63. See Reinhold Niebuhr, *The Essential Reinhold Niebuhr*, ed. Robert McAfee Brown (New Haven, Conn.: Yale University Press, 1986), 113-116. Niebuhr is, even as he draws the distinction, insufficiently careful in distinguishing the functions of love as an indiscriminate principle and as a discriminate principle. At times he suggests that love as an indiscriminate principle functions to draw persons to enact greater possibilities within history. This confuses the discriminate role of love—which properly informs and motivates the Christian concerning possibilities within history—with the indiscriminate role of love—which properly convicts the Christian within history of sin and reminds of the impossibility of perfectionist projects. Niebuhr's tendency to confuse these functions leads him at times to confuse imperfection (which convicts one of sin) with sin itself. For example, Niebuhr writes in the above cited article that "it is not possible to eliminate the *sinful* element in the political expedients" available in history. This is, at best, infelicitously stated. He would have done better to write that it is not possible to eliminate the

imperfections in the political expedients available in history. The fact that God has permitted that we live in a world where such is the case points attention toward our past sin (see his comment here upon the "tyranny against which we contend") and current tendencies toward sinfulness (see his comments here on the nature of "all historic struggles") even as we seek the best possibilities in history.

64. "The church would do more for the cause of reconciliation if, instead of producing moral idealists who think that they can establish justice, it would create religious and Christian realists who know that justice will require that some men shall contend against them." Reinhold Niebuhr, *Love and Justice*, 43.

65. As Langdon Gilkey writes, Niebuhr's emphasis on the perfection of God's transcendent act in Christ "abrogates neither the divine logos and the judgment based upon it, nor the power of the divine being." *On Niebuhr*, 185.

66. There is a certain parallelism between Augustine's claim that creatures within history "cannot help loving peace of some kind or other. For no creature's perversion is so contrary to nature as to destroy the very last vestiges of its nature" (Augustine, *The City of God*, 869) and Niebuhr's claim that love *is* the law of life, and as such "it may have its tentative triumphs even in history; for human history cannot stand in complete contradiction to itself." (Niebuhr, *The Nature and Destiny of Man*, 2:49).

67. Niebuhr, *The Essential Reinhold Niebuhr*, 116-18.

68. We might imagine an analogy here with a situation in which two groups of three persons are each given the task of arranging themselves so as to create a perfect square. One group may arrange itself with one person lying on the floor while the two others take positions standing at the head and feet of the first, thus using (relatively) right angles and the lengths of their bodies to create the impression of a square while leaving one side of their representation empty. The other group may decide that having a closed geometric shape is more important than the presence of (relatively) right angles in approximating a square, and thus contort their bodies so as to produce a (relatively) closed, but more rounded figure. In this process the two groups may discuss the criteria they each employ in the process of approximating the square. Some regulative principles (such as "being a closed shape," and "having right angles") may present themselves as stable criteria for judging between competing approximations. The ideal square is relevant to judgments about the approximations. It always remains a critical principle and an ideal against which the approximations are judged. But, criteria cannot be simply deduced from contemplation of the square, nor can one simply apply the requirements of "being a square" to the situation. Criteria must arise from the practice of finding what approximations are possible.

69. On Niebuhr's relation to later narrative theology, see Robin Lovin, *Reinhold Niebuhr and Christian Realism*, 89-105.

70. Niebuhr, *The Nature and Destiny of Man*, 2:252; *The Essential Reinhold Niebuhr*, 143; "The Problem of a Protestant Social Ethic," *Union Seminary Quarterly Review* 15, no.1 (November, 1959), 7-11.

71. "On a Certain Blindness in Human Beings" in *Essays on Faith and Morals*, 284.

Chapter 3
From Idealism to Covenant Love

Ramsey emerged from his doctoral work in 1943 prepared to shore up the perception of the structure of moral reality against atomistic, relativistic errors. He scanned the landscape of contemporary moral theology and was disappointed by what he found. Some Barthian and existentialist theologians had taken up the freedom of God as a primary category in their ethics.[1] Moral duties, on their account, were created by God's will in the moment of action.[2] No general norms for human action were acceptable from this viewpoint. Human sin prevented such refined knowledge of the good. Thus, norms had to be cast off in favor of God's immanent demands. Ramsey, sensitized by idealism, perceived the defects in this position. It was grounded in the denial of any essential moral order. It rejected categories denoting right and wrong which were necessary to any public dialogue about morality, and thus raised the specter of voluntaristic chaos. This was, Ramsey writes, "theological intuitionism—intuitionism on stilts!"[3]

Ramsey's theological works can be read as a continual struggle against all forms of ethics that Ramsey suspects of beginning without appreciation for the essential moral structure of particular relationships and particular kinds of acts within these relationships. Ramsey's arguments in this struggle are eclectic, drawing upon any available resource in his efforts to maintain order in moral discernment and discussion. He was a brilliant bricoleur and a master of immanent criticism. He was unafraid to use John Rawls' concept of rules of practice, and William Frankena's concept of deontology for his own purposes. He was even willing, in his later writings, to take up the language of basic goods when arguing with Catholic theologians. This chapter shall focus upon Ramsey's recovery of the language of natural law and his work on relating the concepts of natural law to the demands of love in the Christian tradition. While there is, across Ramsey's career, a great deal of development in Ramsey's conceptual scheme, I shall argue that there is also quite a bit of consistency in Ramsey's basic orientation against atomistic moral relativism and in the shape of his own preferred ethics for maintaining moral order. In some ways, the evolution of Ramsey's thought can be read as the continual refinement of a set of ideas that he had developed in a rough form even in his dissertation. In my explication of the development of Ramsey's efforts to articulate these ideas, I will begin with a short treatment of those elements within the Christian natural law tradition on which Ramsey draws. After this, I will develop an account of three phases through which, in my judgment, Ramsey's approach to love and natural law develops: his earliest phase in which he sought to establish a relatively clean distinction between theology and natural law ethics, his ultimately untenable dialectical phase represented in *Basic Christian Ethics*, and his final efforts to provide a comprehensive Christian account of the insights he had previously recognized in idealistic ethics. I will suggest that it was his thought in this last period that allows him to make common cause with certain interpretations of Catholic natural law and a qualified Thomistic deontology. Throughout, I will argue, Ramsey's concern for order and security in moral discourse guides his approach to the concepts of love, natural law, and the relation between the two.

The Natural Law Tradition

In retrospect, Ramsey's recovery of natural law language within the Protestant tradition makes a great deal of sense. Ramsey had, during his graduate work, been introduced to the concept of natural law from the perspective of the idealistic tradition. Placing this tradition in dialogue with theology was a relatively easy step. Developed during a renaissance of neo-Platonism in Germany, the idealist tradition drew from both classical Greek and contemporary Lutheran influences. The natural law tradition, by coincidence, had also developed in relation to neo-Platonism in its earliest stages, and, in a truncated form, survived into the thought of the earliest Reformers. The Christian tradition, as this tradition had embraced and developed natural law, was bound to provide a wealth of resources in defending the concept of an essentially structured moral reality.

In much of contemporary discourse, the Christian natural law tradition is paradigmatically identified with the work of Thomas Aquinas. Aquinas begins with the axiom that the world is a harmonious order created by God. As participants in this creation, and ultimately in the right reason of God, humans have access to the principles of practical reason which guide habitual actions toward the true good. These principles are the content of the natural law. The first principle is self-evident: "good is to be done and promoted, and evil is to be avoided." This principle itself does not provide a great deal of content. Thus, it must be filled out with secondary principles which are accessible through inclinations embedded in human nature.

Within this teleological framework, Thomas' approach to determinations concerning the morality of particular actions is highly structured. The essential form or object of an act, denoted by its properly delimited description as a particular kind of act (e.g. this is an act of murder), may or may not be compatible with the structure of human nature. A lack of compatibility is sufficient to establish the immorality of any particular action.[4] Other aspects of the act, such as the relatively good or bad outcomes of the act, are only to be considered after the morality of the object of the act has been determined. A final positive conclusion regarding the moral acceptability of any particular act depends upon a positive conclusion regarding the moral quality of each aspect of the act.

This kind of careful act analysis and description would find a place in Ramsey's later writings, as would the broader picture of a generally harmonious moral order expressed in terms of primary and secondary principles. Despite a rather circuitous route, Ramsey does eventually find commonality with this most Catholic of saints. But, while Aquinas may be the primary referent in most accounts of Christian natural law, he was not Ramsey's first, or primary, source for his theologically grounded account of natural law theory. This distinction belongs to the apparently less likely Martin Luther.

Reacting to what he saw as Pelagianism in natural law thought, Luther stressed the distinction between law and gospel. These two, he taught, have different sources, contents, and functions.[5] As he writes, "you have heard that our works are good and not good, that they are justice and not justice. Both statements are true, but each in its own realm (*foro*). There are two different justices; the one is of the law, achieved by our own forces or works, while the other is imputed to us by God's mercy through faith."[6]

The law is, for Luther, a broad category which in various senses includes the codes of Mosaic law, natural law, civic law, and the patterns of order embodied in the vocational and institutional structures of society. In principle the proper content of the law is accessible, independent of revelation, to those with sufficient reasoning capabilities.[7] Indeed, Luther himself does not focus upon the content of this law inasmuch as he does not find it to be a proper topic for a person primarily concerned with the revealed grace of God. As one commentator notes,

> Luther regards the details of natural law, like the details of civil justice or of polity, as not within his proper competence as a theologian, and what he has to say about it is limited. He must as a theologian see that it remains within its proper realm, but it is finally up to reason and philosophy to determine its content.[8]

As the source of access to this law is carefully delimited, so is the content of the law. Reasoning associated with the natural law produces knowledge of what constitutes right outward action, but cannot provide, or provide an account of, right motives for action. The law is, within history, enforced upon the majority of the populace by those means of order imposed by God's providence for the purpose of restraining the chaos unleashed by the sinful tendencies of humanity.

For the religiously sensitive person, the law also serves a second function. In revealing the standard of righteousness to which humanity cannot motivate itself, the law functions to "reveal unto man his sin, his blindness, his misery, his impiety, ignorance, hatred and contempt of God, death, hell, the judgment and deserved wrath of God."[9] But in revealing this, the law poses a problem that the law cannot itself solve. It is only an act of revelation and grace from the Word of God, mediated through the gospel, that is able to impose righteousness upon the inward dispositions of the person, thus pointing the self toward its proper goal in love of neighbor and God.[10] This grace, however, does not challenge the law. The gospel may lead one to take actions beyond what the law requires, but it never contradicts the requirements of the law as this is applied in any person's public life.

Thus the law and the gospel are set apart in terms of source, content, and function. The natural law informs one of the right form of action while the work of God through the gospel informs one of, and acts upon one to evoke, proper motivation in action. These are truly separate. "The Christian, as Christian, knows no more about the law in its civil use than does the pagan. When the Holy Spirit reveals to him its spiritual use, this tells him nothing about the content of the law as such; it simply reveals what in modern language might be called the nature of the commitment demanded."[11] But law and grace are not simply to be contrasted with one another. Love, when assigned by God to rule one's will, moves one spontaneously to obey the dictates of the law in public life. The Christian and non-Christian both, in accord with the natural law, work to fulfill the demands of their public vocations. The Christian is unique in doing this for the right reason; out of love for her or his neighbor rather than fear of the consequences of failing the law.

It is this Lutheran conception of the natural law from which Ramsey begins his theological project. Drawing eventually upon both the Thomistic and Lutheran streams of natural law theory would provide a certain tension in Ramsey's moral theology. Throughout his career he would wrestle with the relation between interior and exterior conditions in determinations of morality. He would also, in drawing upon the natural law tradition, have to defend it against charges of conservatism and inflexibility, often couched in the language of the agapic transcendence of Christian moral norms. The concerns behind these charges, Ramsey would find, must be harmonized with a system which is able to articulate the stability of moral order, lest they function to erode the perception of the essential moral reality to which human practice properly aspires. In what follows, I will trace three phases of Ramsey's thought in dealing with these tensions.

The Space Between Theology and Ethics

Ramsey's earliest treatment of natural law is of a piece with his work in his dissertation. There, drawing on an immanent critique of idealism, he had argued that idealism provided the proper framework for thinking about moral actions, but suffered from an idolatrous identification of self, society, and the Absolute. Perhaps not coincidentally, this conclusion matched with the Lutheran strain in Ramsey's thought.[12] The idealistic framework for ethics could provide for a proper framework for determinations of right outward action, but was insufficient for providing an inward transformation of the orientation of the person. The Christian and the idealist may agree on service to the structured common good, but the Christian would serve this common good as a means of service to neighbor while the idealist would serve the common good as a means of service to the true self. As in Luther's picture, here Christian theology is seen as informing one's motivation, not the shape of one's outward action.

Ramsey was soon to find this a helpful formulation in combating the problem of Barthian intuitionism as well. If theological intuitionism constituted a threat to the perception of a structured moral reality, Ramsey hoped the removal of theology from a direct role in producing external moral norms might clear up the intuitionism. Thus, Ramsey undertakes in his earliest treatment of the natural law to clarify the role of theology in ethics. As Ramsey writes:

> Faith cannot add one iota of *content* to the moral law, save as faith renders more impartial and sensitive the employment of the reason; and any additional ethical knowledge secured thereby must be judged by the reasonable conscience alone. A Christian cannot appeal to special intuitions or revelations of the will of God which countermand the rational moral law.[13]

This position allows Ramsey to place great stress upon the natural law known by reason, which at this stage Ramsey identifies with the moral structure proposed by idealism. Theology functions to ease biased egoist passions that obscure one's efforts in the search for the moral structure of society. But this theological corrective does not challenge the basic ethical structure of society as pictured in idealism nor does it challenge the duties and rights that idealism proposes. Contra Kierkegaard and in agreement with Hegel, for Ramsey Abraham is not justified in defying social norms by killing his son, no matter what the voices in his head tell him to do. Thus, the structured order of ethics is protected from the chaos rampant in contemporary theology.

This solution is short lived as a comprehensive account of the relation between theology and natural law for Ramsey. Later formulations will attempt to stress the extent to which Christian love works through and transforms natural law, and Ramsey will eventually ground Christian moral duty in the example of God's own covenanting activity. In these formulations, Ramsey will rely upon theological symbols that serve to support, rather than to relativize the moral order. Still, Ramsey's early position sheds light on the framework of thought behind some of Ramsey's later arguments against the threat of what he took to be relativizing theology run amok in the field of ethics. This kind of "theology" may be useful in transforming the inner life, but it should not be confused with "ethics."

This continuing distinction between "theology and "ethics" in this latter sense can be seen in Ramsey's reaction, in the 1960s, to Paul Lehmann's claim that Christian action in a time of war is guided by the fact that it is "bracketed by the dynamics of God's political activity on the one hand and God's forgiveness on the other." In response Ramsey contests:

> All of this is theology and I will not presume to assess whether it is a good or sufficient statement of Christian theology. But it is not ethics, even if these are wholly valid perspectives and however much that may have *indirectly* to do with ethics. . . . It is rather a religious attitude appropriate to all our works, from which of course important consequences may flow for the moral life. To take in trust the risk of trust is relevant to all choices; it has therefore little or no light to shed upon any particular choice or upon the *problem* of *choice* itself. It does not tell us how to get on the track (or do the good), but only sustains our trust and hope that we are, or, if not, God is.[14]

The reality of moral distinctions within history is thus protected in this early phase, and at points in Ramsey's later thought, through a Ramseyan application of Luther's approach to natural law. The relativizing tendencies of theology are indirectly relevant inasmuch as they may transform the inner motives of the person, but this does not directly influence the determination of what constitutes right action.[15]

Basic Christian Ethics, An Untenable Dialectic

Basic Christian Ethics was, during Ramsey's own lifetime, his most popular work. This is ironic inasmuch as it represents a way station in the midst of a massive transition in Ramsey's thought. The book is full of Ramsey's explorations of fruitful tensions that in this work often come only to unsatisfactory resolutions. What is clear is that Ramsey's emphases have shifted from his earliest approach in relating natural law and theology. Between his earliest articles and his work in composing this book, Ramsey has recognized the power of Barthian demands for the distinctiveness and dominance of Christian theology in moral discernment,[16] and Niebuhrian calls for a more critical edge to Christian moral theology.[17] Any convincing account of moral theology, Ramsey now recognizes, will have to be able to show how its project fits within the frameworks established by these positions. As such, Ramsey reassesses the adequacy of his earlier formulation. *Basic Christian Ethics* can be read as Ramsey's effort to show that his own position is able to fulfill the demands of these great theologians without abandoning its emphasis upon the basic moral structure provided by idealistic ethics.

Love Transforming Natural Law

Making a more substantive claim for distinctively Christian ethics entails, for Ramsey, a focus on the "dominance" of what Ramsey takes to be the central principle of Christian ethics: the imperative of love. Love here finds itself in continuity with the "theological" content from Ramsey's earlier thought. It is understood in terms of the proper inner orientation of the person. But, Ramsey comes here to stress two facets of love which he had not earlier: the way in which love demands attention to the moral distinctions available within history, and the "dominance of love" conceived in terms of its freedom from any particular account of these distinctions.

First, Ramsey stresses the extent to which love requires one to pursue the historically realizable good of the neighbor. Unlike Niebuhr's conception of love, which stresses love's relevance to, but also its essential distinction from prudential and preferential decisions in history,

Ramsey's conception here stresses the extent to which the motivation of love enters directly into the preferential decisions necessary within history. Ramsey reads Jesus' stringent teachings on the requirements of love not as revelations of the impossibility of love in history, but as particular *applications* of love within the narrow field of one-on-one relationships. These relationships provide a perfect crucible for revealing other-orientation of the self because in these relationships this orientation leads directly to obviously self-sacrificial outward actions.[18] Within the matrix of relationships between multiple persons, the correlation between motive and outward action would not be so clear. In situations in which multiple relations are at stake, Ramsey argues, the Christian love directly requires discrimination and preference between persons and goods.

> Christian love, itself absolutely non-resistant in one-one neighbor relationships, may be required to change its tactic to resistance when concerned for the fate of more than one neighbor. Itself non-preferential so far as concerns only the agent's own 'personal welfare,' Christian love *for the neighbor's* sake may actually prefer certain persons to others.[19]

Thus, Ramsey's first significant move is to stress the way in which Christian love is applied to action through the immanent moral distinctions of history.

The second move in Ramsey's attempt to construct a more distinctively Christian ethics is to stress the dominance of love over any particular account of the good. He pursues this in terms of love's freedom. While love demands and enters as a motivational component into prudential and preferential schemes of justice, Ramsey focuses here on the fact that love is not to be simply identified with any one of these schemes as known within history. Love requires one to be oriented toward the *true* need of one's neighbors in history, and thus love's requirements are separable from any particular construction of the needs of one's neighbors which may or may not correlate with their true needs. While love may enter into relationships with natural law if it finds some system of natural law palatable, it can also, if it finds no palatable account, proceed on the basis of an *ad hoc* perception of the need of the other.[20] This picture of love and natural law appears to promote a dialectical model of their relation. Such is the freedom of love from natural law that it always adopts natural law only to the extent that the natural law fits with the real need of the neighbor. Thus love, in its freedom, is to serve as a principle of criticism in what H. R. Niebuhr would later call Ramsey's project of "Christ transforming natural law."[21]

The flip side of Ramsey's treatment of the freedom of love is found in the indeterminacy of love. Love is free inasmuch as it is an inner orientation which can be, but is not necessarily, yoked to any particular account of the good. But love is also itself, characterized in its freedom, empty of any substantive content for guiding external behavior. Thus, love is always dependent upon some external source in order to know what constitutes the good of the neighbor.

> How shall the neighbor's real need be determined, and what adjustment should be made among the competing needs and claims of many neighbors? Impelled by its own concern for more than one neighbor to find *some* answer to this question, biblical justice makes coalition with various rational norms of justice or natural law, but concordats it makes with none.[22]

It is at this point that Ramsey finds his opportunity to advocate for his own ethical preference. Christian love does not, in the contemporary period, have the need to scrounge in an *ad hoc* manner for perceptions of the good. There is a system of natural law which meets the requirements of Christian discernment: philosophical idealism. As such, Ramsey argues that "Christian ethics must make common cause" with this ethical system, which represents "the best insight available at the present stage of thought."[23] Drawing on an idealistically inspired reading of the Christian tradition,[24] Ramsey then lays out the many ways in which idealism provides the best possible fit for Christian love among the alternative accounts of natural law available in modernity.

The (Lack of) Commerce between Love and Natural Law

Thus Ramsey produces an account of a distinctively Christian ethics that is able to maintain the structure of morality provided by idealistic philosophy. Unfortunately, this project is not entirely successful. Ramsey's conception of the dominance of love in terms of its freedom leaves major problems for his conceptual scheme. If this freedom is stressed too much, it becomes clear that love is functionally blind, and thus unable to transform or discriminate amongst available accounts of the good.[25] If this is corrected by stressing the robustness of the transcendent norm of love, there is always the danger of undermining the immanent structure of ethics.[26] In the end, *Basic Christian Ethics* could only be a way station within Ramsey's ongoing project. Ramsey had been unable to coordinate the commerce between the divine transcendent measure of love and the secular philosophical account of the structure of the good and the right. Any solution to this dilemma would require a shift in the conceptualization of Ramsey's starting points.

From Love and Law to Covenant and Creation

Over the next decade Ramsey would continue to struggle with the relation of love and natural law.[27] By the early 1960s Ramsey was prepared to again redraw the lines of his analysis. Before, Ramsey had set out to relate free, Christian love and structured, idealistic natural law. Now, Ramsey made a set of moves that allowed him to present natural law and love as correlated ordered realities springing from the same source and aiming at the same end. Achieving this meant delving into the Christian tradition to find within it much of the content he had up to this point located within the sphere of non-Christian idealistic ethics. Two developments are critical to understanding Ramsey's new position. First, one must understand Ramsey's concept of love as expressed within covenants. Second, one must grasp the new context for understanding progress in the relation between creation and covenant.

Covenant Love

Themes of faithfulness and covenant had been present, even while understated, in *Basic Christian Ethics*. Developing his arguments for the common cause between Christian and idealist ethics in that work had required Ramsey to cultivate those elements in the Christian tradition that found most resonance with the idealistic position. Thus, the concept of covenant emerged as a vaguely significant concept even in his earlier work. It was only later that Ramsey would bring the implications of a covenant understanding of love to full force in his own thought.

Ramsey's concept of covenant as developed in his later career bears great resemblance to some of the idealistic concepts with which Ramsey was working even in his dissertation. The idealists had maintained the goods of moral continuity and individuality by claiming that each person was constituted by a certain identity with the Absolute and the society even while maintaining a respect for her or his distinctive existence, her or his difference, within the Absolute. Ramsey had, as I have suggested, rejected this formulation even within his dissertation. Claims for identity with the Absolute overstated the transcendence of the individual, collapsed the individual too completely into the community, and were ultimately idolatrous. Still, Ramsey was influenced by the means by which the idealists maintained order in the midst of the apparent moral chaos of individuality. From the 1950s through the 60s he would work to find a way of producing a similar formula in Christian theological terms.

Drawing upon the concept of covenant allowed Ramsey to produce a Christian parallel to idealism's identity in difference.

> The covenant is not a relationship with disappearing terms. It is not a pure internal relation with no irreducibly different beings to be related to each other. There is distance in the relations, and relatedness in the distance. Thus, the idea of *covenant*-bond stands between or beyond the idea of *contract* (in which only the surfaces of selves are engaged in action with one another), on one hand, and, on the other, the idea of *union* or merger of beings.[28]

The Christian notion of covenant, as developed here by Ramsey, finds continuity with the idealistic notion of identity in difference inasmuch as it embraces both the continuity of individuals within a structured relational existence and the distance between those individuals involved. But unlike the idealistic picture, covenant is constituted by individual difference held in tension with particular, structured, faithful relationship rather than identity. It is the requirements for maintaining covenant relationships that are now identified with love in Ramsey's thought.

This shift in Ramsey's treatment of love is significant on many levels, not the least because it locates structured and discriminating relationships at the heart of love within history. In Bosanquet's idealism the mind of the Absolute had been expressed through a socially common reservoir of ideas that functioned to structure relationships which were progressively realized within society.[29] With the concept of covenantal love relationships, Ramsey is furnished with a parallel. God's action provides a template for conceiving of the importance of particular stable relationships of persons in the world. Covenants are *particular* relationships of distinct persons. Each is marked by its own moral structure. The "onlook" of Christian ethics, grounded in its account of covenant love, drives one to stress those "canons of loyalty" that structure these particular relationships in history.[30] As Ramsey would later write: "We are born within covenants of life with life. By nature, choice, or need we live with our fellowmen in roles or relations. Therefore, we must ask, What is the meaning of *faithfulness* of one human being to another in every one of these relations? This is the ethical question."[31] At times Ramsey even goes so far as to suggest that in some cases the essential structure of particular relationships can be derived directly from a consideration of love.[32] Viewed as such, love is not distinguished by its freedom from the structure of natural law, as it had been in *Basic Christian Ethics.* Rather, love itself, within history, comes to be correlated with the actions necessary to maintain the *essential* structure of the roles and relations among persons which are being worked out within history.

Covenant and Creation

The relationship between love and natural law also shifts in this period. Again one can see the influence of idealism. Idealism had managed the apparently chaotic process of history by locating historical change in relation to the rolling out of the Absolute within history. The Absolute was the source of the status quo order and of the reformation of this order. No part of history was left to the rule of chaos. All change within a society was understood in terms of the past order provided by the Absolute and the progressive improvement of this order in continuity with the further unrolling of the Absolute in history.

In Ramsey's work from his dissertation through parts of *Nine Modern Moralists*, it was possible to read him as arguing that Christians had to deal with two different and largely unrelated sources for considerations of morality: the Christian resource of love and the secular resources of idealism. These proved troublesome to relate. With Ramsey's new relationally structured conception of love as covenant, he was now prepared to place natural law and love in a more constructive relationship.

Drawing on Barth, Ramsey writes in *Christian Ethics and the Sit-in* that "in the Christian view creation is the external basis of covenant, creation is the promise and makes possible the history of God's covenant dealings with mankind; which His covenant is the internal basis, the meaning or purpose of the creation."[33] This is Barthian language, but

Ramsey's use of it would reinstate moral arguments grounded in the given order of creation that Barth would have found questionable.[34] Creation here constitutes all necessary external conditions for the realization of ordered covenant relations between and among persons within history. Life in the creation allows one access to some of the content of covenant relationships as they obtain in history. Paradigmatically, Ramsey points to physical sexuality as a condition for the realization of marital covenant relations, but his use of the category of creation extends further so as to encompass the whole of the external legal, social and vocational order of human society.

> The state and its law as an ordinance of creation, natural justice, human and legal rights, and social institutions generally, so far as these have a positive purpose under the creative, governing, and preserving purposes of God—all are the external basis making possible the actualization of the promise of covenant; while covenant or fellow humanity is the internal basis and meaning of every right, true justice, or law. This enables us to see why the requirements of charity, or of steadfast covenant-love, and the requirements of justice, or of natural right, are ultimately inseverable.[35]

The natural law here is transformed into a theological concept of creation. The structures in which creation consists are provided both to allow for covenant relations and adjusted to protect these relations against sins of those who would seek to break covenant.

Following chapters will investigate the implications of this move for Ramsey's approach to social institutions. Here it is important to note its implications for dealing with moral norms produced within human communities. Manifesting themselves as a part of God's work to make possible and protect essential covenant relationships, these norms are available as part of the *jus gentium* which is "first expressed in social patterns rather than in personal judgments."[36] They represent the conditions which God provides for producing the best possible order available under the present conditions of sin. Any apparently needed changes in moral norms are best understood not as breaks from the order provided in these principles, but rather as extensions within one's understanding of what these principles require given a new situation. Thus both the established moral order and any transformation of that order are to be understood in terms of the continuity of God's action within the process of change.[37]

With love and natural law so conceived, all of history comes to be viewed as the unrolling of the will of God as essential covenant relations are progressively realized within the evolving confines of phenomenal history. As James T. Johnson writes, Ramsey belongs at this point to a conversionist tradition. "Though sin persists, faith knows that the work of redemption has already begun, and that charity is present in human history to reorder it gradually but effectively *from within*."[38] The meaning of love is grasped in the progressively unfolding understanding of what is required in protecting and advancing the status of covenantal relationships.

> In Christian ethics, at least, *agape* works by many a principle through principle and to defined-principles in its ceaseless endeavor to unfold the meaning of the life of charity. These are always feature-relevant specifications of love. . . if we use the analogy of reasoning by *genus* and *species*, this is not a matter of mere classification or derivation. A better analogy would be an evolutionary one, if biological *species* are thought to arise from some thrust forward or ahead. In some such way principles of faithfulness are unfolded from the elevating and directing power of divine charity. This and our intervening principles are capable of producing from within Christian morality itself deeper meanings, clarifying explanations or stipulations for the 'upbuilding' of the actions and the moral agency going on ordinarily.[39]

Ramsey's Thomism

It is perhaps ironic that an idealistically inspired usage of Karl Barth's formula allowed Ramsey to find common cause with a strain of Catholic moral theology. But regardless of the pedigree of the overlap, Ramsey did find in his later writings a great deal of affinity with certain readings of the Thomistic tradition. By correlating the essential internal structure of covenant relationships with the external structure of institutions, laws, and actions, Ramsey finds a significant field in which he can deploy many of the tools for moral analysis developed within the Thomistic natural law system.

Like Thomas before him Ramsey believes that the world is morally structured and that this essential structure is humanly accessible. While the primary structures of this world are relationships, the meaning of these relationships can be specified in terms of the particular actions constitutive of these structured relationships, or constitutive of deviation from these structured relationships. For instance, adultery is constituted by an action which fails to conform to the structure of faithfulness within the bonds of a marriage covenant.[40] Thus, one can, on principle, reject all instances of adultery.

Within this system Ramsey finds Thomas Aquinas' approach to the analysis of action helpful.[41] With Thomas, he affirms that the first question to be asked when determining the rightness or wrongness of any action is "How is this action properly described?" If an act is properly described in terms which denote a violation of faithful covenant relationships, it cannot be the right action to undertake. Only after a determination of the rightness of the action in terms of its fit with the structure of faithfulness to the particular covenant relationship has been made should other morally relevant features such as motive and consequences of the act be brought under consideration.

Ramsey's peculiar usage of Thomistic categories, and his own use of the term, gave him a reputation as a deontologist. This also made him a popular target for arguments within the protestant community, which in the twentieth century was quite well aware of the dangers of insufficiently developed accounts of duty. But Ramsey was not unaware of the dangers of deontology when understood as a rigid system of superficial external requirements. His mature position gave him resources to respond to these challenges. In his most careful moments he articulated reasons why his brand of relationally based deontology did not have to fall into this trap.

First, Ramsey's focus on the importance of the essential relationship behind the external conditions for the relationship leads him to embrace principles which are not tied directly to physiological descriptions of actions.[42] For example, the concept of adultery is to be understood as denoting a break from the structure of the essential covenant relation of marriage partners rather than in terms of the legitimacy or lack thereof of particular external sexual acts. In some situations—for instance if a woman can only escape from a prison camp and return to her spouse by becoming pregnant by a guard—Ramsey suggests that faithfulness to the marriage covenant may require a sexual act with a person outside the marriage covenant itself.[43] Thus, Ramsey always attempts to keep principles in service to the essence of particular relationships, the demands of which may confound oversimplified expectations.

Second, Ramsey, when he is being careful, embraces a model of moral reasoning in which there is always a deliberative space between a principle and its application to particular situations. Principles can be specific, but they are always arranged so as to define particular *kinds* of action. What principle to apply in a particular situation, and exactly how it is to be applied is a matter left to the prudence of the applicant. The "subsumption of the case," as Ramsey calls this process of prudential application, cannot be governed by rules, but must be left to the prudence of the person in the moment.

Thus, Ramsey came to articulate a unique form of Protestant natural law. A journey begun with Luther eventually brought Ramsey to an appreciation of the usefulness of Thomas Aquinas as well. Always in the background absolute idealism cast a shadow reminding Ramsey of the dangers of moral relativism and pushing him to search for an ethics that reestablished a strong Christian claim for moral order within history.

Conclusion

Unlike Niebuhr, Ramsey's early encounter with idealism sensitized him to the dangers of atomistic moral relativism. Without a structured moral reality behind the chaos of life, the meaning of morality itself would be thrown into question. Ramsey's early attempts to relate idealistic "natural law" ethics and Christian love failed to achieve his goals. He was eventually driven to draw upon elements within the Christian tradition that could bear the load that idealism had been carrying in his thought. Love and law were not to be contrast, but rather to be correlated. Love does not challenge moral order established in society, but rather is the true source and end of moral order.

This produces a system of thought which both overlaps with and diverges from Niebuhr's. These two systems have striking commonalities. Niebuhr believes that the relative order of historical society is frustrated and imperfect, but expressive of the relative peace available within the *saeculum*. The inhabitants of history are drawn to reform this order so as to better approximate loving relations. For Ramsey history has been skewed by sin, but within history humanity is still called to embody the order of loving covenant relationships as it exists before the eschaton.

But the emphases produced by their two systems send them at times in different directions. Niebuhr stresses that love, while relevant to history, always also stands over against the order in history at any moment. The self in its spiritual freedom extends beyond the order provided by nature and historically contextual reason. History is a realm of clashing goods which must be balanced not on the basis of presumably common ideas or essential relationships, but by the practices which are found to best approximate the ideal which ultimately stands outside of history. One within history ought to make responsible decisions among these goods, but must at the same time keep in mind the reality of those goods that must be sacrificed, the imperfection of her or his resolution to the conflict, and the openness of her or his position to criticism. Ramsey, on the other hand, stresses the immanence of love. Love works within the order of history and transforms it from the inside. Love expresses itself in essential relationships which can be grasped through the use of contextual principled human reason. Absolute adherence to the conceptual structures of these essential relationships is constitutive of morality.

Like the idealism and pragmatism which had shaped them in their early lives, Niebuhr and Ramsey have produced systems of thought built upon different guiding metaphors. Niebuhr's relevant transcendent ideal stresses the need for constant responsible criticism, lest one fall into the moral fanaticism of identifying her or his own position with God's. Ramsey's immanent transformism emphasizes the need for morally continuous relationships and loyalty to the essential order of morality, lest atomistic moral chaos erupt in history. These emphases are not contrary to one another, but they do bring about a certain tension between Ramsey and Niebuhr's approaches to morality. It is to this tension, and the illuminations it offers, that we now turn.

Notes

1. Ramsey was opposed to what he took to be the relativism in the Kierkegaardian notion of the "teleological suspension of the ethical." His work can be read as a rejection of Kierkegaard's construction of the moral in terms of the "religious." The last period of his work can even be read as an effort to produce an account of the significance of *sittlichkeit* grounded in Christian theology.

2. For this trend in Barth's ethics, see Robin Lovin, "Karl Barth: The Ethics of Obedience" in *Christian Faith and Public Choices* (Philadelphia, Pa.: Fortress Press, 1984), 18-44.

3. Ramsey, "Natural Law and the Nature of Man," *Christendom* 9, no. 3 (Summer, 1944): 374-79, also *Basic Christian Ethics*, 338. Ramsey's opposition to Barthian "intui-

tionism" is echoed in Niebuhr's criticisms of Barth's position, even while Niebuhr and Ramsey conceive of Barth's position in different terms. Ramsey's reading of Barth's position stresses the danger of intuitionism which may underwrite moral relativism. Niebuhr, as we have seen, finds reason to be concerned about a mode of fanaticism in Barthian moral theology.

4. In the short space available I am not able to provide a complete exegesis of Aquinas with proper attention to those schools of thought that draw different accounts of his ethics. I have, in lieu of this, offered here a short summary of that picture of Aquinas with which Ramsey seems to have been most familiar. For a fuller account of Aquinas' approach to the morality of actions, see Daniel Westberg, "Good and Evil in Human Acts" in *The Ethics of Aquinas*, ed. Stephen J. Pope (Washington D.C.: Georgetown University Press, 2002), 90-102.

5. See Martin Luther, "Commentary on Galatians," in *Martin Luther: Selections from his writings*, ed. John Dillenberger (New York: Doubleday, 1962), 139-40, also "Concerning the Letter and the Spirit," and "The Bondage of the Will," in *Martin Luther's Basic Theological Writings*, ed. Timothy F. Lull (Minneapolis: Fortress Press, 1989), 75-103, 188-208. Aquinas had already laid the groundwork for Luther's shift in emphasis with his discussion of the old and new law. See Pamela M. Hall, "The Old Law and the New Law," in *The Ethics of Aquinas*, 194-206.

6. Quoted in F. Edward Cranz, *An Essay on the Development of Luther's Thought on Justice, Law, and Society* (London: Oxford University Press, 1959), 104.

7. Luther also stresses that, since sin has weakened the power of reason, the repromulgation of the law in scripture is an important source in clarifying determinations of right. See J. B. Schneewind, *The Invention of Autonomy: A history of modern moral philosophy* (New York: Cambridge University Press, 1998), 26.

8. Cranz, *An Essay on the Development of Luther's Thought*, 106. See also, John T. McNeill, "Natural Law in the Thought of Luther," *Church History* 10 (1941), 220-21.

9. Luther, *Martin Luther: Selections from his writings*, 140.

10. Martin Luther, "Two Kinds of Righteousness," in *Martin Luther's Basic Theological Writings*, 155-64.

11. Cranz, *An Essay on the Development of Luther's Thought*, 110. However, compare this account to Ernst Troeltsch's more active picture of the interaction between love and natural law in Luther's thought. Ernst Troeltsch, *The Social Teachings of the Christian Churches*, trans. Olive Wyon (New York: The Macmillan Company, 1931), 528-47. One way to read the theological development across Ramsey's career is to see him as shifting from a theology like that pictured in Cranz's interpretation of Luther to one more like that provided in Troeltsch's interpretation of Luther.

12. Ramsey's most explicit acknowledgments of his debts to Luther come after he has shifted away from emphasizing the distinction between the source of natural law in reason and the source of proper motivation in theology, but it is not to be doubted that Luther's thought provides the ground both for this emphasis and for his later emphasis on the continuity of loving motivation to be found in all moral actions. His early reliance on Luther is revealed in his comment that "In sin man is under God condemned, and in faith he is saved, by the 'law of Christ,' i.e. by the confident abandonment of self which alone may ideally sustain the impartiality requisite for obedience to God through moral law apprehended by reason." See "Natural Law and the Nature of Man," 378. Ramsey's use of the "law of Christ" suggests a parallel to Luther's understanding of this phrase in his exegesis of Galatians 6:2. As Luther writes: "This is what makes caring for the body a

Christian work, that . . . we may be sons of God, each caring for and working for the other, bearing one another's burdens and so fulfilling the law of Christ [Gal. 6:2]. This is a truly Christian life." See Luther, "The Freedom of the Christian" in *Martin Luther's Basic Theological Writings*, 617.

An interesting exchange was prompted by a letter from Roland Bainton to Ramsey in 1950 in which Bainton comments upon Luther's understanding of natural law. "As grades in virtue," Bainton writes, "I wonder whether Luther is not very close to Aquinas because Luther readily concedes that the natural man is capable of the civic virtues. He is perfectly well able to be a good father and a good magistrate. The specifically Christian virtues are distinguished from the natural virtues by contrast between act and attitude. Thou shalt not kill is natural virtue and possible to any. Thou shalt not be angry is a Christian virtue and is unattainable." Roland Bainton to Paul Ramsey, 11 March 1950, Box 2, Paul Ramsey Papers, Duke University Library. To this Ramsey replies that "What you say about Luther is . . . certainly to the point. I have had occasion to insist upon this so far as the natural law is concerned, as it advances the secular authority; but it had not occurred to me to relate this to the doctrine of virtue of personal character." Paul Ramsey to Roland Bainton, 17 March 1950, Box 2, Paul Ramsey Papers, Duke University Library.

For Ramsey's use of Luther in stressing the continuity of loving motivation despite the apparently different external activities demanded by morality in different situations, see Ramsey, "The Theory of Democracy: Idealistic or Christian," *Ethics* 56, no. 4 (July, 1946), 263-64. At one point in his later life Ramsey would go so far as to call himself a "Methodist Lutheran." See Paul Ramsey, "Two Extremes: Ramsey Replies to His Critics," *Dialogue* 6, no. 3 (Summer, 1967), 218.

13. Ramsey, "Natural Law and the Nature of Man," 375. See also Ramsey's parallel comments in *Basic Christian Ethics*, 339.

14. Ramsey, *Deeds and Rules*, 91. It seems probable that something like the distinction between the inner working of theology and right determining function of ethics was in Ramsey's mind when he announced at the 1973 Society of Christian Ethics meeting that "anybody who takes my theology seriously has got to have his head examined. I am not a theologian; I am an ethicist." Cited in John P. Crossley, foreword to *Paul Ramsey's Ethics: The power of 'agape' in a postmodern world*, by Michael C. McKenzie (Westport, Conn.: Praeger, 2001), x.

15. Ramsey never fully leaves the distinction between the external function of the natural law and the internal function of love. This distinction is still reflected in his work in *Basic Christian Ethics* and *Christian Ethics and The Sit-In* (New York: Association Press, 1961), but the content of the two is subtly shifted in each presentation to set them in different relationships.

16. Echoing Barth, Ramsey contends that any adequate Christian ethic "must first of all discover in the strange, new religious world of the Bible the source of the ethical perspectives peculiar to the Hebrew-Christian heritage." See Ramsey, *Basic Christian Ethics*, 2. See Karl Barth, "The Strange New World Within the Bible," in *The Word of God and the Word of Man*, 28-50.

17. "The relation between Christian love and existing social institutions," Ramsey writes, "may be summed up as the constant criticism and reshaping of the institutions of society in the course of using them. And the relationship between Christian love and *other theories of social ethics* may be summed up as the constant criticism and bending

of these social policies in the course of using them." Ramsey, *Basic Christian Ethics*, 349.

18. In *Basic Christian Ethics* Ramsey grounds his reading of Jesus' ethics in the belief that Jesus held a confused eschatology which presupposed belief in the immanence of the eschaton. Given this belief, Ramsey holds that Jesus articulated the requirements of love in terms of what would be required if a person lived in the moment when all neighbors but one were "apocalyptically removed" from the person's concern. See Ramsey, *Basic Christian Ethics*, 24-45. I do not focus on this emphasis here because, in the end, it is not essential to Ramsey's treatment of love or Jesus' ethics. Later Ramsey revises his view of Jesus' eschatology while maintaining that Jesus' ethics functions in the way described above. See Paul Ramsey, *Nine Modern Moralists*, 248.

19. Ramsey *Basic Christian Ethics*, 158. See also Ramsey's comment on the prudence of the early Christians. *Basic Christian Ethics*, 212.

20. Ramsey, *Basic Christian Ethics*, 79.

21. Ramsey, *Nine Modern Moralists*, 7.

22. Ramsey, *Basic Christian Ethics*, 346.

23. Ramsey, *Basic Christian Ethics*, xxxiii.

24. For example, Ramsey's construction of the concept of the *imago dei* and his development of the shape of covenant in *Basic Christian Ethics* both reflect the influence of the idealistic concept of 'identity in difference' which Ramsey has adapted into the concept of 'morally continuous relationship in difference.' Humans, Ramsey writes, are created in the *imago dei*. The *imago dei* is not a facet simply of the person's individuality (simple difference). (249) Nor is the *imago dei* a sign that the person is properly an undifferentiated facet of the divine (simple identity). (252) It is only in a relationship with God which entails both moral continuity and difference that the person is properly seen as standing within the *imago dei*. Similarly, when treating covenant he contrasts the genuinely "Hebraic" covenant with the Hobbesian contract that overstates the difference of those in the society, and the Rousseauian general will which too radically collapses the members of society into identity with the divine will. (367-88)

25. On the failure of Ramsey's formulation here, see Charles Harris, "Love as the Basic Moral Principle in Paul Ramsey's Ethics" *Journal of Religious Ethics* 4 (Fall, 1976), 239-45; also William Werpehowski, "Christian Love and Covenant Faithfulness," *Journal of Religious Ethics* 19 (Fall, 1991), 103-13.

26. Ramsey was still very much concerned about intuitionism. See *Basic Christian Ethics*, 337-40.

27. *Nine Modern Moralists* represents another way station in Ramsey's evolving approach to Natural Law and Love. While the content of Ramsey's thought there is basically the same as that in *Christian Ethics and the Sit-In*, his guiding metaphor is different. In *Nine Modern Moralists*, he would write of the Egypt of natural law in relation to the Exodus of love. Although he would continue to use it occasionally, this metaphor failed to produce the success of Ramsey's use of Barth's formulation concerning creation and covenant.

28. Ramsey, *Christian Ethics and the Sit-In*, 36.

29. As Ramsey writes in his dissertation, for the idealist "*Sub specie aeternitais*, absolute reality is eternally present, but *sub specie temporis*, it appears as a goal to be achieved in the future. The whole is a system whose relationships would exist all at once did not something hinder them, thus forcing the connections of this system to express themselves according to a development in time." Ramsey, "The Nature of Man," 355.

30. Paul Ramsey, "The Case of the Curious Exception," in *Norm and Context in Christian Ethics*, ed. Gene Outka and Paul Ramsey (New York: Charles Scribner's Sons, 1968), 81.

31. Paul Ramsey, *The Patient as Person*, xlv.

32. Thus Ramsey claims that love itself, from its own "inner logic" independent of natural law, is said to produce moral principles. In fact, this inner logic is said to require the whole of the Christian just war theory! See, Paul Ramsey, *War and the Christian Conscience* (Durham, N.C.: Duke University Press, 1961), 9-10.

33. Ramsey, *Christian Ethics and the Sit-In*, 22.

34. As David Attwood notes: "Ramsey borrowed his language in order to use it in social and political ethics in a way that Barth never did, and indeed would have resisted." *Paul Ramsey's Political Ethics* (Lanham, Md.: Rowman & Littlefield Publishers, Inc., 1992), 22. As I shall suggest in the next chapter, the concept of the content of creation Ramsey uses is shaped largely by Emil Brunner's treatment of the "orders of creation."

35. Ramsey, *Christian Ethics and the Sit-In*, 26.

36. Ramsey is quoting here from Maritain. See Ramsey, *Nine Modern Moralists*, 221.

37. There is an overlap, albeit imperfect, between these notions in Ramsey's thought and H. Richard Niebuhr's idea of ethics as consisting in response to all action that comes upon oneself as the action of God upon us. See H. Richard Niebuhr, *The Responsible Self: An essay in Christian moral philosophy* (New York: Harper & Row, 1963), and Paul Ramsey, "Is God Mute in the Goldwater Candidacy" *Christianity and Crisis* 24, no.15 (Spring, 1964), 175-78. There is also an overlap between Ramsey's approach here and the idea of an "ontology of peace" developed in some contemporary theological circles. See John Milbank, *Theology and Social Theory: Beyond secular reason* (Cambridge, Mass.: Blackwell, 1991).

38. James Turner Johnson, *The Just War Tradition and the Restraint of War: A moral and historical inquiry* (Princeton, N.J.: Princeton University Press, 1981), 106. Italics mine. Johnson attributes such a position to Reinhold Niebuhr as well, but this oversimplifies the disagreements between Ramsey and Niebuhr. See the chapter's conclusion below.

39. Ramsey, "The Case of the Curious Exception," 91.

40. See Ramsey, "The Case of the Curious Exception," 87-93.

41. The roots of this type of analysis seems to have appeared first in Ramsey's article "Right and Wrong Calculation," *Worldview* 2 (December, 1959), 6-9. His analysis was later informed largely through the work of Catholic scholar Joseph Eric D'Arcy. See Ramsey, *Deeds and Rules in Christian Ethics*, 192-225. He is most explicit about the relation between his own analysis and that of Thomas in Paul Ramsey, *Speak up for Just War or Pacifism*, 104-5.

42. This is the grounding for the flexibility that Donald Evans helpfully highlights in his account of Ramsey's "*liberal* M-approach" to absolute rules. See Donald Evans, "Paul Ramsey on Exceptionless Moral Rules" in *Love and Society*, 19-46.

43. Ramsey, "The Case of the Curious Exception," 88.

Chapter 4
A Constructive Dialogue

The previous two chapters explicate two different renderings of Christian moral theological language. While Niebuhr and Ramsey were still indebted to the philosophies in which they had been trained, they were theologians. From the rich resources of the Christian tradition, Niebuhr and Ramsey draw theologies which seek to address the moral dangers they perceive, in distinctively Christian terms. While there are vast differences between the ways that Niebuhr and Ramsey use theological symbols, it is harder than one might expect to identify clear contradictions between their modes of discourse.

Comparative criticism between these two positions often poses a problem of translation. Both Ramsey and Niebuhr have comprehensive moral worldviews and linguistic frameworks to articulate these worldviews. As in the comparison of any differing languages, a particular term in the lexicon of one framework does not necessarily have a one-to-one correlation with a similar term in the lexicon of the other. Ferreting out differences in the ways these two languages select certain issues for concern is a difficult task. Generous interpretation and a careful attention to the use of terminology are necessary in any approach to comparative criticism. In this chapter I will trace out one case in which Ramsey and Niebuhr themselves had problems in grasping the meaning of each other's language. I will then suggest a set of mutual criticisms which arise from a dialogue between these two positions.

Problems of Translation: The Language of Love

Problems of translation between their two positions were enough to stump even Ramsey and Niebuhr themselves in their own dialogue. Unable to understand the importance of the impossibility of love in Niebuhr's ethics,[1] and assuming that love must represent the same content in both of their moral schemes,[2] Ramsey proposed the now popular reading of Niebuhr's conception of love as identified with the external activity of self-sacrifice.[3] Niebuhr, on this reading, was carrying out a Ramseyan project of correlating the motive of love with those particular external actions it requires in history, but became confused when transitioning between the stability of loving motivation and the diverse preferential actions this stable motive requires in history. Niebuhr's confusion, on this reading, led him to identify the motive of love with one fixed external activity: self-sacrifice. Then, recognizing the inappropriateness of this particular act within many instances of history, Niebuhr was forced to accept the paradoxical impossible possibility of love. The impossibility of love is thus reduced by Ramsey to an avoidable "Gordian knot" produced by Niebuhr's "somewhat mistaken strategy" in treating love.[4] The upshot of this reading, Ramsey concludes, is a misconception of love which focuses on love's implications for the self rather than for the neighbor. As Ramsey informs his reader, in Niebuhr's writings "'sacrifice' and 'suffering' tend to overcome affirmation of life in the meaning of love."[5]

There is some truth to Ramsey's analysis. Self-sacrifice is central to Niebuhr's conception of love in at least two senses. First, *Agape* entails a greater concern for the neighbor than for the self.[6] Second, the enactment of perfect love depends upon a trust in God which leads to a lack of anxiety about one's life, one's social connections, or one's culture. It is such trust in something beyond history which makes actual acts of self-sacrifice possible in particular situations. These are some of the subjective requirements of love which Niebuhr believes the self inevitably fails to live up to in most moments within history.

But if Ramsey is right in his analysis, Niebuhr went beyond this. Not only did Niebuhr mean that love required these "self-sacrificial" dispositions. Niebuhr went on to conclude that love is to be identified with actual external sacrifice of the self in every instance of conflict. This would be a deeply problematic position, and one that should not be attributed to Niebuhr unless there is no more generous reading available.

While Niebuhr at times seems to confuse these issues in ways that support Ramsey's reading, there are significant points at which Niebuhr's writings clearly belie Ramsey's interpretation. For instance, in *An Interpretation of Christian Ethics*, while deploying the *symbol* of self-sacrificial love to inform the Christian's view of the world and to break the narcissistic egoism and alter-egoism of the self, Niebuhr is clear that one should not derive from love a requirement of external acts of self-sacrifice. Even for the ascetic saint, the "disavowal of the natural relationships and responsibilities of ordinary life . . . *can be no more than a symbol* of the final ideal of love, under the tension of which all men stand."[7] The reason it can be no more than a symbol is that this disavowal "leads to the destruction of life itself." No matter how right the disposition of the actor, the outward act of self sacrifice, performed by a mere human being, fails in living up to the inclusiveness demanded of a perfectly loving act. Self-sacrificial actions undertaken by mere humans are often the best symbols of a divine love which refuses to choose sides due to its inclusiveness. In some cases, such actions will also be the best approximations of love available. But these acts should not be confused with the perfect act of love in Christ.

Passages like this suggest that the impossibility of love is not a conclusion Niebuhr draws from a facile reading of the implications of neighbor oriented motives within history. The impossibility of love arises from Niebuhr's identification of love with the perfect act in which God in Christ orients Godself toward the fulfillment of the need of every person in need.[8] On this reading Niebuhr's conception of love entails perfect orientation of the act toward the good of every neighbor. This requirement of *perfect* orientation, not the unsuitability of self-sacrifice in some cases, is the reason for love's objective impossibility in Niebuhr's scheme. This love is a transcendent principle that functions as an indiscriminate and discriminate measure of criticism. It cannot be bent so as to be simply identified with either sacrificial or non-sacrificial actions within the bounds of history.

The reasons for the differences between Ramsey and Niebuhr's two accounts of love on this reading are not to be located in the confusion of one author or the other. These differences are related to the moral dangers to which pragmatism and idealism had sensitized them. Ramsey and Niebuhr each draw upon facets of the symbol of Christian love in protecting against these moral dangers, but since they are dealing with different moral dangers, they also conceive of love differently. Ramsey finds love to be identified with the unrolling of moral order within history. Love is said to be identifiable with the very texture of this order, and acts of love are acts of obedience to the order. But Ramsey, in his careful moments,[9] recognizes that our access to this order is imperfect. As he often quotes from H. Richard Niebuhr, we live in a world where the "vision every man and ever nation has is 'a view of the universal'; it is not 'a universal view.'"[10] Niebuhr draws upon the image of the perfect love of God in Christ to remind humanity of its imperfection and the imperfection of each of its projects. The impossible norm of love serves as a constant lure for progressive action and a constant principle of criticism against any particular order or project of reform. Actual duties are not identified with love, but are rather conceived of as the approximations of love within a broken world. Knowledge of these duties arises not from an application of love to the contingencies of history, but from a love *informed* analysis of the realistic possibilities for realizing relatively stable values in history.

The upshot of this analysis is that neither Ramsey nor Niebuhr lacks categories for expressing either the need for a strong set of actual duties or the imperfection of all human projects in providing such a set. But, their frameworks for talking about these duties and this imperfection place emphases in different areas. Their conceptions of the moral world select out different moral consideration for special attention. Niebuhr's framework is oriented against the dangers of closing off moral claims from responsible criticism while Ramsey's is constructed so as to protect the moral structure of reality. The emphases of each system echo the distinctive moral dangers to which Ramsey and Niebuhr were sensitized by pragmatism and absolute idealism.

These moral languages and the emphases they place on certain facets of moral analysis are not neutral. They at times illumine and at times obscure the perspective of the moral actor who speaks the language. As such, the insights available to moral actors using one linguistic framework may prove profitable to those using the other. It is not clear that any synthesis of the two languages can be produced. But below, I suggest some of the insights and dangers of each system which are thrown into relief in a constructive dialogue between the two.

Niebuhr

The strength of Niebuhr's analysis lies in its focus upon the narrative within which responsible Christian historical actions are to be located. Every act is contextualized by Niebuhr in a story of human frailty and sin which strips away pretentious claims to self righteousness that might obscure one's perspective on historical activity. Niebuhr's ethics also excel in pointing attention to the virtues necessary to appropriate calculations of proportionality and consequence. Christian humility, criticalness, and responsibility are necessary in reining in those who seek to enact projects aimed at ends beyond historical possibility, those who are led by the height of their goals to produce naive accounts of the costs involved in achieving them, or those who deny the reality of costs entailed by their action due to the perceived righteousness of their action. These are the tools necessary to combat moral fanaticism.

But Niebuhr's emphasis also leaves some weak points in his own analysis and language. First, Niebuhr's focus upon the brokenness of history at times leads him to an overly pessimistic realism about the possibilities for morally motivated reformations of human practice. His treatment of "total war" during World War II is a case in point. Total wars are those in which societies mobilize their entire resources in order to win. In such wars, Niebuhr thought, it may be necessary to undertake acts of massive and indiscriminate destruction in order to prevail. The responsible person within history, he suggests, must accept and deal with the inevitable forces of history that bring such horrendous options.

> . . .it would be hazardous to draw absolute distinctions between what is, and what is not, permissible in a total war. The melancholy necessities of total war were invented neither by the Nazi nor by us. They are consequences of a technical society that makes the harnessing of the total resources of a society for the destruction of the foe possible and therefore necessary. The necessity follows the possibility because once the instruments of total war are unloosed they will guarantee defeat for the side that fails to use them, whether from want of resolution, or failure of organization, or moral scruple.[11]

Niebuhr's analysis here is, at least, overly simple.[12] If the ends of the war did not justify the means, which would at least be the case in most situations, it would be imperative for the Christian to withdraw from participation in the war. There are, as Niebuhr recognizes in his calmer moments, times when acceptance of defeat is the best approximation of love possible within history.[13] Even if nations cannot recognize this, Christians within the nation can. Niebuhr's broad argument here gives too little attention to the power of moral reasoning that might lead the Christian to decide at points that the ends do not justify the means necessary in this or that situation.

Looking back, we can also see that Niebuhr's analysis of this situation was overly pessimistic concerning the effectiveness of moral reasoning in shaping, albeit indirectly, policy and strategy decisions within war. The presence of massively destructive technology had not so radically effaced the possibility of more limited wars as Niebuhr suggests. There are several economic and technological conditions that contribute to the possibility of contemporary limited war. The importance of these conditions should not be underestimated as manipulation of these factors can provide some means of protecting against outbreak of another total war.[14] But the power of moral reason in contributing to the shift to contemporary limited war should also be recognized. Cultural shifts recognizing human rights, the laws of war, and the reality of war crimes have mixed with the influence of work produced by scholars like Ramsey to contribute to a global culture that is more sensitive to the moral problems of limiting the means of war. In the latter half of the twentieth century, national prestige and political viability have come to be tied to the perception of selective targeting in ways that Niebuhr would not have predicted. Niebuhr's pessimism about the possibilities for history prevented him from foreseeing or participating in such developments. This is a fault that should be noted by all later Niebuhrians.

Second, Niebuhr's particularism meant that he never took part in the developments in casuistic categories arising from the dialogue among contemporary scholars. As such Niebuhr's approach to moral problems never takes advantage of the rich descriptions of the interactions of intent, object, motive, target, consequences, and types of duties that informed these casuistic accounts. While Niebuhr often deploys an intuitive grasp of such factors, they rarely raise to the level of an explicit facet of his analysis of actions. Niebuhr's own approach to particular cases would have benefited from the richer description of acts available through the use of these casuistic categories. Such analysis could also have allowed him to present a more developed account of the shape and content of moral determinations concerning the balance of goods intrinsic in acts and the goods available as outcomes of acts.[15]

Third, Niebuhr would have benefited from a greater appreciation of the usefulness of principled moral language in general. While there are several places in his work in which Niebuhr articulates the need for principles in guiding moral action, Niebuhr's treatment of principled approaches to morality most often focuses on the ways in which this language has been used to absolutize the peculiar or unjust order of particular societies throughout history. This is an important lesson, but principled language can also be used for more positive purposes, which Ramseyan analysis is quick to point out. Rules of conduct can serve as protections for certain enduring goods which humans in the heat of the moment are often tempted to abandon for the sake of short range satisfaction. Rules are also useful in governing those situations where following the rule generally and leads to the realization of a better balance of goods and there are epistemic limitations to telling whether any particular case is a rare exception. Finally, there are times in which the establishment of rules is a necessary step in creating the trust necessary to improve strained relations. Niebuhr proposes no barriers to the usage of such principled guidelines, and his writings suggest his openness to such norms. Unfortunately, his primary focus never led him to develop this mode of moral reasoning.

Finally, at times, in his effort to stress the relativity of goods, the brokenness of history, and the humility necessary to proper moral determinations, Niebuhr makes claims which appear to level the importance of moral distinctions within history. In his discourse on particular issues Niebuhr deploys the language of sin and guilt in various frameworks. Unfortunately, at times he fails to distinguish between the imperfection of an action and the sin and guilt entailed in undertaking the action. Here, he suggests that participation in imperfect actions constitutes sin, and imparts guilt. Since all activities within history are imperfect, within this framework they all appear to entail sin and guilt. Thus, moral choice requires opting for the least sinful, or the least evil activity, and thus taking on the least guilt.[16] The effect is to provide a sliding scale of sin and guilt on which all actions fall, thus relativizing the moral difference between them and failing to adequately treat issues of intentionality behind particular actions.

The motive behind this language game is not malign. Niebuhr is attempting to use Christian language to remind the participant in history of the limitedness of human activity, and the imperfection of all human action in the light of Christ's perfect act. Unfortunately, Niebuhr's confusion here leads to exactly the kinds of problems Ramsey is concerned about. Confusing these ideas leads to the appearance of relativism. Acts within history may be imperfect, but this does not mean that they are sinful or entail guilt *per se*. If a person chooses the best possible action available to her or him, the act chosen cannot be an act of sin. It cannot make a person morally guilty. By allowing, and at times advocating for, actions that he is willing to call sinful, Niebuhr opens himself to the charge that he does not recognize the reality of moral boundaries.

As I have suggested in the last chapter, Niebuhr had more subtle ways of relating imperfection, sin and guilt. When he is careful, Niebuhr is clear that the imperfection of present options function to remind one of past sins and the current temptation to sinfulness. Such is the function of love as an indiscriminate measure. Humans, Niebuhr believes, would have lived without the need to make choices between imperfect options if it had not been for sin and sinfulness. Thus the imperfection of historical alternatives stands as a reminder of human sinfulness, and ought to chasten participants in history. But this does not make it acceptable to continue sinning. There must be some possibility of avoiding sin and guilt even within the imperfection of history. In making these distinctions Niebuhr should have more consistently applied the discriminate criticism associated with love to make clearer the moral distinctions that do make a difference within history. Unfortunately, at some points he confuses the indiscriminate and discriminate usages of love, and falls into confusing imperfection *per se* with sin and guilt. There is a danger here that if one focuses too much upon the sin and guilt *which brought* the situation that one will not make enough of the ideal of avoiding sin and guilt *in* the situation.

A helpful corrective is offered by Ramsey's emphasis upon the ideal possibility of moral relational continuity, even within situations that morally require imperfect actions.[17] In some extreme cases, the moral relationship in such situations may be primarily maintained by subjective orientation. When moral obligation requires one to sacrifice goods that are usually considered constitutive of a relationship, maintaining faithfulness to the relationship demands at least that the actor orient her or his will so as not to *directly* target the sacrificed goods for destruction. For instance, in Ramsey's example of the woman trapped in the prison camp, it may be morally obligatory to sacrifice the good of physical monogamy with one's husband, but while sacrificing this good, the woman should not think of sex with the prison guard as the goal of her action.[18] Instead she ideally maintains subjectively faithful marital relations by conceiving of undertaking the act as a means of returning to her husband.

Even such a subjective measure is significant both in terms of assessing the intrinsic value of the act itself and in terms of the framework it allows one to develop when speaking of morality. A focus on the existence of ideal possibilities for ongoing relationships within compromising situations can be the grounding for an extension of the robustness of the moral requirements in which these relationships consist. The recognition that in war soldiers ideally exist in moral relationships with their enemies shifts the way that one thinks about war, even while it does not necessarily preclude the sacrifice of those goods that are necessarily destroyed in the process of war. Because there is no area in which relationship ought to be totally broken, it becomes clear that moral analysis is not a question of whether there should be bounded moral relationships that guide action in particular situations. Moral analysis is rather a question of how, in terms of internal and external features, to delimit the moral boundaries which are demanded in these particular relationships.

Provided that such analysis can be held in tension with the recognition of the significance of those goods which at times must be sacrificed while undertaking moral action in history, and provided that such analysis does not fall into the mistake of preemptively cutting off moral argument concerning the shape of these relations, there is nothing that prevents the Niebuhrian from embracing the insights this analysis offers. Indeed, Niebuhr himself at times struggled to articulate such a notion when he approached the issue of the relation between combatants in war. In one notable deviation from his usual practice of stressing the impossibility of love, he even attempts to draw upon the language of love to describe the ideal possibilities for continuity in this most strained relationship.[19] Unfortunately, his lack of sufficient categories for articulating the subtle relationships possible under such extreme pressures limits his ability to explore these relationships. A more astute student of these categories may be able to succeed in this Niebuhrian project where Niebuhr himself failed.

All of these suggestions for reform in Niebuhrian analysis focus upon the immanent demands for approximating love within history. Niebuhr's efforts to keep these immanent demands open to criticism and his stress upon the imperfection of all historical measures prevented him from sufficiently developing accounts of the measures to be used in approaching particular acts. Niebuhr's analysis often charges into the fray of application wielding accounts of values that he assumes, but does not systematically articulate. Drawing upon insights available in dialogue with a Ramsey, Niebuhrian analysis would be forced to take up the task of articulating these values more carefully.

Ramsey

The strengths and weaknesses of Ramsey's emphases provide a mirror reflection of Niebuhr's. Ramsey was a talented casuist. Drawing razor sharp moral distinctions, his effort to categorize, or in his words "anatomize," moral action produced a body of work to be profitably reflected upon for generations to come. Ramsey stresses uncompromisingly the reality of determinations of right within history, and the need to articulate the morally significant facets of action that guide our moral discernment. Still, his focus on bolstering the perception of order within ethics also contributed to the neglect of some areas in Ramsey's ethics.

While Ramsey was, in his more careful moments, clear that Christian ethics cannot be reduced to an account of absolute principles,[20] his emphasis on and search for security in an ordered moral world often leaves the impression that Ramsey has an overly narrow conception of what constitutes ethics and moral reasoning. The view of theological concerns which grew out of his early reliance on Luther is a case in point. By stressing the cleavage between the inner orientation of the person and the quality of the outward act, Ramsey obscures the significance of the relation between being a good person and knowing and doing right actions. This emphasis at times leads Ramsey to a bifurcated view of human existence that leaves important facets of human morality outside the realm of ethics proper. As he argues, the account of divine forgiveness, justification, and justice which transcends the bounds of humanly applicable principle is "relevant to all choices; it has therefore little or no light to shed upon any particular choice."[21] This account is, according to Ramsey, part of theology and not ethics.

Such a position says too little about the ethical import of how one views and situates oneself in the world. It understates the significance of the narratives and accounts of virtuous actions which inform humans about what it means to be a good person. These narratives, virtues and dispositions carry important moral implications for the process of perceiving the morally relevant features of a situation as it unfolds. While these considerations may not lead directly and unambiguously to the articulation of types of acts to be designated morally righteous or morally wrong, they are central to the goodness of human life in which one is called upon to apply any such articulations. One can here profitably generalize comments that William May has written concerning Ramsey's principled treatment of medical ethics.

> . . . patients are not merely decision makers but also, at least in some way, authors of their lives. And authors do not write in a vacuum, but in the setting of those great shaping narratives, those mythic forms, that help supply them with their perceptions of the world and themselves, and give them some cues for their behavior. Ramsey and other ethicists of his generation trafficked chiefly in quandaries and searched for principles and policies to order practices in the setting of large institutions—an important task indeed. Others, subsequently, have turned to narrative ethics in order to flesh out and shape the stories of the patient as person.[22]

In continuity with the broader idealist tradition, Ramsey also had problems articulating the moral significance of calculations of proportionality and consequence.[23] When pushed on the subject, he would admit that such calculations were "subjects for moral evaluation."[24] But, his perspective on the nature of such calculations often led him to understate their moral status. The particularities of these calculations did not, in Ramsey's thought, easily correlate with the stable conceptual structure of faithful relationships elaborated in principled reasoning.[25] Since he conceived morality primarily as the working out of these divine conceptual structures in history, calculations of the remaining variables of proportion and consequence are often downplayed or excluded altogether from the sphere of moral reasoning. "Moral reasoning," Ramsey writes, "is always a matter of surrounding the particulars of action by increasingly specific general terms—i.e., increasing illumination—for the direction of concrete actions."[26] Thus, Ramsey has a tendency to find, as he writes in another article, that "moral considerations are behind the eyeballs . . . they precede the exercise of calculating reason."[27]

Ramsey also has the tendency of overestimating the security of principled claims while stressing the insecurity of claims grounded on calculations of proportionality or consequence. As he moves from a dialectical ethic and toward an ethic stressing the immanent ordering work of God, the epistemic chasm between these two kinds of judgments tends more and more to widen in Ramsey's writings. For "Christian ethics has," Ramsey comes to believe, "more reason for knowing something significant about proper conduct than we have the competence to count up all its remote effects, subject as these are to erosions, reversals, and glacial changes of history yet to come."[28]

There is a great deal of truth in such a conclusion. Even while the particular understandings of all principles should be held open to criticism, the use of principles that have been tested by time and culture often provides guidance even when other factors seem impossible to reckon. But Ramsey's confidence in principled judgments seems to go beyond such an account of the relative security offered in tradition tested judgments. In his most robust statements, his confidence in principled determinations seems to be tied to an idealistically inspired account of the source of principled forms of moral knowledge.

Somehow, Ramsey suggests, by contemplating the application of principles growing out of covenant relations, the human could gain guidance from her or his intellectual participation in the unrolling of God's conceptual order in history. Principles are descriptions not of particular acts, but of the structure of ideal covenant relations that lie behind phenomenal life. Principles thus have reservoirs of "implicit" meaning which can illumine the requirements for right action even in phenomenally novel situations. Knowledge of these implicit meanings arises, Ramsey writes, "with" but not "from" experience of the particular situation. In this context Ramsey speaks of "the power of morality itself to make an imprint upon human life, the capacity of moral principle to mold and shape our lives and to specify *out of its own nature* the moral terrain." Taking part in principled moral reasoning, he suggests, is part of "living in thought the sort of human life which God is shaping into the divine righteousness;" grasping intellectually the "the meaning of the life of charity" unfolded by Christian agape.[29] Thus, principled judgments take on much of the character of revealed Christian truths, available through the participation in God's ongoing work of ordering the world. Ramsey's confidence in these moral determinations at times even leads him to trespass into the deliberative space between a principle and its application, publicly drawing applied conclusions from principled judgment where he criticizes others for similar practice with judgments of proportionality and consequence.

Niebuhr's emphasis upon the historical relativity and limitedness of human reason is helpful in countering some of Ramsey's excesses. Regardless of the various plausible arguments for *relatively* greater security available in principled judgments, many of which were also deployed by Ramsey, the religious dimension to Ramsey's confidence overstates the participation of sinful humanity in God's unfolding reason and presents too strong an account of the security of particular principled judgments. In Ramsey's own writings, this dimension of Ramsey's thought leads to an oversimplified view of both the historical and practical complexity involved in producing principled judgments.

For example, in approaching war, Ramsey suggests that "Christian love *of its own inner logic*" apart from any natural law consideration is impelled to affirm "just war doctrine," conceived in terms of the obligation to protect the oppressed neighbor and the absolute imperative of noncombatant immunity.[30] Afterward he would stress that noncombatant immunity arose as an absolute in the just war tradition on the basis of distinctively Christian reflections on the requirements of loving intent. Presented as such it appears that Ramsey's conclusion is clearly supported both by reason and by unambiguous tradition.

These claims are, at least, oversimplified. As Charles Harris suggests, nothing inherent in the logic of a neighbor oriented disposition *per se* requires just war doctrine.

> The first deficiency of the love-principle is that it does not determine what the primary good for others is in a situation in which physical force is being exerted. Ramsey assumes that the primary good which can be offered to one who is physically attacked is assistance against the attacker. But why should this be so? What is the basis for the primacy of the physical good of assistance against attack? Alternatives are clearly possible. Why not, for example, say that the greatest good that can be done for the one in distress is to help him bear his suffering in love?[31]

Ramsey is here, Harris suggests, surreptitiously drawing upon adventitious principles to fill out his own conclusion. There may be, and I believe there are, good reasons for suggesting that Ramsey has selected the correct good in his own approach, but there is nothing inherent in the logic of love itself that necessitates this selection.

Further, as James Turner Johnson's careful historical study of the just war tradition has shown, the development of the principle of noncombatant immunity drew upon the Christian focus on right intent only in a complex interaction with notions of honor and shame within chivalric culture, originally self-defensive Church decrees protecting the clergy from being directly attacked, and a concern for avoiding waste of resources on imprudent targets. Johnson goes on to write:

> To regard the fourteenth-century version of just war theory on noncombatantcy as a morally ideal statement for all time is to make the same error of judgment often made about just war thought as a whole; it is not a moral absolute, demarcating the limits of that which is ideally, inflexibly and eternally just, but a time bound and culture bound formulation of a moral floor upon human conduct in war.[32]

Ramsey's work to shore up the structure of moral reality in this case leads him to the recovery of a significant principle of military ethics. But here, as elsewhere, his theologically grounded overconfidence in the security of principled judgments also obscures the fragility of his own conclusions when deploying principled reasoning.

In contrast to his approach to principled judgments, Ramsey's approach to calculations of proportionality and consequence overstates the insecurity and lack of structure in such determinations.[33] Ramsey's moral sensitivity to relativistic moral systems led him to react zealously to several moral errors he saw in contemporary society. In continuity with the broader idealistic tradition, he positioned himself fervently against the error of "technological reason" which quantified all goods as if they were simply commensurable. He also battled against reductive consequentialism which collapsed moral accounts of action into accounts of the motives which drive the actor. Both do present serious dangers in moral reasoning. But, Ramsey has a tendency of overreacting to these dangers, shying away from any systematic account of proportional decisions, and focusing too narrowly upon the indeterminacy of claims about the future.

These concerns mix in Ramsey's analysis with a distaste for what Ramsey perceived as naive liberal Christian demands for reforms and actions that attempted to apply transcendent principles directly to political situations in ways that threatened the immanent moral order of history. In his reaction to this threat, Ramsey uses Niebuhrian/Kierkegaardian rhetoric in his battle to maintain the immanent moral order. Those who attempt to discern what God is doing in the future ought to be treated, Ramsey suggests, with a dose of skepticism. It is only a form of deluded messianism, Ramsey writes, that "describes the proper political act in terms of one or another alleged discernment of the times and the seasons."[34]

While this is Niebuhrian rhetoric, it is, at best, a one sided Nieburianism. Niebuhr's critical edge is ideally composed of transcendent criticism oriented to some extent both toward the status quo order and progressive movements. This critical movement in Niebuhr's thought was always conjoined with a strong account of the kind of action in history which one was willing to undertake and a will to take responsibility for tough calculations of proportionality and consequence. Ramsey, in his 1960s arguments against liberals, uses Niebuhr's rhetoric in a different context, stressing the criticism of what he takes to be naive progressive programs while begging off from providing an account of the proportional and consequential reasoning necessary to historical responsibility in the Niebuhrian sense.

The upshot of these anti-consequentialist and proportionalist concerns and rhetoric is ultimately to make the shape of such calculations enigmatic from Ramsey's perspective. All too often these calculations come to seem, in Ramsey's analysis, "almost, if not altogether, incorrigible to moral reasoning."[35]

In his most polemic moments, the religious dimension of his confidence in principled judgments and lack of confidence in judgments of proportionality and consequence comes to the fore. Such is the case in one of his criticism of the procedure employed by the United Methodist Bishops when approaching the subject of nuclear war.

> When the Bishops lighted upon the Concerned Scientists as their chosen experts, and made foundational these scientists' plausible or implausible predictions of futurelessness and the self-destruction of the human species, they built their house upon shifting sand. Not only are computer models mutable; commonly experienced events or supposed future events are also mutable. *Among them the rock of our salvation is not to be found. An adequate Christian outlook or onlook upon the future cannot be drawn from common events; right and wrong do not depend upon eventualities for foundation.*[36]

Statements like this reveal both Ramsey's zeal in establishing a secure foundation for the reality of the moral structure of history and the hazard of overstatement in his polemic mood. He is right that the rock of our salvation is not to be found in the adequacy of our calculations of consequence or proportionality. But, no matter how much more relative security it may contain, it is to be hoped that salvation is also not to be found in the adequacy of our grasp of principled judgments. This is a fact that Ramsey recognizes in his less polemic and more qualified moments. As the rock of our salvation, Niebuhr would remind us, God sent God's unique son to achieve that which no rule within history could.

Thus, Ramsey's approach to moral determination excels in articulating in detail the morally relevant features of particular acts. This is an important corrective in Protestant culture which has a tendency toward voluntaristic conceptions of the good or the right. But such analysis must be supplemented with an emphasis upon the explicitly moral considerations dealing with a wider set of concerns about how one perceives the world. A viable moral system also requires a more even handed treatment of deontic and prudential moral considerations than Ramsey produces.

Conclusion

Niebuhr and Ramsey draw from the Christian tradition in ways that allow them to treat the moral problems to which their earlier philosophical training had sensitized them. Drawing on the multivalent symbol of love Niebuhr and Ramsey are able to construct Christian moral languages that protect against fanaticism and atomistic relativism. In the end they are left with overlapping but divergent Christian perspectives on the world. These perspectives often share the strengths and weaknesses of the philosophical systems to which they are related.

This is only part of the Christian reconstruction of the idealist/pragmatist debate that Niebuhr and Ramsey took part in. Their views of society and war further show ways in which their later works remain influenced by these philosophical schools. Their doctrines of sin can also be read as efforts to re-describe the moral dangers of fanaticism and atomistic relativism in Christian terms. It is to these further developments that we now turn.

Notes

1. John Crossley writes of one encounter in which Ramsey was challenged concerning the "uniqueness of the love of God in Jesus Christ." Crossley recalls that Ramsey replied that "the uniqueness of Christian love was not that it called all other ethics into question, but that it was unique because it was so rare." See, John Crossley, foreword to *Paul Ramsey's Ethics*, by Michael C. McKenzie, xii. As one might expect if the disagreement is partially grounded in translational problems, Ramsey himself is able to express similar sentiments to some of those found in Niebuhr's "impossibility of love" when he himself stresses the impossibility of an exact imitation of Christ. See Ramsey, *Speak Up For Just War or Pacifism*, 113-114.

2. The Ramseyan flavor of Ramsey's reading of Niebuhr on love is revealed by his language in describing Niebuhr's account of love; a language which parallels his own account of love as a motive which can be yoked to diverse and preferential actions. He states that in dealing with love "we are here dealing with the motive or intention of the act." Ramsey, *Nine Modern Moralists*, 136. Ramsey also continually attempts to read Niebuhr as proposing a scheme in which regulative principles follow from a consideration of love applied directly to history. In the first edition of his essay on Niebuhr, Ramsey suggests that these principles follow "'in a necessary manner' from reflecting upon the nature of man as man and the love requirements of his quintessential freedom." Paul Ramsey, "Love and Law," in *Reinhold Niebuhr: His religious, social, and political thought*, 98. By the time he revises his essay for *Nine Modern Moralists* it has become clear that this was a flawed interpretation. As such he attempts to correct his statement by arguing that regulative principles "follow in some manner if not 'in a necessary manner'" from such considerations. Ramsey, *Nine Modern Moralists*, 126.

3. For others who locate self-sacrifice at the heart of Niebuhr's concept of love see Joseph L. Allen, *Love and Conflict*, 90, and Gene Outka, *Agape: An ethical analysis* (New Haven, Conn.: Yale University Press, 1972) 24-34, 169-75. There are times when Niebuhr seems to suggest that self-sacrifice is the central content of love, but these passages must be carefully exegeted. For instance, Niebuhr writes that the love of Christ is found in "*His* disinterested and sacrificial agape." Niebuhr, *The Nature and Destiny of Man*, 2:71. On my reading this makes sense inasmuch as Christ's act on the cross is the only act which could be a purely loving self-sacrifice because this act saves all in need. Niebuhr also writes that "it is impossible to *symbolize* the divine goodness in history in any other way than by complete powerlessness." Niebuhr, *The Nature and Destiny of Man*, 2:72. Here it is important to maintain a distinction between the symbolizing of love and the approximating of love in Niebuhr's thought. Self-sacrificial symbolic acts may remind humanity of its sin and God's offer of salvation, and thus draw the self beyond the self in its anxiety. But even these acts should not be confused with the actualization of love in history, which is properly only available to Christ. (See Chapter 7 below on prophetic pacifism). Approximations of love are those acts that seek to realize the social goods for which God has provided in history.

4. Ramsey, *Nine Modern Moralists*, 136, 139.

5. Ramsey, *Nine Modern Moralists*, 135.

6. In this sense, both Ramsey and Niebuhr find self-sacrifice to be central to love. See Ramsey's comments on self-sacrifice as an "*inner* attitude" in *Nine Modern Moralists*, 135.

7. Niebuhr, *An Interpretation of Christian Ethics*, 168. Italics mine. See also Niebuhr, *The Nature and Destiny of Man*, 2:88, and Niebuhr, *Faith and History*, 184. The only act that can be more than a *symbol*, even while it is a symbol, of this divine goodness is found in Christ's action in its trans-historical dimension. See Niebuhr, *The Nature and Destiny of Man*, 2:71-72, and Niebuhr, *Love and Justice*, 276. Ramsey seems to interpret Niebuhr as claiming that taking part in such powerlessness is *a direct requirement of historical participation* in divine goodness. For Niebuhr, such participation is impossible.

8. In his course lectures on Christian Ethics, Niebuhr favorably cites a New Testament scholar who finds that the Aramaic statement reflected in Matthew 5:48 would have better been translated "let your love therefore be all inclusive as God's love includes all." Niebuhr continues on to note that this is the problematic starting point for all Christian social ethics. "Because social ethics deals with all the ambiguities of tolerable harmony, tolerable justice, etc., etc. And that's why both the Catholic Church and the Protestant Church have difficulty in relating these ultimate demands to the proximate demands of a social ethic." Niebuhr, "Ethics of Jesus," Compact disk of a lecture by Reinhold Niebuhr delivered in 1960, CD N665, 34, The Reinhold Niebuhr Audio Collection (Richmond, Va.: Union Presbyterian School of Christian Education).

9. As I shall argue below, at times Ramsey makes the mistake of overstressing the implications of this imperfection on judgments of proportion and consequence while understating its impact on deontic reasoning.

10. Ramsey, *The Just War*, 179.

11. Reinhold Niebuhr, *Love and Justice*, 190.

12. Ramsey's claim that "war first became total in the minds of men" is also an oversimplification. See, Ramsey, *The Just War*, 160. The shift in modern conceptions of war was a product of a complex interaction between shifting cultural factors and the evolution of weaponry and transportation. See James Turner Johnson, *Ideology, Reason, and The Limitation of War: religious and secular concepts, 1200-1740* (Princeton, N.J.: Princeton University Press, 1975), and Johnson, *Just War Tradition and the Restraint of War*. As I shall suggest below, Ramsey's polemic tendencies led him at times to oversimplify the extent to which principled moral reasons shine a clear light on the moral decisions faced in history.

13. See Chapter 7.

14. Phillip Bobbit, for instance, suggests that the way that nation states organize their economic strategies may play a large role in determining the level of violence in future wars. See *The Shield of Achilles: War, peace, and the course of history* (New York: Alfred A. Knopf, 2002), 213-342, 667-816.

15. While Niebuhr never developed a fully articulate system for describing the intrinsic values of particular acts, he was not unaware of these values. In an essay criticizing the practice of obliteration bombing during World War II, Niebuhr notes that the "theory that the bombing of workers' homes represents an indirect destruction of industrial power" is not sufficient to justify this bombing. See "Is the Bombing Necessary," *Christianity and Crisis*, 4 (April 3, 1944), 1.

16. See for instance Niebuhr, *Love and Justice*, 223.

17. It is important to note that I do not take the following account to be identical with Ramsey's framework for thinking through these moral conflicts. I am interested here in

his general emphasis on relational continuity, and not all of the particulars of the ways he would conceive of these relationships and their structures.

18. See Chapter 3 above, and Ramsey, "The Case of the Curious Exception," 88.

19. See Niebuhr, *Love and Justice*, 218-21.

20. See Ramsey, *Deeds and Rules*, 162, *The Just War*, 398-403.

21. Ramsey, *Deeds and Rules*, 91.

22. William May, "The Patient as Person: Beyond Ramsey's Beecher Lectures" in *The Patient as Person*, by Paul Ramsey, xxxvi.

23. On Ramsey and such calculations, see Charles Curran, *Politics, Medicine, and Christian Ethics: A Dialogue with Paul Ramsey*, 52, Donald Evans, "Paul Ramsey on Exceptionless Moral Rules," in *Love and Society*, 39, 44, David Little, "The Structure of Justification in the Political Ethics of Paul Ramsey," in *Love and Society* 146-49, and Joseph Allen, "Paul Ramsey and his Respondents since *The Patient as Person*," *Religious Studies Review* 5, no. 2 (April, 1979), 89-93.

24. Ramsey, "Some Rejoinders," 206. Elsewhere Ramsey writes that his project should be construed as the rejection of a reduction of ethics to consequentialist and proportionalist calculation "without in any sense minimizing the significance of calculation, in its proper place, both for morality and for political decision." Ramsey, *War and the Christian Conscience*, 5. See also Donald Evans, "Paul Ramsey on Exceptionless Moral Rules," in *Love and Society*, 44

25. See Ramsey, "The Case of the Curious Exception," 126. In one instance concerning the ethics of experimentation he writes: "The principle of an informed consent is a statement of the fidelity between the man who performs medical procedures and the man on whom they are performed. Other aspects of medical ethics—for example the requirement of a good experimental design and of professional skill at least as good as is customary in ordinary medical practice—treat the man as purely passive subject or patient. These are also the requirements that hold for an ethical experiment on animals. But any human being is more than a patient or experimental subject; he is also a *personal* subject—every bit as much a man as the physician-investigator. Fidelity is between man and man in these procedures." Ramsey, *The Patient as Person*, 5.

26. Ramsey, "The Case of the Curious Exception," 76. Ramsey's account of the content of "moral reason" cannot be fully separated from his view of the structure of society which will be discussed in the Chapter 6 below. As we shall see, Ramsey attempts to distinguish between the kind of reason properly used by the moralist qua moralist or the Christian qua Christian, and the spheres of reason which are properly reserved for persons as they function within other specialized fields.

27. Ramsey, "Force and Political Responsibility," in *Ethics and World Politics*, ed. Ernest Lefever (Baltimore, Md.: Johns Hopkins Press, 1972), 52.

28. Ramsey, *War and the Christian Conscience*, 11

29. Ramsey, "The Case of the Curious Exception," 90-91. Italics mine. This concept of the guidance of God in particular spheres of moral reasoning can also be seen, albeit more vaguely, in Ramsey's transformism as showcased in *War and the Christian Conscience*. There he writes: "the nature of that City in which men together attain their final end is divine charity, as a consequence even earthly cities began to be elevated and their justice was infused and transformed by new perspectives, limits, and principles." Ramsey, *War and the Christian Conscience*, xxi.

30. Ramsey, *War and the Christian Conscience*, 9-10. Italics mine.

31. Charles Harris, "Love as the Basic Moral Principle in Paul Ramsey's Ethics," 243.

32. James T. Johnson, *Just War Tradition and the Restraint of War*, 150

33. In one treatment of calculations of proportionality and consequence as regards war, Ramsey notes that such calculations suffer under "the greatest uncertainty" and as such establish rather than remove "the possibility of conscientious disagreement among prudent men." Ramsey, *The Just War*, 195. Such a statement would not be so striking if it were not the case that Ramsey was at the same time arguing that the strategy adopted by the insurgents in Vietnam (if it was properly described by Ramsey himself) had "enlarged the target" for legitimate attack so broadly that the principle of discrimination no longer provided a main source for limiting acts within the war. Ramsey, *The Just War*, 435. This "principled judgment" was at least as great a source for "conscientious disagreement" as the calculations of proportionality others were undertaking.

34. Paul Ramsey, "Politics as Science, Not Prophecy," in *Worldview* 11, no. 1 (January, 1968), 18.

35. Ramsey, *The Patient as Person*, 240. Here Ramsey is speaking specifically of "the larger questions of medical and social priorities." There are exceptions to this skeptical trend in Ramsey's thought. While criticizing radical American liberals in the Vietnam era for those mistakes Ramsey believes "they have *done* and have *foreseeably* done," Ramsey argues that "in charity one should assume the best of every one, and among other things that they are rational about the political consequences of their words and deeds." See Paul Ramsey, "Political Repentance Now!" *Christianity and Crisis* 28, no. 18 (October 28, 1968), 247.

36. Ramsey, *Speak up for Just War or Pacifism*, 26-27.

Part II
Political Society

Chapter 5
Providence, Sin, Institutions, and Authority

The American transcendentalists were pioneers in the area of civil disobedience. Henry David Thoreau's famous essay on the subject grew out of his dispute with the United States government over the nation's participation in the Mexican-American War and slavery. For Thoreau, the state was due obedience only insofar as the individual found it to be representative of justice in its policies. The pragmatists moderated many of the transcendentalists' ideas concerning self-sufficiency. Freedoms had to be justified in terms of social benefit, and all individual views were fallible. But the pragmatists maintained a picture of society that stressed the need for continual criticism of social institutions, and authorities. As possible loci of fanaticism, these structures had to be held open to the public eye, and the public needed to be empowered to critically assess its own order. Institutions were not conceived as given, natural features of the landscape, but rather as collective experiments in social human life. Social policies were to be legitimated by democratic procedure rather than the pronouncements of authorities. Structures were good only inasmuch as they served to facilitate relatively harmonious human life, and they could be set aside if they failed to do so. All institutions and authorities, the pragmatists emphasized, could be called to account.

Absolute idealism began from a different set of concerns. Kant had attempted to liberate people from imposed structures of authority by allowing them to appeal to abstract human reason. The principles of moral reason, he thought, transcended social structures and delivered a universal moral code. Hegel was troubled about the atomistic individualism of Kant's conception of rational autonomy. He found that, left to their own abstract reason, individuals had an amazing capacity to wish to universalize even the most selfish and immoral maxims. The upshot of Kantianism was thus revealed to be a form of atomistic relativism. To solve this problem, Hegel took up Kant's category of rational autonomy and turned it on its head. The order of the state, he posited, is an expression of the ultimately rational Absolute. Therefore any rationally autonomous person finds her or his freedom exactly in obedience to the structures of the state in which she or he is reared. In this way Hegel reinstituted a premodern sense of reverence for institutions and authorities on modern grounds.[1] Rationality required obedience to the given structures of the state. This was not an argument in favor of totalitarianism. Hegel himself lived in a constitutional monarchy. Later idealists in England and America worked to show that this picture could be compatible with liberal democratic values, stressing the structured demands of rights and responsibilities in democratic societies. In these pictures, however, obedience and reverence were always primary concerns. Only with these factors emphasized could there be room for freedom within the order of society.

Given their exposure to these two schools of thought, it is not surprising that Ramsey's and Niebuhr's later theologies take different courses when relating to social institutions and authorities. But as usual, Niebuhr's and Ramsey's frameworks are grounded in theological rather than philosophical accounts of reality. This chapter explores the distinctive conceptions of providence and sin in Niebuhr's and Ramsey's works and draws out how their development of these doctrines reflect the concerns and shapes of the idealism and pragmatism in which they were trained. In the first section of the chapter I will suggest that Ramsey's and Niebuhr's doctrines of providence underwrite different perspectives upon social institutions. The second section of the chapter treats their distinctive understandings of sin and their perspectives on those with authority and power within a given social structure. Finally, I will offer some of the mutual critiques I find arising from a critical dialogue between the two positions.

Throughout, I will argue that Ramsey's and Niebuhr's respective theological systems function to illumine the institutional manifestations of those moral dangers in relation to which each is sensitized. While Niebuhr recognizes the enduring and often beneficial nature of social institutions, his understandings of providence and sin draw attention to the dangerous fanatic tendencies inherent in uncritical participation in any particular social unit and in the wielding of political power. While Ramsey recognizes the need for continual transformation of institutions, his understandings of providence and sin lead him to emphasize the dangers of atomistic individualism and treachery against the structure, authority, and projects of one's community.

Providence and Social Institutions

Both Ramsey and Niebuhr recognize that history is encompassed by the providential work of God. As such, both find an important role for God in establishing order within history. Both also provide means for talking about God's action in challenging or transforming social orders in the light of the requirements of love. But their views of providence also diverge along predictable lines given Niebuhr's and Ramsey's early formation. Niebuhr's framework tends to emphasize God's historical judgment, which stands in tension with any contemporary order and any program for progress so as to hold these open to criticism. The social order in history is not an expression of the conceptual structure of God's mind so much as it is an imperfect means of mediating between the relative goods available in sin-skewed history. Like the pragmatists, Niebuhr shies away from essentialist analysis in favor of seeing institutions as experimental structures that exist due to, and gain their value from, their present usefulness in the process of human history. Historical institutions are temporary structures meant to maintain a relative justice in the *saeculum*, but all of these structures will eventually be dismantled by God's judgment before the coming of perfection in the eschaton. Ramsey's framework, on the other hand, stresses the extent to which God works through institutions, even in their continual transformation, so as to stress the importance of immanent divine guidance and the demands of this order. Similar to the idealists, Ramsey pictures the history of institutions as a history of the action of God in unfolding and perfecting the conditions for the ideal relational order that will be consummated in the eschaton. In what follows, I will present how these emphases work out in terms of Niebuhr's and Ramsey's theologies.

Institutions and God's Historical Judgment

Niebuhr is not unaware of the importance of institutions within history or the work of God which allows for and sustains such institutions. "The vast variety of historic organisms, the richness of their elaborations of human potentialities, the wealth of their many cultural forms and social configurations are," Niebuhr writes, "certainly a testimony to the divine providence under which they have grown."[2] Within history, social institutions are part of the "common grace" of God through which the self is drawn out of the self toward concern for ever more inclusive circles of persons in the world.[3]

Niebuhr is also attuned to the dangers of ignoring the "organic" and culturally conditioned divisions inherent in historical society. These provide a structure to society which is resistant to being dissolved into any homogenizing account of the common good. Resisting homogenization is not a purely negative function. It is the diversity of the institutions and cultural forms within history that often prevents the collapse of the wider society into tyrannical forms of power. The balancing of power among different groups in the society provides a modicum of justice within history. Naive programs of reform that seek to abolish these divisions are, Niebuhr reminds, bound to fail, bringing more damage than they alleviate.

But Niebuhr is also aware of the dangers involved with identifying any particular historical institutional order too closely with God's ultimate will. All achievements of history are imperfect. All are products of creation involving God's providence and sinful human contributions.[4] There are no perfect solutions to social problems within history and every particular solution, embodied in a particular institution or set of institutions, will be used by sinful humanity against its better possibilities. As such, when writing of God's action within history, Niebuhr tends to stress not God's creative action in institutional forms but God's judgment of these institutions.

The Old Testament recounts the story of God's use of the orders represented by Assyria and Babylon in meting out God's judgment against Israel.[5] In these stories God is not to be simply identified with the orders represented by these powers. These orders are themselves due for judgment. This divine act shows both God's use of historic order, and God's judgment against historic order. This is the dialectic which shapes Niebuhr's view of providence. While God is active within the orders of history, all orders within history are corrupted by sin, and God is never to be simply identified with such order. Thus, while the growth of social institutions is a sign of providence, "their destruction is a vindication of the eternal judgment, which they are unable to deny with impunity."[6] God's providence is most excellently revealed in those historical occasions that remind the Christian that all of these particular forms of institutional power are passing away, not only in the eschaton, but under the judgment meted out by God even now.[7] God's is both active within and critical of all those forms of order available in history.

Such an emphasis leaves Niebuhr critical of those theologians who focus upon God's action in buttressing immanent order within history. His reaction to Emil Brunner's concept of the "orders of creation" is a case in point. There "must be something in the order of creation which makes it normative," Niebuhr writes. "But it is difficult to find this normative principle because man is a historical creature and there are no purely 'natural' forms in his life which have not been subjected to both the freedom and the corruption of history."[8] Niebuhr argues that even the institution of marriage, the closest thing to a "natural" human institution, has been humanly shaped and thus corrupted within history. Further, the shape of this partially corrupted institution has been, in the Christian tradition itself, wrongly linked with absolute claims for the particular form of order it represents. It was this mistake that made "the Christian community tardy in recognizing the fact that a woman in a modern culture must have the freedom to add another vocation to that of motherhood because it regarded the biological limits as more fixed than they are."[9] The human claim to know the divinely sanctioned form of marriage thus became an impediment to the realization of greater possibilities in the lives of women. Thankfully, though not perfectly, this misconception has, over time, slowly come under the historic judgment of God.

Thus, Niebuhr stresses the extent to which God's ultimate will should not be identified with any institution lest the believer become enthralled with the institution and fail to expect God's judgment over and against it within history. This does not prevent an appreciation for the relative orders available within history. In most cases the responsible Christian must work through the orders available in history. But the

Christian always participates in such orders with a religious reservation. History for Niebuhr is a realm of ironic reversals wherein putative progress often finds itself judged by God. The greatest danger is for one to fanatically close her or himself off from hearing this judgment.

God's Saving Work through the Orders of Creation

Ramsey's approach to providence is, needless to say, somewhat different. Ramsey is, as we have seen, not unaware of the dangers of theological conservatism. He does endorse Brunner's concept of the "orders of creation." But he believes that by locating the orders within the whole creative, preserving, and redemptive action of God, it is possible to retain a continual stress upon God's work *within* the orders of society without falling into conservatism.[10] Like the idealists, Ramsey finds that history is best conceived as constantly caught up in God's ordering activity. God's work in the orders includes God's work in transforming those orders so as to provide for the best actualization of essential covenant relations in history. As such, Ramsey recognizes the possibility of transformative moments in which "love *immanent within* the orders also will sometimes require that they be shattered and reconstructed."[11] With this understanding in place, Ramsey denies that a theological ethic grounded in the orders of creation manifests any conservative tendency. He avers that whoever finds in this ethic "only a static ethic of creation or a pessimistic view of sinfulness is himself probably one of those fanatics and sentimental enthusiasts whom Brunner rightly opposes."[12]

But while Ramsey's framework allows for transformative change, the image it presents suggests a significantly different emphasis from Niebuhr's own view. This difference in emphasis emerges in Ramsey's approach to the prophetic tradition. Ramsey's reading of the prophetic tradition focuses on those stories in which particular prophets call for actions which were not justified within the limitations of history. As such, he tends to identify the prophetic movement with naive progressive political projects, overzealous claims to be able to foretell the outcomes of policy decisions, and efforts to identify one's position with God's perspective and action.[13] In contrast to the prophetic tradition thus construed, Ramsey stresses the role of God in providing and maintaining social institutions even as they are transformed. In practice, this means focusing upon the extent to which love must be "refracted" through existing institutions while advances in loving society must be worked out in the "interstitial spaces" within and between existing institutions.[14]

It is within this framework that Ramsey approaches the civil rights movement of the early 1960s. Here Ramsey recognizes the need for a transformation of the social structure of American life on the grounds that such is required to allow for a more genuine realization of covenant relations between the diverse ranges of American citizens. But Ramsey also stresses that movements for change must be grounded in respect for the form of order that exists in the present. To the extent possible, the protester should remain within the bounds of the laws that govern relations within the society. If one comes to a point where she or he finds she or he is morally required to break the law, one should submit to the punishments which follow from the law she or he has broken.[15] Institutional restraints are product of God's providential will emerging through the dialogue and consensus of the community. Thus, these restraints should be respected even when challenged in the name of God's immanent transforming activity.

Ramsey's own emphasis upon understanding extant institutions in terms of God's efforts to provide the best possible order within the limitations of history lead him to react against conceptions of society that focus upon the imperfections in extant institutional forms. In one case, Ramsey responds to Helmut Thielicke's comment that "the world between the fall and the judgment is not only empowered to set up states; it is *condemned* to do so." Ramsey retorts that it is better to say that in the post-lapsarian world we are "condemned to be able to do *no more than* govern one another through an opposed–system in which power is restrained by further power."[16] Thus presented, the stress falls upon the positive role that the state plays within God's unfolding providential plan. Caught up in the framework of God's providence the immanent structures of social institutions function to protect from sin and guide toward salvation.

Ramsey's view of providence is thus tied up in God's ever present action within the structures of the world. Life is lived in the space within the structure that God has provided and is refining. Humans are bound to this order, both protected by its current shape and obligated to participate in its continual transformation. Respect for the whole of God's work in this order demands nothing less than thorough attention to the ways in which God moves through the structured immanent demands of life within history.

Sin and Society

These pictures of providence provide a glimpse into the different emphases of Niebuhr and Ramsey as they approach social institutions and authorities, but the picture provided thus far is insufficiently rich to capture the full depth of these emphases in Niebuhr and Ramsey's thought. To further clarify their perspectives it is necessary to carry our inquiry to a doctrine central to both Ramsey's and Niebuhr's theologies: the doctrine of sin. Both Niebuhr and Ramsey have quite robust accounts of the shape of sin, though, as is the case with other doctrines, they are overlapping but divergent accounts. As we shall see below, Niebuhr draws upon the insights of Kierkegaard's analysis and stresses the danger of idolatry especially as expressed in the "worship" of historical social organizations. Ramsey provides a deontic twist to Kierkegaard's understanding of sin and is influenced by a Roycean conception of sin as treachery against a common social cause. An understanding of these divergent starting points illumines the tension between the Ramseyan and Niebuhrian approaches to criticism of social institutions and the systems of authority inherent in those institutions.

Sin as Idolatry

When approaching the issue of sin, Niebuhr turns to another great scholar who wrestled with issues central to the Augustinian tradition: Søren Kierkegaard. Like Niebuhr, Kierkegaard had been a polemicist against moral reductivism and dogmatism. In the Hegelianism imported into Denmark during the nineteenth century Kierkegaard recognized reductive accounts of the sources of moral knowledge and expansive claims concerning the completeness of moral knowledge.[17] Setting the stage for Niebuhr's later pragmatically influenced Christian realism, Kierkegaard questioned the hubris of human schemes of thought that claimed intellectual ownership of ultimate reality.

> If a dancer could leap very high, we would admire him, but if he wanted to give the impression that he could fly—even though he could leap higher than any dancer had ever leapt before—let laughter over-

> take him. . . . To be a human being has been abolished and every speculative thinker confuses himself with humankind whereby he becomes something infinitely great and nothing at all.[18]

He reacted to this hubris with theological, psychological, and philosophical analyses designed to show that any self-contained and self-sufficing system of human thought would inevitably fail to grapple with the reality of existence in relation to a transcendent God. Also like Niebuhr, Kierkegaard's reaction to these reductive tendencies was grounded in theology. "Existence itself," Kierkegaard writes, "is a system for God, but it cannot be a system for any existing [*existerende*] spirit."[19] Hegelianism, Kierkegaard suggests through his pseudonymous authors, fails to live up to Christian theological demands exactly because it reduces the "ethical" to the contingent, partial norms of societal reason within history and is unable to recognize the judgment of God which exists beyond and at times in contradiction to historical human institutions and purposes.

Niebuhr's understanding of sin develops upon the insights of Kierkegaard's work.[20] According to Niebuhr's doctrine, the human, as a finite but free individual, is able in her or his freedom to access an inchoate vision of her or his telos. But this telos is, as we have seen above, fragile. Anxious about the possible failure of the self to realize its potential, the self is placed in an existentially vulnerable position. It is possible to accept one's finitude and fragility with trust that God will provide for fulfillment, but such is inevitably not the route followed by humanity within history. The sinful self denies her or his own finitude in the effort to secure enough power, knowledge, and virtue to insure her or his own fulfillment. In the process he or she enters into idolatrous practice. With willing ignorance, the self sets her or himself up as God and overestimates his or her grasp, or construes some finite institution, practice, or system of value as ultimate and comes to "worship" this false god.[21] The sinful person, unwilling to rely on God's efforts to fulfill her or his nature, falls to reductive and perfectionist impulses which lead the individual to claim the power to control the whole of the moral world or to withdraw from the wider world so as to maintain faux purity. The roots of both sectarian and paternalistic fanaticisms that the pragmatists had pointed out are thus located, by Niebuhr, not in epistemic errors but the original sins of humanity.

The understanding of sin as idolatry highlights the fact that there is no simple "solution" to this problem. In its worship of the idol, no part of the self is left unaffected by sin. Neither reason, nor appetites, nor emotion is safe from abuse. Each can be used by the sinful self to obscure its own sinfulness. The sinful person may use reason to form morally corrupt rules and enforce an immoral order by means of advocating strict obligation to these rules. A person may find her or himself drawn by feelings of patriotic devotion even toward a corrupt national organization. No appeal to any part of the self provides a refuge in which self-criticism becomes unnecessary.

The individual is not, however, simply lost to sinful impulses. Niebuhr does not believe that sin blots out all moral knowledge.[22] Within the individual is a sense of that which is lacking in every self-driven effort to achieve fulfillment. In moments of reflection, the self in its spiritual dimension is able to transcend itself and perceive this sinful self as object.[23] From this perspective above the sinful self, one is able to recognize her or his lack of fit with sinful action and existence. This moment then provides insight into the proper reformation of action in the next moment. But, following Kierkegaard, Niebuhr argues that the perspective provided in this self-transcendent moment is never identifiable with a closed systematic account of the ways in which the self fails in reaching her or his ideal state. If it were conceived as providing such, the transcendent moment would itself offer another temptation to sinful moral fanaticism.

On the one hand, the perspective should never be identified with a God's eye view of the good or the right. One must remember this in order to avoid mistakenly thinking that "its present ability to judge and criticize the undue and unjust claims of the self in a previous action is a guarantee of its virtue in a subsequent action."[24] It is true that each resource within the person provides insight into the truth of morality and the corrupt actions of the self in the past. But, being finite and tinged with sin, none provides an absolute and unquestionable knowledge of the good or the right. As such each must be kept under constant self-criticism.

On the other hand, the self-transcendent perspective is always something more than the systematic account of life provided by any particular finite set of institutions, practices, and systems of value to which one might have bound oneself. "The man who searches after both meaning and fulfillments beyond the ambiguous fulfillments and frustrations of history," Niebuhr argues, "exists in a height of spirit which no historical process can completely contain."[25] The self is never so all-consumed by the reductive tendencies toward moral fanaticism as to be incapable of gaining a critical perspective upon the organic, cultural, and institutional frameworks in which she or he is located.[26]

It is noteworthy that this scheme for understanding sin covers much of the same content covered by the idea of fanaticism. Idolatry is constituted by an overreaching of the self or the community that holds itself outside of criticism. Both paternalistic and sectarian forms of idolatry are denied in Niebuhr's theology as modes of idolatry. But unlike the pragmatic concern for fanaticism, Niebuhr's concept of sin is grounded in the Christian belief in an eternal order maintained by God. Niebuhr opposes the pretentiousness of humans who confuse their own claims with Gods on distinctly theological grounds.

Within this framework, the sinfulness associated with the structure of social groups within history was one of Niebuhr's special concerns.[27] Social groups can provide a psychological and sociological buffer between those inside and those outside the group, thus stymieing the perception of a neighbor's needs which are more immediate in intimate personal relations. Social organizations always rely upon symbols, myths, and ideologies to unify their members.[28] These symbol systems, in their function of eliciting loyalty, tend to overstate the goodness, sufficiency, and power of the social entity itself thus tempting individuals to idolatrous worship of the system. They also create an epistemic context in which the group always understands its own perception of the good in ways that it can never grasp another group's perception thereof. Unlike individual relations, within which disputes may be adjudicated by a relatively dispassionate higher social authority, inter-group relations, especially at the highest levels, are often governed by brute power. Finally, the level of power and correlative greater possibilities available to particular social organizations is always a temptation to pride on the part of the group and its leadership. The greater plausibility of self-deceptive group pretensions mixed with the real limitations of the possibilities for the group can lead to destructive grasps for power. For all these reasons, Niebuhr keeps a critical eye on the function of institutions and their structures of authority. Sinful pride and idolatrous pretensions, as Niebuhr notes, may not be *necessary* within group actions, but they are "an *inevitable* concomitant of the cohesion of large political groups."[29]

This does not mean that Niebuhr finds that an absolutely superior epistemic position is granted to the oppressed social critic. Social critics too must be checked in their own self righteousness, especially when they attempt to push for reforms that attempt to apply the absolute measures of the Kingdom of God directly to history. But Niebuhr does find in the prophetic Christian tradition a preference for criticisms leveled at those in positions of power and authority.

> The strictures of the prophets against the mighty, accusing them of pride and injustice, of both the religious and the social dimension of sin, are consistently partial. Prophetic judgment is leveled at those 'which oppress the poor, which crush the needy" (Amos 4:1), those who "lie upon beds of ivory, and stretch themselves upon their couches, and eat lambs out of the flock, and the calves out of the midst of the stall" (Amos 6:4), who "swallow up the needy, even to make the poor of the land to fail." (Amos 8:4)[30]

The idolatry of the powerful is thus the first target of the Christian critic.

Sin as Treason

Ramsey is no stranger to the Kierkegaardian understanding of idolatry. Kierkegaard's analysis was central to the "theological" (as opposed to "ethical") portion of Ramsey's earliest response to idealism. The identity between the self, the society, and the Absolute in Hegel's thought was the paradigm case of Kierkegaardian idolatry. Kierkegaard's argumentation is central to Ramsey's project of reforming the motive for service to the structured common good.[31] But Ramsey was much less inclined toward Kierkegaard's thought in the field of ethics. Within the realm of ethics, Ramsey found Kierkegaard to be a threat to moral stability. Along with many other scholars influenced by the idealistic tradition, Ramsey reads Kierkegaard's challenge to the "ethical" not as a challenge to reductive accounts of moral duty and value, but rather as a proposal for intuitionist ethical positivism. The suspension of the "ethical" becomes a challenge to the reality of the moral law itself. Ramsey thus reads Kierkegaard as one of the sources of the confused "theological intuitionism" which he battled throughout his career.

It is this complex relationship with Kierkegaard that lies in the background of Ramsey's first deviation from Niebuhr's theory of sin. In *Basic Christian Ethics* Ramsey presents the Niebuhrian theory largely as it is presented above, but one shift in his treatment leads to a subtle realignment of the doctrine so as to fit within a moral scheme directed against the danger of moral relativism rather than moral fanaticism.

When speaking of the nature of the self-transcendent moment, Ramsey redescribes the kind of knowledge available to the individual, and thus recasts the shape of sinfulness.

> After the doing of any deed [the person] judges his previous act *in terms of universal norms*; he stands within the image of God or under a standard of righteousness which he acknowledges has bearing upon him. He confesses that in doing A or B or C he loved the deed too much, or himself in the deed to much. However, when he begins to orient his thinking and planning toward the doing of his next deed . . . *he ceases to apply universal norms* to himself, or he twists them so as to make an exception of himself.[32]

Ever so subtly, Ramsey here turns Kierkegaard's emphasis on its head.[33] In the transcendent moment, Ramsey stresses the systematic nature of the knowledge available to the sinner. If one knows her or his action to be wrong, then he or she must know this *kind* of action to be wrong. Therefore, she or he is taking part in a kind of systematic thought about morality in the moment of transcendence. Sin now takes on the shape of individualistic rebellion against the moral structure which he or she knows when not making an exception for her or himself in the moment of action.

Thus, Ramsey finds that an appeal to generalizable principles constitutes a primary protection against sin. In his early work this strategy for controlling sin is expressed in terms of Rousseau's notion of the generality of application necessary to any truly just standard for public action.[34] In Ramsey's later, more explicitly Christian formulation, the need for rules could be articulated as an expression of the protection of covenant relations.

> Man's competence to know the good is, of course, not to be denied. . . . But we can also grasp the fact there is another law in our members, and we can anticipate the consequences of this even in metaethics (in rule-strengthening rules of moral reasoning that allow this to be taken realistically into account). At least, this is part of Christian theological *normative* metaethics—not only to call the fidelities to be done but also to exhibit the fact that faithlessness in ourselves needs governing by ordinances ever to ensure that we keep covenant.[35]

But Ramsey is not satisfied even with this revised "Kierkegaardian" theory of sin. Standing by itself it is, he suggests, too focused upon the origins of sin in the individual. Thus, in the last section of his treatment of sin in *Basic Christian Ethics* Ramsey attempts to push past Kierkegaard to an account of the social origins of sinfulness. For aid in his quest, Ramsey turns to the insights of the idealist tradition in Rousseau and Royce. For our purposes it is Royce's understanding of sin that is most important.[36]

For Royce, the self is individuated through the process of receiving unique positive and negative attitudes from the community. One's community brings one into existence by selectively treating one as individually right or wrong in specific situations. But in becoming a conscientious individual, the self is placed at that same time within a state of "original sin" because the self as individual conceives of itself as apart from the cause of the society which has produced her or his individuality and inevitably (in the Niebuhrian sense) rebels against the cause of the society. The only solution to the situation is to be "saved" by willed loyalty to some social cause. There is still, however, a danger even beyond this salvation. After willing the cause, the individual may again, in an act of actual sin, separate her or himself from the cause by an act of treachery. Thus, Ramsey suggests, the society itself, through the process of individuation, plays a significant role in the arousal of original sin.

The whole Roycean account is thus presented by Ramsey as an account of the social "origin" of original sin. But the implications of this theory of sin are greater than this suggests. This theory not only proposes a different understanding of the origin of sin, but also a different shape for sin itself. In contrast to the understanding of sin as idolatry, sin in the Roycean model is understood primarily in terms of treason against the will of God as expressed in the will, political processes, and structures of society.[37]

While Ramsey is not unaware of the sinful abuse of institutions or power, he, following out some possible implications of this view of sin, most often focuses on the kind of sin tied up with exempting oneself from the established moral and societal order. As he writes in 1961, the "sinful man affirms that, as an individual item, he has his humanity, his natural rights and justice due him, radically without his fellow man, half without him, and on some other basis than a man's true manhood *with* other men."[38] Correlatively, Ramsey finds that the "restraint and remedy of sin" should first be sought in the structure of social institutions.[39] It is loyalty to the delimited roles, relations, and rules of society which provides the best protection against falling into individualistic indulgence.

> Sin croucheth at the door of man's life with his fellow man. Created for life in covenant community, man has always already broken this covenant for which he was made in his fellow humanity. . . . We recognize man's propensity not only to be neutral or without his fellow man, but to stand in relation to him only for oneself. This means that the achievement of more abundant expressions of fellow humanity in the social order generally, no less and even more than in marriage, needs 'garments of skin' (Gen. 3:21) with which God by his own hands clothed naked human relations. This is a symbol for God's restraining grace in every impersonal and coercive institution and in the legal order, by which he intends for our good always to preserve a tolerable fellow humanity against the ravagements of sin.[40]

Ramsey also tends to stress the need to support the leaders of the society and the policies of the society, especially when a unifying communal cause has been undertaken. His approach to war as a social cause provides a good example. As he notes, in the run up to a war, citizens, functioning as "magistrates," properly operate under a presumption against war, debating and challenging the choice of this particular cause.

> Once the decision is taken, however, and the foreign policy of a nation has undertaken a particular political use of armed force the presumption shifts in favor of the justice of the war that these processes have authorized. It shifts because there is a shift to a *presumption favoring the established or legitimate political processes* by which the decision was made. Before, the individual was a 'lesser magistrate' . . . Now, the individual is a 'subject' . . .[41]

Perhaps for similar reasons, Ramsey often exhibits a tendency to defend the work of public officials from criticism. The authority of public officials is grounded in the established procedure and order of the community of which they are the leaders. As such, they stand in a special place in God's unfolding plan of history. In some sense, they are endowed with their power by the providence of God, so as to participate in their roles in restraining sin by enforcing the general will. In a suggestive passage, Ramsey reflects on some of the wartime duties of a king in Augustine's thought.

> The reason Augustine required declaration of war on the part of the highest official authority was because the existing political authority has the responsibility for that combination of wills or agreement as to goods necessary to the earthly life of a multitude if it is a people. The king, more than any individual or party, could be expected to be the voice of this alignment of wills, and he is therefore charged with the responsibility of preserving it.[42]

This does not, especially within the social order of a democracy, leave public authorities outside of the sphere of criticism. They must not overstep the bounds of their given role and betray the general will of the society. But it does mean that public officials are the persons with the primary responsibility for determining the way in which the community's common principles will be applied in political practice. "A statesman," Ramsey writes, "has the high and lonely responsibility of choosing what shall actually be done from among a number of possibilities, any of which might have been."[43]

There may be many disagreements about the particular applications the politician chooses, but even if the politician is in the wrong, there is not necessarily any sin involved. Not every political disagreement, and indeed for Ramsey very few political disagreements, concern betrayals of the common moral order of the community. There is no necessary sin, for example, in the politician undertaking a policy that ends up to have been disproportionate. One may undertake an act which is disproportionate for reasons of ignorance of the outcome of the action, thus committing a factual, but not a moral error. It would only be a sin if the act was undertaken *as a* disproportionate act.

> Concerning a great many choices it has to be said that only a deliberately or inflexibly imprudent decision would be wrong, or an uncharitable exercise of prudence. The principle of prudence (amongst Christian's teachings) definitely refers the matter in question to the magistrate or to the political process for decision; and the Christian as such can say no more than that this is the case.[44]

Only an intentional *betrayal* of the principle of proportionality is properly sinful. Since political officials find themselves in that role within the social order to which responsibility has been given, they must make decisions even in the midst of much confusion. Given the great burden they face, and the lack of security available to them in the process of applying socially common principles, public authorities should be given a benefit of the doubt, and the social cause they choose, once chosen, should be approached with presumption of correctness.

Ramsey also goes further in suggesting that even when sin may be involved, in public life one ought to "turn the other cheek" as it were in relation to possible violations on the part of one's neighbors, especially those in positions of political responsibility. In response to Niebuhr's own critical perspective on temporal authorities, Ramsey retorts:

> Perhaps where we fall short of the ideal of love in private and in public life is a subject that should be approached confessionally, throwing the mantle of charity over the sins of others, as Luther said, and not curiously spying them out, much less laying down in advance for them or for ourselves how far sin must abound.[45]

The reference to Luther seems to be to his commentary on Galatians 6:2.

> Love . . . is mild, courteous, patient, not in receiving, but in giving; for it is constrained to wink at many things, and to bear them. . . . if we bear and wink at our own vices and offences which we daily commit, let us also bear other men's faults, according to this saying: 'bear ye one another's burdens,' &c., and: 'Thou shalt love thy neighbor as thyself.[46]

Christian love requires that one maintain the given covenantal/institutional relationships inherent in society, even if this means bearing much of the burden of the covenant oneself when one's covenant partner fails.

Ramsey's approach is, however, not so 'charitable' when treating those whom he perceives as irresponsibly criticizing authorities from outside the given institutional system. During the late 1960s, as social movements critical of the governing authorities developed, he would lament the "truncated view of 'original sin'" being applied in Christian public discourse. This view is, he writes, "applied to produce only a concept of the 'arrogance of power'—forgetting that such an authentic view of man would entail in politics an *equal or greater suspicion* to be cast upon the 'arrogance of conscience' and moral self-righteousness."[47] It is the individual, standing apart from the social structures of authority and actual social responsibility for her or his criticisms, that must be reined in, lest sin corrode the order God has provided. Atomistic individualism is thus properly controlled only by a presumption in favor of social authority.

Criticism

It is important not to overstate the divergence between Ramsey and Niebuhr in these areas. As noted above, both agree that God is active both in maintaining and transforming social structures, even if they emphasize different aspects of God's action. Similarly, the understanding of sin as treachery is not to be cast as diametrically opposed to the understanding of sin as idolatry. Like most facets of Ramsey's and Niebuhr's theologies these divergent accounts provide different ways of talking, but overlap with one another significantly. In fact, the overlaps between the two views were at times significant enough to allow Ramsey to continue deploying the language of idolatry even while his application of the understanding of sin reflected his more Roycean framework. For instance, Ramsey maintains Kierkegaardian rhetoric when arguing for epistemic humility against those who ground their criticism in their calculations of proportionality and consequence, two forms of reasoning which Ramsey identifies with individual prudential discernment.

Correlatively, the differences between Niebuhr's and Ramsey's approaches to social institutions and authorities are relative differences. Niebuhr is not disavowing the order of society or calling for a rejection of the structures of established relationships. In some moods, he is even able to speak of the "government as a divine ordinance," and reverence for the "majesty of the law which coordinates the vitalities of a nation."[48] Nor was Niebuhr calling for weak or timid authorities. In the run up to World War II, he lamented the "weakness of democracy" in which America's authorities were blinded by the inertia of their own electorate and failed to "anticipate perils which the common man cannot see."[49] On the other side, Ramsey is never arguing for authoritarianism. Nor is his work lacking in democratic spirit. As we shall see in the next chapter, Ramsey was a stalwart defender of the structured relationship embodied in the democratic practice. Even when, in the above citation, Ramsey moves the citizen from the role of magistrate to the role of subject, the shift is a qualified one. The subject bears a *presumption* against any argument critical of the social policy, but does not bear an obligation to endorse a clearly immoral policy. One should take Ramsey at his word when, in responding to criticism of his approach to authorities, he notes that there are times when "we may be called upon, as Calvin said, 'to spit on the heads of magistrates.'"[50]

Still, one should not write off the import of the differences in emphases that these doctrines bring to bear on Niebuhr's and Ramsey's moral theologies. As with their views explored in the last section, the strengths and weaknesses of their own positions on social institutions and authorities are reflective of the moral dangers to which each is attuned.

Niebuhr, in his efforts to maintain a critical eye upon social actions, at times draws too straight a line between the sacrifice of certain goods entailed in social life and the moral ambiguity of the group and its leadership. As a proof of the fact that social failures are greater than those of individuals Niebuhr points out that group actions tend to fall farther short of the realization of pure love than do individual actions. The state, for instance, is required to take part in coercion, war, espionage, and other actions which are stark contradictions of the ultimate law of love. Summing up, Niebuhr quotes Camillo Cavour: "If . . . we did for ourselves what we do for our country, what rascals we would be."[51] Unfortunately, this is another mistaken example of the confusion of the functions of love as an indiscriminate and discriminate principle.

Niebuhr is right that the objective failure of our social organizations to live up to the law of love is morally significant. Through the lens of the Augustinian Christian narrative, the wretched necessities of history provide reminders of the brokenness of history and of our own participation both socially and individually in bringing about that brokenness. The necessity of such wretched activities is always part of the judgment of God perceived in history, and as such each person should recognize her or his own guilt when she or he is brought to the necessity of sacrificing genuinely human goods in the process of approximating love in history. Thus, social reality always stands under the judgment of love as an indiscriminate measure, convicting the world of sin. Niebuhr is also right to stress the reality of those goods which are sacrificed in many social activities. Without a rich appreciation for these goods, it becomes too easy to underestimate the cost of sacrifices for the social cause. But, as Ramsey was quick to point out in his own criticism of Niebuhr, and as Niebuhr recognizes in his more careful moments, this does not mean that all acts that sacrifice goods are themselves acts necessarily born directly out of sinful pretense. In the light of the discriminate measure of love, social acts may be found to represent the best approximation of love available at some period in history. One's original and past actual guilt may be revealed in that she or he finds her or himself in the position where she or he must have recourse to coercion, deception, or the infliction of some other harm, but this does not necessarily make the coercive, deceptive, or harmful act itself an act in which one incurs guilt.

A similar confusion is to be found in Niebuhr's treatment of the equality of sin and the inequality of guilt. The problem arises from Niebuhr's efforts to hold in tension both the sinfulness of all humanity and the need for greater criticism of those with greater power. Unfortunately, he decides to articulate his insight in terms of a distinction between universal sin and particular guilt. "Guilt," Niebuhr suggests, "is distinguished from sin in that it represents the objective and historical consequences of sin, for which the sinner must be held responsible."[52] Behind this formulation is a powerful argument for why those in power should be held under special scrutiny. Even if all are equally sinful, not all are equally dangerous. This in itself is an important addition to the reasons for criticism of authorities already provided in Niebuhr's account of idolatry.

Unfortunately, despite the insights it represents, the formula produces more confusion than clarity and fails to represent the subtlety of Niebuhr's own moral analysis.[53] Assessments of guilt, as this term is recognized in common usage, must depend on much more than the objective historical consequences of action. Motive, intent, and other conditions enter into any defensible analysis of the morality of an act or of the guilt a person incurs in any particular action. Further, the subjective state of a person, as Niebuhr recognizes when careful, is capable of degrees of selfishness which ought not to be leveled within the concept of the equality of sin. Thus, the Niebuhrian must seek some more subtle means of reproducing Niebuhr's insights on this point.

But Ramsey's ethic is also skewed in its approach to authorities. The Niebuhrian insight into the relation between power and the need for criticism should have been Ramsey's own. One might creatively paraphrase Ramsey against his own eventual conclusion: "Christian love, itself throwing an absolute mantle of charity over the sins of others in one-one relationships, may be required to change its tactic to curiously spying out the sin of those in power when concerned for the fate of more than one neighbor."[54] Unfortunately, Ramsey's tendencies took him elsewhere.

Ramsey is right that criticism of public authorities and policies can become a forum in which those without direct responsibility for outcomes are free to lob impossible challenges at those who are willing to take up public service. A culture grounded primarily in criticism may (perhaps, however, only in the most refined of academic discourses) devolve into a perverse nihilism in which the most successful polemicist is the one who finds a way of denying all positive claims, even, absurdly, her or his own. Concerning the rejection of these types of criticism Ramsey and Niebuhr have no disagreement. Ramsey is also right, as Niebuhr would agree, that no critic should hold her or himself outside of the range of criticism by any epistemic claim to indefeasible knowledge secured by prophetic insight or special social perspective. These are genuine insights from Ramsey. But these insights must be held in tension with the reality and dangers of the self-deceptive idolatrous pride, ideology, and social inertia concomitant with group actions and often manifested in the activities of social authorities. Ramsey's theological and polemic focuses did not allow him to develop a sufficient account of these forces,[55] or an appropriate counterweight to his own criticism of social critics.

This is one part of a larger problem in the balance of Ramsey's general approach to morality and public institutions. Having focused upon sin as individualistic treason against the moral order and structures of society, Ramsey tends to understate the ambiguity of appeal to rules and structured accounts of social relationships. He is correct to note that there are times in which an appeal to "rules of practice" is essential to determinations of right and wrong. For example, all other things being equal (or not *radically* unequal), vote tampering should be condemned by all who exist in democratic relationships regardless of whether such tampering helps one's favored candidate to win. There is a need for such things as civic virtue, faithfulness to one's word, and recognized obligation to enduring stable relations on all levels of human life. But, this side of the eschaton, human appeals to rules of practice are no sure protection against sinfulness. Unjust structures can be maintained by appeal to a wrongly constructed duty. Rule strengthening rules and efforts to shore up social institutions only protect against sin if it is the right rule or institution that is strengthened, and in human practice knowing which rule to strengthen and which to reject always requires an appeal to prudence. Ramsey's treatment of the usefulness of rules and institutions in protecting against sin often obscures the ambiguity involved in drawing upon principles and social institutions, and overstates the security they provide in steering a clear moral path through life.

Conclusion

This chapter has explored the subtle differences between Niebuhr's and Ramsey's approaches to the moral status of institutions and forms of loyalty properly due to these institutions and the authorities within these institutions. Predictably, while their systems of thought overlap, Niebuhr's theology presents a more reserved view of the reverence due to institutions and authorities than does Ramsey's. Again, an analysis of their positions reveals theologies which are grounded in Christian traditions, but also influenced by their early philosophical encounters with pragmatism and idealism. These differences continue in Niebuhr's and Ramsey's divergent but overlapping conceptions of public dialogue and Christian responsibility within that dialogue. The next chapter delves into these differences.

Notes

1. See Charles Taylor, *Hegel and Modern Society*, 81.
2. Niebuhr, *The Nature and Destiny of Man*, 2:305.
3. Niebuhr, *Faith and History*, 175.
4. As Langdon Gilkey writes: "Though he does not say so, Niebuhr agrees with Whitehead and Hartshorne that human freedom entails the capacity to be 'cocreator' with God, to introduce new forms into temporal sequence that had not been there before." *On Niebuhr*, 200.
5. See Niebuhr, *Essays in Applied Christianity*, 161.
6. *The Nature and Destiny of Man*, 2:305.
7. Niebuhr finds the same theme played out in the later works of Augustine. It was, Niebuhr writes, Augustine's insight that "destruction is the very law of life of the 'city of this world' and that pride is the cause of its destruction." *The Nature and Destiny of Man*, 1:215.
8. Reinhold Niebuhr, "The Concept of Orders of Creation in Emil Brunner's Social Ethic," in *The Theology of Emil Brunner*, ed. Charles W. Kegley (New York: Macmillan, 1962), 266.
9. Niebuhr, "The Concept of Orders of Creation, 267.
10. Ramsey, *Nine Modern Moralists*, 205.
11. Ramsey, *Nine Modern Moralists*, 205. Italics mine.
12. Ramsey, *Nine Modern Moralists*, 205
13. See Ramsey, *Speak Up for Just War or Pacifism*, 192-95, *Who Speaks for the Church*, and "Politics as Science Not Prophecy." It is important to note that Niebuhr does

recognize such tendencies in the prophetic tradition as represented in the Bible. But these tendencies never become central to his interpretation of the prophetic tradition. See Niebuhr, *Faith and History*, 128.

14. Ramsey, *Nine Modern Moralists*, 231, and *The Just War*, 498. See also the treatment of Ramsey, idealism, and change in Chapter 1.

15. Ramsey, *Christian Ethics and the Sit-In*, 83-98.

16. Ramsey, *Speak Up for Just War or Pacifism*, 186. Italics mine.

17. For a general account of Kierkegaard's critique of his society and Hegel's thought, see Merold Westphal, *Kierkegaard's Critique of Reason and Society* (University Park, Pa.: The Pennsylvania State University Press, 1991). For a treatment of contemporary continental debates that would be useful for Niebuhrian dialogue, see J. Aaron Simmons and David Wood (ed.) *Kierkegaard and Levinas: Ethics, Politics, and Religion* (Bloomington, Ind.: Indiana University Press, 2008).

18. Søren Kierkegaard, *Concluding Unscientific Postscript to "Philosophical Fragments"* trans. Howard V. Hong and Edna H. Hong (Princeton N.J.: Princeton University Press, 1992), 1:124.

19. Kierkegaard, *Concluding Unscientific Postscript*, 1:118.

20. See *Essays in Applied Christianity*, 124-25. A careful exegesis of Kierkegaard and exploration of his relation to Niebuhr is far beyond the scope of this book. Perhaps it is sufficient here to say that Niebuhr appreciated the concepts of self-transcendence and idolatry proposed by Kierkegaard inasmuch as they remind the person that her or his will is more than the will of any finite institution and less than the will of God. If Kierkegaard ever fell into the kind of otherworldly perfectionism Niebuhr found in Barth's writings, Niebuhr disagreed with his position on these points. See Niebuhr's treatment of "essentially universal principles" in *The Nature and Destiny of Man*, 2:254.

21. Niebuhr, *The Nature and Destiny of Man*, 1:203-7.

22. There is always in the human a "point of contact" with the divine and the virtuous. Niebuhr, *The Nature and Destiny of Man*, 1:220, 2:64.

23. Niebuhr, *The Nature and Destiny of Man*, 1:277.

24. Niebuhr, *The Nature and Destiny of Man*, 1:227.

25. Reinhold Niebuhr, *The Children of Light and the Children of Darkness*, 85.

26. See Lovin, *Reinhold Niebuhr and Christian Realism*, 154. Ramsey too admits the possibility of criticisms of the "rules of practice" under which society is governed. However, as should be expected, he emphasizes the need for stability within the rules of practice and the burden upon one who wishes to change them. See Ramsey, *Deeds and Rules in Christian Ethics*, 135-37.

27. Niebuhr's earliest statements on the relation of individual and group morality are overstated. In Niebuhr's early Marxist period he suggests a "frank dualism" between group morality and individual morality, and attributes the relative immorality of groups to their lack of "capacity for self-transcendence." Niebuhr, *Moral Man and Immoral Society*, xxv, 271. These claims overstated the moral dichotomy between groups and individuals and overlooked the fact that the group does not exist (and thus it has *no* transcendence) apart from the individuals that compose it. Individuals run the group, and these individuals do have access to self-transcendence. Niebuhr eventually recognized both errors. Individuals were, as Niebuhr would later note, more corrupt than he sometimes suggested in his early work, and groups had more capacity for moral action. See *Man's Nature and His Communities: essays on the dynamics and enigmas of man's personal and social existence* (New York: Charles Scribner's Sons, 1965), 22; also John Bennett,

"Reinhold Niebuhr's Social Ethics," in *Reinhold Niebuhr: His religious, social, and political thought*, 61. Niebuhr also notes in later writings that "strictly speaking, only individuals are moral agents, and group pride is therefore merely an aspect of the pride and arrogance of individuals." *The Nature and Destiny of Man*, 1:208. These corrections in Niebuhr's thought did not, however, weaken his stress upon the fact that groups provided temptations to idolatry and thus proper subjects for continual criticism.

28. Any comprehensive study of Niebuhr's view on social organizations would also highlight his use of Karl Marx, another critic of Hegel's. Niebuhr's use of Marx has been widely noted elsewhere.

29. Niebuhr, *The Nature and Destiny of Man*, 1:210.

30. Niebuhr, *The Nature and Destiny of Man*, 1:223.

31. See Ramsey "Natural Law and the Nature of Man" and "Existenz and The Existence of God: A Study of Kierkegaard and Hegel" *Journal of Religion* 28, no. 3 (July, 1948): 157-176.

32. Ramsey, *Basic Christian Ethics*, 312. Italics mine.

33. It is not clear how conscious Ramsey was of this shift. From his earliest work, he reads Niebuhr's work on the self-transcendent moment as treating a moment in which the self "has a memory of innocence and is able to *frame universal principles of action* which the self can never fully carry out." See "The Idealistic View of Moral Evil," 586. Italics mine. See also "Natural Law and the Nature of Man," 373.

34. Ramsey, "The Theory of Democracy: Idealistic or Christian," 257.

35. Ramsey, "The Case of the Curious Exception," 118.

36. Ramsey, *Basic Christian Ethics*, 319-25.

37. The language of sin as "betrayal" and as "treason" is central to Ramsey's own explication of Royce's view of sin. Ramsey does not tend to use this exact language elsewhere, but the concept remains central to his understanding of sin. See Ramsey, *Basic Christian Ethics*, 322-23.

38. Ramsey, *Christian Ethics and the Sit-In*, 31.

39. Ramsey, *Basic Christian Ethics*, 328.

40. Ramsey, *Christian Ethics and the Sit-In*, 48.

41. Ramsey, *The Just War*, 275.

42. Ramsey, *War and the Christian Conscience*, 39. Interesting here is the way in which Ramsey treats Augustine's revised definition of earthly justice. He suggests that Augustine believed that societies in history are "bound together by agreement of will and purpose" rather than by true justice in relating everything to God. Ramsey, *War and the Christian Conscience*, 23. By stressing the commonality of wills in Augustine's historical sociology rather than emphasizing the plurality of overlapping wills in historical society, Ramsey produces a picture suggestive of society as expressive of a socially common general will.

43. Paul Ramsey, "Force and Political Responsibility," 47-48. Ramsey would, when attempting to counter criticism of his position, point out that in passages treating the "magistracy" he meant to include all citizens as magistrates. See Ramsey, "Some Rejoinders," 187. This is indeed Ramsey's explicit intent in several passages, but his defense understates his own tendency to also distinguish between the general populace and those in roles of established political authority. He certainly was capable of speaking in terms of "the different measures and kinds of responsibilities possessed in modern states by statesmen and by individual citizens." See Paul Ramsey, "The Just War Theory on Trial," *Cross Currents* 13, n. 14 (Fall, 1963), 484. I take his comment here on "the

statesman" in her or his "high and *lonely* responsibility" to be an example of an instance in which his writing suggests a distinction between those in official positions of authority and those who are members of the general magistracy. See also his above distinction between magistrates and subjects, and his comments on the need to stand in awe before "'decision makers,' or rather before the majesty of *topmost* political agency." Ramsey, *Who Speaks for the Church*, 153. Italics mine. For further commentary on the shape (or lack thereof) in Ramsey's conception of political decision making see the next chapter.

44. Paul Ramsey, *Who Speaks for the Church*, 136. See also Ramsey, *The Just War*, 524.

45. Ramsey, *Nine Modern Moralists*, 137.

46. Martin Luther, *A Commentary on St. Paul's Epistle to the Galatians*, ed. Philip S. Watson (Westwood, N.J.: Fleming H. Revell Company, 1953), 540.

47. Paul Ramsey "Election Issues 1968," *Social Action* 35, no. 2 (September-October, 1968), 27. Italics mine.

48. Reinhold Niebuhr, *Essays in Applied Christianity*, 87.

49. Reinhold Niebuhr, "The War and American Churches," in *Christianity and Power Politics* (New York: Charles. Scribner's Sons, 1940), 47.

50. Ramsey "Some Rejoinders," 188. Ramsey is reacting here to a critique in David Little, "The Structure of Justification in the Political Ethics of Paul Ramsey," in *Love and Society*, 160. The reference to Calvin seems to be to his commentary on Daniel 6:22, in which Calvin writes that "earthly princes lay aside their power when they rise up against God, and are unworthy to be reckoned among the number of mankind. We ought, rather, utterly to defy them [*conspuere in ipsorum capita*, lit. 'to spit on their heads'] than to obey them." Cited in John Calvin, *Institutes of the Christian Religion*, ed. John T. McNeill, trans. Ford Lewis Battles (Louisville, Ky.: Westminster John Knox Press, 1960), 1519, *n.* 54. It should, however, be noted that I know of no time at which either Calvin or Ramsey so expectorated.

51. Niebuhr, *The Nature and Destiny of Man*, 1:209.

52. Niebuhr, *The Nature and Destiny of Man*, 1:222.

53. See John Bennett, "Reinhold Niebuhr's Social Ethics," 54-55, William Wolf, "Reinhold Niebuhr's Doctrine of Man," in *Reinhold Niebuhr: His religious, social and political thought*, 240-41, Reinhold Niebuhr, "Reply to interpretation and Criticisms," in *Reinhold Niebuhr: His religious, social and political thought*, 437, and Ronald Stone, *Reinhold Niebuhr: Prophet to politicians* (Nashville, Tenn.: Abingdon Press, 1972), 99-100.

54. See Ramsey, *Basic Christian Ethics*, 158.

55. Ramsey's own critique of Niebuhr focuses upon those points in which Niebuhr seems to, as I suggest above, confuse the objective failure of society to live up to the ideal of love and the subjective rightness of particular social actions. Ramsey never approaches the more subtle arguments Niebuhr has suggested concerning the subjective temptations to idolatry presented by group actions, or the need for criticism proportional to power. See Ramsey, *Nine Modern Moralists*, 135-40.

Chapter 6
Pluralism, Social Principle, and Christianity

In the last chapter, I explored Ramsey's and Niebuhr's philosophically influenced and theologically embedded perspectives on loyalty to social institutions and authority. In this chapter I explore Niebuhr's and Ramsey's perspectives on democratic dialogue and Christian responsibility in this dialogue. Since Ramsey and Niebuhr lived in a democratic context, and since the majority of their writings on social dialogue focus upon dialogue in democratic settings, this chapter will focus upon their conceptions of democracy and democratic discourse. The chapter does range beyond this framework where it is useful to establish the boundaries of some important idea, as when Ramsey discusses the Church's responsibility at the doorstep to Auschwitz. But in general I am interested in Ramsey's and Niebuhr's conceptions of public discourse in the context where they understood themselves to be acting.

Not surprisingly, the accounts Ramsey and Niebuhr produce reveal the influence of their early encounters with pragmatism and idealism. For Niebuhr, who follows in the more pragmatic tradition of stressing the need for a beneficial diversity in society, democracy is conceived as a polity that at its best protects a responsible pluralism. The strength of democracy is found in its ability to maintain corridors of humble and critical dialogue amongst persons with truly distinctive identities without demanding an abandonment of these distinctive identities in the process.

Democracy manifests a openness to this critical dialogue even when the dialogue turns to investigate and criticize the society itself. Democracy is the polity which at its best resists efforts to make the ideas of any of its members into a communal ideology.

For Niebuhr, the Christian is well suited to participate in democratic practice as a Christian since she or he is, by virtue of her or his Christianity, a humble, critical, and responsible member of society. The Christian as such will recognize that being a Christian does not give her or him any revealed access to facts about the world as it stands, knowledge about the likely success or failure of particular strategies, or moral principles that are not available to other members of the society. Indeed, knowing of the danger of idolatry, she or he will avoid sanctifying any established order or program for political progress. But, the Christian will participate in democracy as a Christian enlightened by her or his relationship with the transcendent God, inspired and shaped by the prophetic tradition of Christian scripture. She or he will, with humble recognition of her or his own fallibility, seek to interpret the world in light of the Christian narrative, and contribute her or his religiously informed perspective to the broader dialogue in the society.

Ramsey's conception of democratic society, in contrast to Niebuhr's, finds affinities with the idealistic conception proposed by Bernard Bosanquet. Democratic societies, like all societies, are constituted by a set of structured relationships which can be articulated in terms of principles, rights, and duties. Every society has a common ethos from which the members of the society emerge and by which they are shaped. This ethos provides those in the society access to the principles around which their lives are organized. The primary moral danger for society is found in a loss of the stability provided by a communal perception of the reality of these principled relationships.

Within society, Christians as Christians are given a very specific task. Christians, as those who are most aware of their own participation in the unfolding of covenant relations in history, are called upon to aid in articulating and heightening those ethos-embedded principles that ought to shape the practice of those in society. But Christians as Christians do not have any special insight into the application of these principles to the evanescent processes of history. Only in their roles as secular magistrates, albeit as magistrates motivated by love, should they participate in arguments concerning the dictates of political prudence in an ever changing world.

This chapter will be divided into three sections. In the first I will develop Niebuhr's and Ramsey's accounts of democracy. I will then move to focus on their approaches to the question of Christian responsibility in democratic society. Finally, I shall offer some mutual criticisms arising from the dialogue between these positions.

Democratic Vistas

Niebuhr and Ramsey were both ardent advocates for the need to maintain and defend democracy in the contemporary world. The overlap between Niebuhr and Ramsey on this point is perhaps best symbolized by their common usage of Niebuhr's axiom: "Man's capacity for justice makes democracy possible; but man's inclination to injustice makes democracy necessary."[1] At the same time, their pictures of democracy should be distinguished with careful attention to the emphases they respectively place upon pluralism and principled commonality within the democracy.

Niebuhr and Democratic Pluralism

For Niebuhr, a certain amount of cultural unity and conformity is a precondition for any functioning democracy.[2] But this unity is not the distinctive mark of democracy, nor is it the strength of democracy. According to Niebuhr, democracy can be seen as "the fruit of a cultural and religious pluralism" that developed out of the Reformation and Renaissance.[3] This pluralism leads to the new heights of relative justice possible in democracies for two basic reasons.[4] First, it provides a relative freedom for human creativity and imagination from the reductive forms of imposed unity which had restricted them previously. Democracy is the only polity thus far in human history that provides for an expression of limited human transcendence over the structures of history within the structures themselves. Second, it ideally provides for the limited views of the good held by any particular part of the community to be offset in practice by views of the good held by others in the society. As such, democratic society depends in large part on the rich and various traditions and identities of those citizens that compose it. Each participant and each subsidiary society within the democracy must proclaim her, his, or its highest insights while at the same time preserving the humility necessary to participate in democratic dialogue. For those who enter the dialogue from religious standpoints, this, Niebuhr finds, demands "a very high form of religious commitment."[5]

Central to democratic practice within this conception is a continuous openness to criticism. As Niebuhr writes, in a democracy "not even the moral presuppositions upon which the society rests are withdrawn from constant scrutiny and re-examination."[6] At times, this scrutiny reveals that traditionally established "absolute rights" are in fact the tools of social oppression and repression. Even those bourgeois conceptions of property rights which were, for many, the moral grounds for the American Revolution have been profitably challenged and reconceived in the ongoing practice of American democracy. Such occurrences offer, Niebuhr holds, sufficient reason for maintaining the openness of democratic society to even foundational critique. But this is not the only reason for maintaining such freedom. Sometimes, he writes, "new truth rides into history upon the back of an error."[7] While early feminism presented, Niebuhr suggests, an overly libertarian conception of the family, it properly pointed out the goods of greater freedom and possibilities for women in society. If such a position had been quashed prematurely because of its errors it would not have been allowed to contribute the insights it bore. For these reasons, pluralism must be given some rein even beyond the bounds of the status quo conception of the common good.

The primary problem of democracy is found in maintaining this fruitful, critical pluralism against collapse into imposed reductive unity. Pluralism is constantly threatened by those who would prematurely seek to establish their own conceptions of order independent of criticism. The problem of maintaining critical pluralism is never completely solved within history, but it is a problem the approach to which is always properly guided by a set of moral virtues and a set of equilibrating formal structures.

Morally, democracies require within their citizens a mixture of criticalness, responsibility, and humility. Such virtues allow the society to maintain "working principles of justice" which are necessary to society even while recognizing that "every historical statement of those principles is subject to amendment."[8] These virtues restrain autocratic pretension that would use democratic practice as a means of pushing one's own morally fanatic project to establish social harmony. They also preserve the possibility for commonality amongst citizens in the democratic society by breaking down the fixed divisions that form when participants uncritically accept any one of the absolute dogmatic alternatives which are constantly vying for power within the society.[9]

While these virtues are necessary, Niebuhr does not, however, believe that they are sufficient to maintain a democracy.[10] In addition to the moral requirements, democracy also entails a set of equilibrating formal structures. There are, in Niebuhr's thought, two main formal threats to pluralism. One is tyranny, in which a centralized power functions to directly repress the vitalities of the pluralist society. The other is anarchy, in which the "capricious disproportions of power" among the various groups within the society eventually allow relatively more powerful groups to implement "forms of domination and enslavement" for those with relatively less power.[11] Democracies must be constructed so as to maintain a careful balance of domestic powers to avoid either tyranny or anarchy. This balance is maintained by a centralized "organizing power" of government that is at once above all of the subsidiary power centers and at the same time partially checked by each of these subsidiary centers.

In this way pluralism is protected from the moral dangers of autocratic pretense and dogmatic sectarianism and from the formal dangers of tyranny and anarchy. Humanity's "capacity for justice," that is, the height of the human's creative potential in its limited self-transcendence, is freed from the constrictions of prematurely imposed reductive unity. Humanity's "inclination to injustice," that is, the human's tendency to pretentious and fanatic abuse of power, is stymied by the intrinsic moral virtues and extrinsic formal balancing of powers in the democratic society.

Ramsey and the Structured Democratic Ethos

Ramsey agrees with much within Niebuhr's approach to democracy. But his own emphases are found in areas quite different from Niebuhr's. In one early article, Ramsey begins by lamenting that Americans have "become so 'liberal' in our religious and democratic thought that literally 'we don't know what to do.'"[12] The problem, Ramsey posits, is that pragmatic liberal methodology neglects the essential structures of liberal society. Pragmatism reduces social policy to the *search for* social policy, and thus is unable to establish substantial norms of justice. This pragmatic "liberalism knows of no experiments that should *not* be tried," and thus "cannot distinguish before the experiment between the pragmatism of a F.D.R. and that of a Mussolini."[13]

True liberalism, on the other hand, Ramsey suggests, makes more substantial claims. Democracy is itself a structured relationship delineable in terms of a set of rights, duties, and expectations for reasonable participation. It is the unifying structure of this social relationship that allows for the possibility of fruitful diversity. Thus, respect for this structure is necessarily foundational to any democratic polity. The sinful human will always seek to make for her or himself an exception to this structure so as to protect her or his own individualistically conceived good against the more inclusive good of the society. Any society that would resist these sinful tendencies must shore up the necessary structures that hold a community of individuals in common so as to allow for a genuinely fruitful critical dialogue among its members. What is needed in contemporary discourse, Ramsey suggests, "is the recognition on the part of contemporary liberals that today the chief enemy is no longer, if ever, the hypothetical ethical absolutist, but the relativist who does not see that there are some things that cannot be fundamentally called in question, because they are presuppositions of all *good* 'calling in question.'"[14] Thus, for Ramsey, the primary problem of democracy is found in defending its unifying ideal structure against the forces of chaos that threaten to tear it apart.

In Ramsey's early works, he finds the resources to maintain the structured unity of democratic society in the writings of the idealists. Drawing on T.H. Green, Ramsey articulates a theory of democracy in which a set of inalienable rights and correlative duties pertain to individuals in light of, and only in light of, their roles in service to the structured common good of the society.[15] This theory includes rights to certain socially beneficial forms of diversity. A large part of democracy is constituted by the right to free speech and the correlative duty to listen with respect. But this diversity must be carefully contained. To maintain the order of society, as Ramsey would later write, every dissenter must be willing to be "overruled by the common voice" of the community.[16] Further, rights cannot be extended so as to cover those acts which would challenge the structure of democracy itself. After all, "no one," Ramsey writes, "has a right to speak freely, and in the speaking to advocate the abolition of free speech."[17]

Correlative with this understanding of the structured common good, rights, and duties entailed in a democracy, Ramsey's early works draw upon Rousseau's concept of the generality of application as a means of locating the essential nature of minimal justice in a democracy.[18] Since the primary danger in a democracy is found in the exemption of the self or one's own group from the general will of the society, it is necessary that all laws be stated so as to be generally applicable to all. Inasmuch as the right to vote provides the best practical mechanism for maintaining such generality in the law against the sinful tendencies of those most directly involved in the legislative process, such is recognized as a constitutive facet of democratic practice.[19]

In Ramsey's later works, without shedding his understanding of democracy as a structured relationship,[20] he tends to speak in terms of a unifying ethos that holds society together. He conceives this ethos in terms that parallel his understanding of the progressively unfolding principled structure of morality. The ethos of a society consists primarily in the common principled conceptual categories which arise in the minds of the populace from participation in the common life in the community.

> The truth is that moral considerations are behind the eyeballs . . . they precede the exercise of calculating reason. . . . The values of a people are the spirit and purposes animating the community, pervading its institutions and voluntary associations, forming consciences, including the consciences of citizen and magistrate alike. The values are in the ethos, the traditions of a people; they are inculcated by the institutions, the laws, the activities of the community . . . Men get to know justice first of all through the *jus gentium* animating the historical community into which they are born; a man's conscience and moral sensibilities have their origin in identity with the purposes of a particular people. To step outside the morality that was handed down to us and then to attain power sets raw power against weak and abstract morality and sets truth and goodness against power. Still, families, schools, churches, and the writers of a nation's songs should not mistake the most telling way in which anyone speaks truth and righteousness to decision-makers in power. That is through their upbringing and moral development in a society whose moral purposes, values and outlook they (perhaps inarticulately) share.[21]

This ethos is the common basis for morality within the diversity of society. It constitutes the ground of moral reasoning in the society. The task of the moralist and, as we shall see below, of the Christian as Christian is to provide an ever clearer articulation of the principles which express the structure of the ethos. It is the "waywardness of the human heart" Ramsey writes, that "works against any *ethos*, customs, or laws that are generally good for all."[22] Indeed, as he states above, the greatest threat to the moral order of society is constituted by one who conceives of and deploys power outside the structure of the common ethos. The possibility for social responsibility is grounded in the recognition of and loyalty to the structured social moral conceptual repository.

Against the backdrop of this moral conceptual commonality there will certainly be differences as individual citizens apply socially imparted principles to the often chaotic phenomenal world. Further, there will be many disagreements as persons draw out those calculations of proportionality and consequence in which political reasoning, as opposed to moral reasoning, consists. Such divergences are to be expected, and, since they fall outside the conceptual space delimited within the common ethos, they are to be accepted largely as good faith disagreements. But this diversity is, when the ethos is properly recognized, always held within the bounds of common morality which defines the limits which political reason cannot cross.

Thus, in each phase of Ramsey's thought democracy is protected from the wiles of relativist individualism which threatens to bring about its dissolution. For Ramsey, humanity's "capacity for justice," that is the human's capacity for loyalty to the general will or common ethos, allows the human within the democracy to contribute to the common good. Humanity's "inclination to injustice," that is the human's tendency to "make himself an exception" within the general will or social ethos, is stymied by the enforcement of the rational order that grounds the diversity of the society.[23]

The Christian's Role in Dialogue

The pattern of overlapping yet diverging approaches appears again in Ramsey's and Niebuhr's treatments of responsible Christian participation in political dialogue. While they each see Christianity as making significant contributions to all political discourse, both Niebuhr and Ramsey are wary of any attempt to claim knowledge of a "Christian" political program. But Niebuhr and Ramsey differ from one another concerning the reasons for this wariness and the forms of proper Christian contribution to public dialog. For Niebuhr, the Christian, to the extent that she or he can live out her or his faith, is an ideal participant in pluralistic dialogue. Christianity gives her or him the humility necessary to avoid linking her or his political project to the security of a God's eye perspective even while she or he is enough aware of the call of God beyond all finite institutions to maintain a critical stance toward these institutions. For Ramsey, the Christian Church and the Christian qua Christian serve chiefly to contribute to and maintain the stability of God's order within history. Participating in God's unfolding order in history, the Christian is prepared to take part in defining that order by contributing to discussions about principled judgments which contribute to the unfolding ethos of the nation. But, the Christian must avoid confusing her or his distinctive role as a Christian with participation in the chaotic calculations of political prudence which are properly reserved for persons functioning as secular magistrates.

Niebuhr and the Humble Christian Prophet

It is, perhaps, overly ambitious to suggest *a* Niebuhrian approach to responsible Christian participation in political dialogue. Niebuhr's own approaches to political developments often appear, in good pragmatic style, as ad hoc responses to the needs of the particular situation. Still, it is possible to outline the dangers Niebuhr sees in relating Christian belief and political policy, and to note some of the means he suggests in protecting from these dangers. In this way one can find Niebuhr's view of Christian political responsibility as located between the twin dangers of prideful abuse of "Christian" reason and irresponsible renunciation of the prophetic role of the Christian.

Christian symbols are highly unstable when deployed by sinful humanity. They are properly understood first in relation to the ultimate story of God, whose virtue, knowledge, and power always exceed that of humanity. As such, their use always offers the occasion for sinful abuse as the finite human seeks to be identified with this virtue, knowledge, and power. These sinful tendencies are most egregiously manifested by those who deploy Christian symbols in an effort to claim their political position as following necessarily from the principles of the Christian faith itself.

By drawing too simple a relation between politics and religion, the Christian Church feeds the tendency of idolatry in the broader society. In the one extreme, Christian claims are used to sanctify ongoing imperfect partisan political projects within history.[24] In another extreme, the perfection of Christ's act is treated as a simple possibility for humans or human collectives within history, thus leading to a naive effort to actualize a perfectly loving political policy. Both options turn Christian ethics on its head, using the security of claims to revelation to stave off recognition of the fragility of human knowledge and potential, and abetting forms of moral fanaticism which should properly be broken by the revelation of God's action in Christ. Practicing one's piety in public, it seems, provides the gravest temptation to hypocrisy.

Such concerns might lead one to wish for the construction of a wall between religion and politics. The Christian qua Christian may appear to have no place in a public debate. This is not, however, Niebuhr's position. Niebuhr does advocate for some distance between Christian and political discourse, but if one stops here she or he misses the other side of Niebuhr's perspective on the public responsibility of the Christian. If the gravest temptation facing the Christian as Christian in public is temptation to offer religious warrants for moral fanaticism and idolatry, the proper responsibility of the Christian must be found in humbly interpreting the narrative of history so as to illumine God's judgment against all fanatic and idolatrous forms of historical morality and culture.

> Must not the church be busy in 'the pulling down of the strongholds, casting down imaginations and every thing that exalteth itself against the knowledge of God and bringing into captivity every thought to the obedience of Christ'? . . . it *does* belong to the 'care' of the church for the world that it so interpret the judgments under which nations stand, and so disclose their divine origin, that there is a possibility of repentance.[25]

Certainly, the Christian as Christian has no special access to information concerning the immediate consequences of political policies, or an absolute grasp of the relative values of particular goods within history. But the Christian does have, Niebuhr suggests, a special perspective that grows from her or his life understood in relation to the Christian God. Unlike those who find their highest source of meaning and value in the finite institutions and goods of history, persons who see all of history in relation to the ultimate judgment and redemption offered by God are responsible for sharing the limited insights this perspective provides with the world.[26] Thus, dealing "as rigorously with the religious and theological presuppositions of social policy as with the details of political and economic theory," the Christian spies out idolatrous tendencies embodied in contemporary social and political movements.[27] Resisting the draw of conventionalism, she or he presses on toward "radical religious protest, which subjects all historical reality (including economic, social and radical injustice) to the 'word of the Lord.'"[28]

No doubt it is a tortuous path that winds between these two pitfalls in the public life of the Christian. How shall the Christian live up to the demands of her or his prophetic vocation without falling to the temptation of pride in the process? How shall she or he maintain humility without withdrawing from the critical task of interpretation which she or he has to share? Perhaps it is even inevitable that the Christian will fall to one of the two dangers at some point, but this does not alleviate the need for each horn of the dilemma facing the humble prophet. Niebuhr does, however, suggest several rules of thumb which might provide some limited guidance for the Christian in her or his work.

First, it is clear that the Christian has access to more clarity concerning general judgments than she or he has about the propriety of particular strategies. In general, as one drives more and more into the details of strategy there is less and less security available for prophetic criticism.[29] The perplexities of choosing particular policies are not to be underestimated and Christian humility demands openness to disagreement without religious rancor aggravating the situation. Thankfully for the prophet, in most cases it will not be necessary for the Christian to delve deeply into strategy as the pretensions of politics are usually bold enough to be readily recognizable at a broader level. Political rhetoric that markets projects to make the world safe for democracy, to spread unqualified freedom or equality, or to implement God's politics all reveal the marks of idolatry long before their particular strategies are revealed in detail.

Second, the role of the prophet is always more negative than positive. "The church," Niebuhr suggests, "ought to be more concerned to bring the goodness of Christ as judgment upon every fragmentary form of human goodness than to find the particular cause which might be identified with Christ."[30] The prophet does not know God's immediate plan for the world, nor does she or he seek to identify her or himself simply with God's action. But the prophet does have assurance of the fact that God's judgment will come against all hubris. The prophetic impetus always leads to a ferreting out of both the pretense concomitant in positions one opposes *and* the pretense in one's own preferred position. If one is able to articulate clearly those goods sacrificed by the enactment of the other's position but unable to recognize the reality of those sacrificed in her or his own preferred position, she or he has failed to carry out the prophetic calling consistently. Further, the Christian does not claim any indefeasible security in her or his own interpretation of God's judgment. She or he recognizes her or his own fallibility and, even when carrying out the Christian duty of prophetism, remains open to criticism.

Finally, Niebuhr suggests that there ought to be a qualified distinction between "the responsibility of individual Christians and voluntary groups, and the responsibility of the church as community of faith."[31] The primary goal of the Church is found in drawing individuals beyond all of the idolatrous centers of society, including itself.[32] As an institution it should focus first upon teaching the specially revealed truth of God's ultimate, indiscriminate judgment and love rather than delving into historical political and moral judgments. Historical groupings of Christians in denominations and other ecclesial formations will, for the sake of unity, coherent polity, and Christian responsibility, be required to provide more substantive moral claims and guidelines based upon their own efforts to correlate the narrative of God's action with the world in which they exist. Their conclusions here function as their own denominational working principles. To the extent possible without abandoning Christian responsibility, at the higher levels of the church these should be general so as to allow room for honest disagreements among Christians within the church on both specific principled and prudential issues. The burden of arguing for more particular judgments falls more quickly upon subsidiary voluntary Christian organizations and upon the individual Christian as Christian than upon the Church itself.

Each of these points provides some guidance to the Christian in the world as she or he seeks to act as a humble prophet. But Niebuhr also recognizes the limited nature of this guidance. No rule provides any final security for the Christian in history. "In actual life," Niebuhr writes, "no clear distinction between moral principles and strategy can be made."[33] Even general judgments offer no final protection from sinful pretense, and there is nothing necessarily apolitical about principled judgments. Indeed in addition to strategic differences, disagreements on principled judgments are often the core of partisan social debates. Ultimately, God revealed only one principle in God's definitive act, the principle of perfect love. While often qualitatively more secure than judgments of strategy, more specific principles are the outcomes of particular human historical creation, and thus defeasible. Further, claims of strategy cannot be completely withdrawn from prophetic criticism. If isolated from criticism, the human's vicious tendencies might find free rein in the sphere of strategy so long as one paid proper tribute to virtue by ostensibly locating her or his strategy under the umbrella of righteous principle. Niebuhr also questions the finality of appeal to consensus, even in the Church. In some trying cases, he suggests, "the church cannot afford to deal merely in vague generalities because it lacks unanimous convictions on the level of political strategy."[34] In the face of Nazism, for instance, the responsible minister did best to call for action even before there was unanimity in her or his congregation. Thus the prophet is, in the final consideration, left to the task of interpretation steered by the virtues of humility, criticalness, and responsibility inspired by the Christian narrative. Christianity does not, as such, Niebuhr notes, offer a "clear moral lead." But it does present "a clear religious insight into the fragmentary character of all human morality."[35]

Ramsey and the Church as a Protector of Order

Ramsey's approach to responsible Christian participation in public discourse finds great resonance with certain parts of Niebuhr's treatment.[36] Like Niebuhr, he warns against the mistake of identifying Christianity with any particular political project. Too many Christians, he writes, act upon ostensibly religious claims without realizing that "conservative and liberal *religious* opinion is the same thing as conservative and liberal *secular* opinion—with a sharper edge."[37] Still, Ramsey's treatment is driven by concerns that are overlapping but not identical with Niebuhr's own, and his own diagnosis of and prescription for the problem of Christian politics led him to quite different conclusions than those to which Niebuhr came.

Unlike Niebuhr's approach to Christian social responsibility, which relies upon a set of permeable rules of thumb and guiding virtues for governing Christian action, Ramsey's approach is grounded in a clean distinction between the spheres of "the Christian" and "the magistracy." While Ramsey at times suggests that there ought to be some distinction between the Church and the individual Christian,[38] his tendency is to treat the Church and the Christian as Christian as existing within the same sphere and thus as fulfilling the same basic function in society.[39] Especially important for our inquiry is Ramsey's explicit claim that he tries to apply to himself *as a Christian ethicist* the same restrictions that he placed upon the Church as a whole.[40] So what is at stake in this distinction, and what are the restrictions that Ramsey finds to be properly applied to both himself as a Christian ethicist and to the Church at large?

For Ramsey the primary problem in contemporary approaches to Christian responsibility is that the Church and the Christian have strayed from their proper place in the divinely imparted social order. The spheres of responsibility occupied respectively by the individual as Christian and by the individual as secular magistrate have been sundered by the action of God. As Ramsey writes, "since the coming of Christ, and in him the establishment of God's universal covenant with all mankind, there now are two cities, not one."[41] The mistake of contemporary Christian political action, Ramsey believes, arises from a rejection of this divinely implemented division of labor.

Acting in their proper function the Church and the Christian do have an important contribution to make to the public good. As those who stand under and participate most self-reflectively in the unrolling of God's order in history, the Church and the Christian as Christian should work to articulate the principled specifications of the essential covenant relationships God maintains for the common good. They should thus find their primary public duty as the Church and as Christians in informing the ethos of the nation.

> [The Churches] should clarify the ground on which government must rest. They ought to open wide the articulation of structural elements in that human reality which statesmanship must govern and the range of alternatives it is legitimate for statesmen to have in mind as they rule by specific decree. They should inform the ethos and conscience of the nation, and thus aid in forming the conscience of its statesmen.[42]

The Church thus properly functions as a protector of the moral order of society.[43] The very essence of the Church, and the unifying characteristic among Christians, is found in common access to and life lived out of the order imparted by God. Recognizing this as their own areas of competence, the Church and the Christian as Christian properly abstain from muddying the clarity and security of this order by wading into the chaotic and indeterminate world of application and strategy which is properly the sphere of competence and responsibility reserved for persons functioning as secular magistrates. The Christian as Christian has no special insights into the facts of any particular case, nor does she or he have any special ability to foretell the future. As such, discerning the situation and calculating proportionality and probable consequences properly fall within the sphere of political reasoning rather than Christian or moral reasoning.

In democratic society citizens may play the role of both Christian and magistrate, but these two specialized roles should never be confounded. In general Ramsey uses the term magistrate to refer to a particular vocation which is, in a democracy, additional to and separable from one's vocation as a Christian. As such, he stresses that he does not mean by setting the prudential calculations of the magistrate outside of distinctively Christian criticism to set political office holders outside the realm of all criticism. One may, while functioning as a magistrate instead of as a Christian, criticize a political office holder for any particular decision.[44] What is of the utmost importance is that the citizen not confuse these roles and claim religious sanction for prudential political judgments.

Unfortunately, Ramsey posits, the Christian vocation has been obscured in the contemporary scene, especially in ecumenical meetings, by the rise of a "truncated Barthian" theology which stresses "Christ in the revolutionary situation" and propounds belief in a Christian prophetic calling that seeks to identify and participate in what "God is doing" to overturn and recast the present order of the world.[45] The upshot of these theological mistakes is the destabilization of the Church and the hampering of its proper role in the world. Disrupting the distinction between sphere of principled Christian knowledge and the sphere of political prudence, Christians exacerbate rather than shore up the world of political discourse. Instead of steadying the ship of politics they carry out "riotous moralizing."[46]

Further, this prophetic approach turns "the church inside out."[47] It does this by carrying the chaos of political calculations to the very heart of the Christian community itself, thus introducing *heresy*—"divisions into the life that may properly be a confession of the faith of the church."[48] The Christian who recognizes her or his delimited vocation, Ramsey suggests, would recognize "the right of persons in their official capacities of magistrates or citizen not to have their consciences faulted, their freedom in the slightest degree overborne" due to disagreements within the realm of political prudence.[49] But in a context skewed by prophetism, Christians encroach upon their neighbor's freedom of conscience by challenging the neighbor's moral status even when she or he is acting on the basis of properly formulated principles, and thus with right intent. Casting contentious claims to and fro "prophets" turn honest disagreements concerning prudential calculations into the purportedly clear signs of sinfulness in their opponents. These "prophets" stand with pretended religious authority outside of the sphere of actual responsibility for policy and call down judgments as if from heaven.

What is needed in the Church, Ramsey suggests, is a "Critique of Ecumenical Reasoning," demonstrating the need for a decisive line between secure principled and insecure strategic judgments.[50] This critique will point out "the contradiction of one another's 'prudences'" which emerge when Christians wrongly wade into "the noumenal—the ambiguous—world of politics."[51] The upshot of this critique is found in the reinstatement of the paramount importance of two standards for Christian proclamation.

First, the Church and the Christian as Christian must find a strong consensus among Christians in order to make any public claim.[52] The Christian should always, Ramsey suggests, "take along with us in our minds a 'counterpart'—a fellow Christian we know who disagrees with us on specific economic, social, and political conclusions, whose particular 'scruples' are different from ours, but who (we cannot deny) thinks about his life and his responsibilities upon the same basis that we do." Even if one comes to a different conclusion than this 'counterpart,' Ramsey suggests, one "could scarcely pronounce against him."[53]

Second, the Church and the Christian as Christian should impose upon her, him, or itself a "self-denying ordinance" requiring "that no more be said in addressing the urgent political problems of the present day than can clearly be said on the basis of Christian truth and insights."[54] In this way, Ramsey suggests, the Church might be able to return to its proper place as a protector of order in the society, beginning by reclaiming the internal order imparted by God and eventually reaching out to steady the chaos of the world to that extent possible.[55]

There is one exception Ramsey allows within the general picture as thus far presented. When pressed by some critics, Ramsey admits that in the face of Nazism and at the gateway to Auschwitz, it was proper for Christians and the Church to call out the specific crimes of the government and to call in the name of "Christian responsibility" for military resistance.[56] Strangely for Ramsey, who usually requires clearly delimited reasons for exceptions to general rules, the character of the reasons behind this exception are left largely amorphous.[57] What Ramsey is clear about is that this exception should not be an excuse for any person in the contemporary world who as a Christian wishes to make particular policy claims. This exception functions primarily to prove the rule.

With prophetism set aside and properly delimited Christian vocation reestablished, it will be possible to assume a proper position in relation to the magistrates whose sphere of responsibility is distinct from that of the Church. Recognizing the courage and fortitude of those functioning as magistrates, sorting through the practically unintelligible ambiguity of prudential calculations, the Church will come to recognize the proper dignity of the magistrate's position. These religious communities, Ramsey suggests, will "stand in awe before people called political 'decision makers,' or rather before the majesty of topmost political agency."[58] As he writes elsewhere:

> Political decision and action is in *the image of God*, who also rules by particular decrees. God does not create a world in general; he creates a specific world out of myriad possibilities that might have been. God says, 'Let there be . . .'; and there is some new shaping event put forth into the world. The political act calls the things that are to be into being from things that are not. In a very real sense, an exercise of statecraft is a creation *ex nihilo*. For all the doctrine and the policy research that went before, a statesman shapes events by decisions or indecisions that go beyond doctrine, that launch out into the unknown and the not-yet, and that do not pop out of research, game playing, or systems analysis. A statesman must actualize what is to be from among a number of legitimate choices, each of which is plausible before the event. He has the high and lonely responsibility of choosing what shall actually be done from among a number of possibilities, any of which might have been. To prove after the event that political decisions were right is rather like speculating what world history would have been if Cleopatra's nose had been longer, or like asking whether God should have created this world and not some other which any half-baked intellect can think of in a thrice.[59]

If there is one thing the true Christian knows, it is that one ought not, on religious grounds, question an act of divine creation.

Criticism

There is more overlap between Ramsey's and Niebuhr's positions than may be apparent on a first reading. Niebuhr was not, in arguing for an understanding of democracy which emphasized pluralism, arguing for an individualistic society which lacked a substantive working definition of justice. Ramsey was not arguing for a collapse of the diversity or ongoing debate which is central to democratic practice. But as in the other areas we have surveyed, their divergent tendencies lead them to emphasize different dangers when dealing with democracy, and thus leave room for a beneficial mutual critique. No doubt, Niebuhr is at times too reticent to deploy rights and duties language when articulating the demands of democracy. On the other side, Ramsey's approach at times overstates the extent to which the society can know the structure of the common good and the extent to which members of the society are able to specify ahead of time which forms of diversity are beneficial. In the time following Ramsey's and Niebuhr's work in these areas, several proposals have sought to synthesize the insights each represents with positive results.[60] In this ongoing discussion of how to conceive democracy the tension between Ramseyan and Niebuhrian insights should not be lost, but neither should their significant areas of agreement be overlooked.

It is also true that Ramsey's and Niebuhr's approaches to Christian responsibility in public dialogue should not be simply contrasted. While they appear to hold opposing positions on the role of prophetism in Christian responsibility, the differences between their two positions are, in part, resolved by acts of translation. For Ramsey prophetism is a social movement built upon pretentious claims to knowledge about prudential and consequential calculations. For Niebuhr prophetism is a movement consisting in the ongoing critique of all human pretension. If prophetism is understood as Ramsey construes it, Niebuhr too is to be read as opposed to much that falls under the heading. If prophetism is understood as Niebuhr construes it, Ramsey's criticisms might be conceived as prophetic. Both Niebuhr and Ramsey recognize that the Christian is not, by virtue of her or his Christianity, endowed with an ability to predict the future or to claim an absolutely unique ability to interpret the facts as they stand in the world. Both agree further that no Christian should identify her or his preferred political project simply with what God is doing in the world.

Still, there are profound differences between their approaches, and differences in the points at which they deserve critique. Niebuhr's approach to the public responsibility of the Christian does not focus enough upon the substantive contributions that the Church, along with other social institutions, ought to make in providing tools for moral reflection.

While Niebuhr was certainly aware of the necessity of institutional and traditional grounding in maintaining Christian virtue,[61] he does not suggest strongly enough the ways in which the Christian Church should be active in reflecting upon moral norms that have been useful to its own tradition and the broader society in the past. Though the Church ought never to rest on its laurels by uncritically repeating these moral norms, it ought to search out the guidance that they may provide in ever new situations.

It is also true that Niebuhr's approach to Christian responsibility does not offer the kind of apparent security in principled Christian proclamation that Ramsey's model claims to provide. On Niebuhr's account, no Christian proclamation on historical morality which steps beyond requiring humble prophetic virtue should ever be taken as ultimately authoritative. One might argue that accepting such a position surrenders too much of the Church's authority and ultimately erodes the significance and distinctiveness of the Christian voice in its role of informing the broader culture of society.

Such is an important criticism, but I find it less than fully convincing. It rests on the assumption that, at least in some sphere, the Christian has a source for deriving moral conclusions that is independent of and secure from the vicissitude of history and sin. Not only does such a conclusion beg the question against Niebuhr's theological insights into the finitude and sinfulness of humanity, it seems an unlikely truth in the light of the actual practice of the historical Christian community. In its history the Christian tradition itself has often, both in its principled judgments and its interpretations of the present situation, been the maintainer of injustice rather than a beacon of rectitude. Attempts to claim such security in one's own purified recovery of the true and comprehensive content of revealed morality seem implausible if not, as Niebuhr would claim, idolatrous.

It is important to note that the absence of such a divinely secured comprehensive account of distinctively Christian morality does not lead Niebuhr to abandon the importance of distinctively Christian contributions to society. Niebuhr's humble prophetism is not an invitation for culture-Christianity. On the contrary, Niebuhr's prophetic movement consists first of a confession against all forms of polytheism or henotheism in which culture-Christianity partakes.[62] It is loyalty first to the One God of Christianity that requires the prophet to resist the collapse of her or his identity into any one historical culture, role, or perspective. The encounter with God requires her or him to approach the world as a humble Christian prophet, but it also guides her or him to keep all of her or his particular claims open to criticism.

Thus I take Niebuhr's approach to Christian responsibility to provide a relatively sound grounding for the public responsibility of the Christian in the world. I do not take Ramsey's to fare quite as well. Despite the ongoing popularity of Ramsey's approach to the public responsibility of the Christian and the Church in some theological circles,[63] this position seems, in my own judgment, untenable for several reasons.

Ramsey's approach to political discourse and the role of the Church within this discourse reflects an overestimate of the moral conceptual similarity among diverse members within society. This overestimation is revealed inasmuch as he suggests that the contentious divisions of politics arise only in the area of policy and strategy. Such a suggestion rests upon the presumption that all political partisans within a society share a substantial and basic identity in their perceptions of the principled conceptual categories that should be implemented in their particular policies. In such a scheme it may take some careful thinking to articulate the content of this shared source in the ethos of the nation, but on the level of principle, as opposed to the level of application, one does not expect to encounter enduring factious disputes.

A parallel assumption is exhibited in Ramsey's treatment of the need for strong consensus in guiding Christian proclamation to provide a stabilizing influence on the world. His hypothetical 'counterpart' is suggestive here. Ramsey's imagined counterpart may disagree on "specific economic, social, and political conclusions" but Ramsey presupposes that she or he will think about responsibility "upon the same basis that we do."[64] Because he assumes the presence of basically similar principled reasoning in the minds of Christians, he assumes that the strong consensus available within the Church will be able to provide a unified account of substantive directions for action, even while Christians will disagree on the particular policies to choose within the bounds provided by these directions.

This underestimates the depth of the plurality of moral perspective represented both within and outside the Christian church and ultimately fails to provide the kind of stability and protection against the politicization of Christian faith at which Ramsey aims. It is hard, in the contemporary situation, to imagine that the sincere differences played out both in Christian and broader political discourse on issues such as abortion or homosexual marriage are always merely the outcomes of different applications of basically similar principles, or that the differences could be simply resolved within history if only one side could articulate itself clearly enough to evoke a recognition of the ethos which is, albeit inarticulately, common in the minds of all in the debate. Ramsey's tendency towards accepting a monistic view of society leads to his assumption that these conflicts are more easily resolvable and less politically volatile than they in fact are. This tendency also leads him to overstate the assurance available to the Church and the world in general through the use of principled reasons.

This mistake is aggravated by Ramsey's willingness to accept a relatively wide range of principles which arise in the course of historical practice as "clearly" grounded "on the basis of *Christian* truth and insights." He himself, as I have noted in an earlier chapter, presumes that the requirements of just war theory are in some way divinely imparted to society through a distinctively Christian mode of thought, and at times he suggests that principled judgments are specially secured by one's or one's community's participation in the unfolding of God's reason in history through contextual principled reasoning. Because of his maximalist understanding of the distinctively Christian character of these principled insights, he supposes that requiring such robust standards of distinctively Christian truth for Christian proclamation will not restrain the Church or the Christian as Christian from its responsibility in making relatively specific principled statements in political, medical, and sexual ethics.

Accepting such a scheme allows Ramsey to overstate the extent to which the divisions within the Church in present history are simply an outcome of a contemporary tendency to make proclamations upon the specific applications of Christian principles. A Church proclamation which identified Ramsey's principled understanding of the moral limitations on abortion as *the* Christian position on the subject would do as much if not more to drive division into the heart of the community of faith as proclamations on particular conflicts. Indeed, as one critic notes, "if the churches confined themselves to saying only what could be grounded directly and firmly in 'Christian truth'—and took this quite literally—they would not say much at all, even in the realm of theory."[65] Ramsey, however, does not seem to worry about those who would feel "unchurched" due to his own principled arguments.

In contrast to Ramsey's overstatement of the distinctively Christian security and assurance available in principled judgments, his explicit treatment of prudential judgments vastly overstates the indeterminacy of such claims. Ramsey's approach here at times suggests that prudential reason is so indeterminate as to appear almost arbitrary. In the noumenal world of politics it seems that all substance on which to ground our judgments is hidden from perception. The upshot is to make the world of prudence appear as a world properly devoid of meaningful moral criticism.

There is some great wisdom to be found in Ramsey's defense of the freedom of conscience. Two persons, and indeed two Christians, can, perhaps especially in the area of prudential judgments, disagree even while both are acting out of right intent. It is a sign of one's own lack of humility when she or he too quickly finds that the root for actual disagreement is to be found in the sinfulness of the person with whom she or he disagrees. But Ramsey's treatment needs to be qualified in two ways. First, it is important to note that freedom of conscience, to the extent that it should be recognized, reaches both to principled and prudential conclusions. It is possible for two Christians arguing in good faith to disagree upon how to conceive of the moral framework for thinking through issues of, for instance, euthanasia or medical experimentation upon children. If concern for this right to freedom of conscience does not prevent us from offering critiques of one another's conclusions in the area of principled argument then such should not prevent us from offering similar critiques in the area of prudential judgments. Second, as Ramsey recognizes when careful,[66] our prudential judgments, like our principled judgments, may be influenced by those virtues and vices that constitute our character. The vice of pride may lead one to overestimate her or his abilities in the process of prudential calculation. The erroneous conclusions to which we come in these judgments can be signs of immorality and in some cases should be called out as such.

In his later writings Ramsey would accept "a degree of fault for describing political futures as systematically indeterminate and rationally incalculable and uncertain, without qualification."[67] He would also in later writings attempt to suggest that proportional calculations were not as indeterminate as some of his earlier writings suggest.[68] But Ramsey would always place a great deal of stress upon the difference in kind between the modes of reason involved in dealing with principles and those involved in prudential forms of reasoning, always focusing upon what he saw as the vastly greater security available to persons deploying principled reasoning. The difference in security is, I would suggest, much more qualified than Ramsey suggests.

Even if there is some line to be drawn between principled and prudential reason there is no line bright enough to allow for an absolute sense of security concerning when Christian responsibility requires Christian proclamation on particular issues and when Christian humility demands reticence in offering a proclamation. This point is illustrated by Ramsey's own allowance of an exception to his general scheme when he sees the Christian facing down Nazism or standing at the gate to Auschwitz.

Ramsey resisted such a conclusion. In one article he notes:

> I hope, that no one dismisses [my work] with the cliché that, because I affirm that actions such as genocide are clearly to be characterized and condemned as unchristian, this opens the door to a series of particular pronouncements that should have been the church's witness before it stood at the gateway to Auschwitz.[69]

Unfortunately, there are deep problems with such a response. Why should the line for Christian proclamation be drawn at genocide? Are there other morally repugnant acts that demand such proclamations? One suspects that Ramsey was here downplaying his own dependence upon prudence in determining how serious an infraction against morality must be to justify accepting the dangers concomitant in allowing distinctively Christian proclamations on particular instances of infraction. But one need not stop here. How shall one recognize "actions such as genocide"? What level of certainty should one have that the application is correct before making the "Christian" application? To answer these questions an appeal to prudence is necessary. If this analysis is correct, Ramsey cannot ahead of time provide an absolute barrier against the prudential arguments that would hold that particular instances of moral failure in the world are appropriate subjects for distinctively Christian proclamation. No doubt, these arguments will provide no indefeasible security to the arguer, but, as I have suggested, some level of insecurity seems properly to be concomitant within every position in any argument, be it principled or prudential.

Thankfully, as one from a more pragmatic tradition might expect, Ramsey's practice is better than his theory. Despite occasional instances in which Ramsey subtly begs the question against his opponents in moral arguments by suggesting their insights are non-Christian,[70] and despite his overly zealous claims concerning the *agapic* entailment of an absolute principle of noncombatant protection, his own general openness to criticism reveals that even when making principled arguments as a Christian ethicist he does not assume that his conclusions are so clearly grounded in Christian truth and insights as to be impervious to critique. Further, in some cases when he has encounters with those whom he takes to be identifying Christian truth too closely with policy conclusions Ramsey counters them with more than his theoretical bright line preventing such pronouncement. He also offers his own prudential arguments grounded in his interpretation of the situation at hand, suggesting why he considers the particular case in question too ambiguous for the given pronouncement.[71] Finally, when Ramsey witnesses what he takes to be a violation of moral principle both significant and obvious enough to warrant it, Ramsey himself, writing as a Christian ethicist, is not inhibited in pronouncing condemnation on the particular instance of immorality.[72] Ramsey would have done well to allow the moral intuitions that led to such actions to carry greater influence in the process of his theorizing.

Conclusion

In critiquing Ramsey's approach to Christian public responsibility, I do not mean to support all of those against whom he was arguing. Ramsey was certainly right to recognize that there is a prevalent error to be found with any group that identifies its own conclusions on policy issues as secured by specifically Christian warrants. Further, while ecclesial bodies should not all be so limited, there is a great need for ecclesial and ecumenical Christian structures which limit themselves to making broad statements on ethics and doctrine while maintaining, to that extent possible, the ties which hold Christians in common. What I do wish to suggest is that Ramsey overstates the security of principled judgments and understates the security of prudential judgments, and on the basis of this overstatement sees fit to allow putatively secure Christian proclamations on the basis of the one rather than the other. If Niebuhr is right, the security Ramsey seeks in Christian moral proclamations, and thus the kind of authority he searches for in Christian moral proclamations, does not exist either at the level of principled or prudential judgments. If the Christian is to contribute something special to public discourse it will not be on the basis of her or his special participation in the unfolding mind of God.

The Christian is the one who recognizes that every particular claim with regards to historical morality is a claim made without ultimate divine authority. The contribution of the Christian as Christian is thus not to be found in the security of her or his particular conclusions, but in her or his life lived out of the virtues of humility, criticalness, and responsibility born of encounter with God in Christ. It is these virtues that should guide Christians even as they, as Christians, correlate the Christian narrative with the situation in the contemporary world and debate with one another on all issues.

Notes

1. Niebuhr, *The Children of Light and The Children of Darkness*, xiii. Ramsey adopts the phrase in 1946 to recommend his own use of idealism in defending democracy, and re-applies it again and again throughout his scholarly work, "The Theory of Democracy: Idealistic or Christian," 260.

2. See Reinhold Niebuhr and Paul Sigmund, *The Democratic Experience* (New York: Fredrick A. Prager, 1969), 73.

3. Niebuhr, *The Children of Light and the Children of Darkness*, 120.

4. One should not overstate the extent to which the ideals of democracy presented here were ever conceived as a concrete reality by either Niebuhr or Ramsey. As they would be first to point out, the actual practices of historical democracies never live up to their ideals.

5. Niebuhr, *The Children of Light and the Children of Darkness*, 134.

6. Niebuhr, *The Children of Light and the Children of Darkness*, 74.

7. Niebuhr, *The Children of Light and the Children of Darkness*, 75-77.

8. Niebuhr, *The Children of Light and the Children of Darkness*, 71.

9. See Niebuhr's comments on the need for "common denominators" in democratic arguments. *The Children of Light and the Children of Darkness*, 98, 117.

10. "The wisdom and the virtue of the citizen is not great enough to affirm justice irrespective of interest. Democracies can remain healthy if there is enough wisdom and justice to affirm the compromises which result when no interest can fully prevail." Reinhold Niebuhr, "Editorials," *Christianity and Society* 16, no. 2 (Spring, 1951), 4.

11. Niebuhr, *The Nature and Destiny of Man*, 2:266.

12. Ramsey, "A Social Policy for Liberal Religion," 495.

13. Ramsey, "A Social Policy for Liberal Religion," 495.

14. Ramsey, "A Social Policy for Liberal Religion," 506. Italics mine.

15. Ramsey, "The Theory of Democracy: Idealistic or Christian," 260, "A Social Policy for Liberal Religion," 500.

16. Ramsey, "Election Issues 1968," 25. As we have seen above, Ramsey also presents a framework for protests which contradict the laws in some extreme cases, so long as these protests show respect for the laws by accepting punishment.

17. Ramsey, "A Social Policy for Liberal Religion," 504.

18. Ramsey, "The Theory of Democracy: Idealistic or Christian," 258.

19. Ramsey, "The Theory of Democracy: Idealistic or Christian," 258; see also Ramsey, *Basic Christian Ethics*, 306.

20. For Ramsey's consistency on this point compare his treatment of the right to free speech and the correlative duty to listen in 1944 and 1968. See Ramsey, "A Social Policy for Liberal Religion," 502, and "Election Issues 1968," 25.

21. Ramsey, "Force and Political Responsibility," 52.

22. Ramsey, *Deeds and Rules*, 20.

23. Ramsey, "The Theory of Democracy: Idealistic or Christian," 260.

24. Reinhold Niebuhr, *Essays in Applied Christianity*, 92. See also Reinhold Niebuhr, "Religious Politics," *Christianity and Society* 16, no. 4 (February 14, 1951), 5.

25. Niebuhr, *Essays in Applied Christianity*, 170-171.

26. Reinhold Niebuhr, *Essays in Applied Christianity*, 87. See also "National Pride vs. The Church," *The Lutheran* 37, no. 6 (November 10, 1954), 12. There is again an overlap between the Niebuhrian and Augustinian positions to be found here. As Rowan Williams notes, in *The City of God*, while Augustine cautiously avoids proposing rule by the saints, one finds "the paradox that the only reliable political leader, the only ruler who can be guaranteed to safeguard authentically *political* values . . . is the man who is, at the end of the day, indifferent to their survival in the relative shapes of the existing order, because he knows them to be safeguarded at the level of God's eternal and immutable providence, vindicated in the eternal *civitas dei*." Rowan Williams, "Politics and the Soul, A Reading of *The City of God*," *Milltown Studies* 19 (1987), 67.

27. See Reinhold Niebuhr, *Essays in Applied Christianity*, 105.

28. Reinhold Niebuhr, "The King's Chapel and the King's Court," *Christianity and Crisis* 29, no. 14 (August 4, 1969), 212; See also Reinhold Niebuhr, "The Christian Witness in a Secular Age," *The Christian Century* 70, no. 29 (July 22, 1953), 842.

29. Reinhold Niebuhr, "Christian Faith and Political Controversy," *Christianity and Crisis* 12, no. 13 (July 21, 1952), 98, "Piety and Politics," *Christianity and Society* 18, no. 3 (Summer, 1953), 4, and "Politics in the Church," *The Lutheran* 31, no. 50 (September 14, 1949), 19.

30. Niebuhr, *Essays in Applied Christianity*, 92.

31. Niebuhr, "Christian Faith and Political Controversy," 98.

32. It is in doing this that the Church is properly a mediator of "saving grace." See Niebuhr, *Man's Nature and His Communities*, 110.

33. Niebuhr, "Christian Faith and Political Controversy," 97-98.

34. Niebuhr, *Essays in Applied Christianity*, 92.

35. Niebuhr, *Essays in Applied Christianity*, 92

36. I focus here primarily upon Ramsey's work in *Who Speaks for the Church?*. Ramsey may be interpreted as having modified his scheme by the time he wrote *Speak Up for Just War or Pacifism*, but I have not included an account of this later development. For an account that does go into this later development, see Philip Turner, "Social Advocacy as a Moral Issue in Itself," *The Journal of Religious Ethics* 19, no. 2 (Fall, 1991), 157-81.

37. Ramsey, *Who Speaks for the Church*, 101.

38. See, for instance, Ramsey, *Who Speaks for the Church*, 170, *n.* 2.

39. Thus he distinguishes between one's vocation as a citizen and as a churchman along the same lines that he distinguishes between the Church and the secular magistracy. See *Who Speaks for the Church*, 157.

40. Paul Ramsey, response in *Speaking to the World: Four protestant perspectives*, by Richard John Neuhaus (Washington D.C.: Ethics and Public Policy Centre, 1983), 21.

41. Ramsey, *Who Speaks for the Church*, 21.

42. Ramsey, *Who Speaks for the Church*, 154.

43. It is hard to convey in any one metaphor the role of the Church in Ramsey's thought. The Church is for Ramsey partially the guardian of order, but simply to say this suggests too passive a relationship, as if the Church were merely protecting the given order in society. Ramsey also wishes the Church to contribute to the refinement of this order from its own position as the self-conscious participant in the unfolding of agapic divine order. In this way, he never abandons the theme of transformism in his theology.

44. See Ramsey, *Who Speaks for the Church*, 49, and "Some Rejoinders," 187-88.

45. Ramsey, *Who Speaks for the Church*, 77, 108.

46. Paul Ramsey, "Two Extremes: Ramsey Replies to his Critics," 219.

47. Ramsey, *Who Speaks for the Church*, 55.

48. Ramsey, *Who Speaks for the Church*, 56.

49. Ramsey, *Who Speaks for the Church*, 108.

50. More pragmatically minded theologians attempted to interpret Ramsey's work as a reminder to maintain the virtue of Christian humility in contemporary discourse. In this fashion, John Bennett interpreted Ramsey's work as "good medicine for those who are *too heedless* in making pronouncements on specific matters of policy." Roger Shinn suggested that Ramsey was advocating "*Christian restraint*" in Christian pronouncements on policy. Ramsey rejects such interpretations as turning the "main current" of his argument into an "eddy." "No one," he writes, "would have labored to bring forth that mouse!" Paul Ramsey, "Paul Ramsey Replies," *Christianity and Crisis* 27 (November 27, 1967), 280.

51. Ramsey, *Who Speaks for the Church*, 46.

52. Ramsey does not draw out exactly what kind of consensus is required, he merely stresses the necessity of consensus. Here I follow Michael McKenzie in using the language of "strong consensus." See McKenzie, *Paul Ramsey's Ethics*, 17. It may be possible to push further with Charles Curran, who suggests that Ramsey means for Christian judgment to rely only upon "a specifically Christian ethical consideration upon which all Christians agree." See *Politics, Medicine, and Christian Ethics*, 45.

53. Ramsey, *Who Speaks for the Church*, 56.

54. Ramsey, *Who Speaks for the Church*, 30.

55. Ramsey, *Who Speaks for the Church*, 144.

56. Ramsey, *Who Speaks for the Church*, 47-49. Notably, Ramsey recognizes Niebuhr as one of the few Christians ever to have the competence required to make such claims.

57. The only clear criteria Ramsey suggests for guiding when such an exception would be warranted is that each pronouncement condemning or approving of a specific instance of action "would need to have the same clear warrant in Christian faith and morals attributable to this one." Ramsey, *Who Speaks for the Church*, 49. This statement is rather strange inasmuch as Ramsey claims elsewhere that there is no such thing as a "Christian" interpretation of facts dealing with particular instances of action. Certainly Ramsey may claim that genocide as a *kind* of action is seen as wrong on specifically Christian grounds, but so long as there is no specifically Christian interpretation of action, this claim does not address the question of why an exception was allowed in this case so that the Church could condemn not only genocide in general, but this specific

instance as genocide. Ramsey goes on to state that some great level of competence is necessary in making the decision to make the exception. This suggests, contra Ramsey's wishes, that the exception is, as I will suggest below, grounded primarily in prudential concerns.

58. Ramsey, *Who Speaks for the Church*, 153.

59. Ramsey, "Force and Political Responsibility," 47-48.

60. See for instance David Hollenbach, *The Common Good and Christian Ethics*, and Jeffrey Stout, *Democracy and Tradition.*

61. See, for instance, Niebuhr, *An Interpretation of Christian Ethics*, 193.

62. There is, I would suggest, a great overlap between Reinhold's work and his brother Richard's in this area. See H. Richard Niebuhr, *Radical Monotheism and Western Culture, With Supplementary Essays* (Louisville, Ky.: Westminster/John Knox Press, 1993).

63. Oliver O'Donovan endorses the deployment of a somewhat different reading of Ramsey than the one I have produced. See, *The Just War Revisited* (New York: Cambridge University Press, 2003), 124 -29. Note also George Weigel's use of Ramsey's argument in the run up to the war in Iraq in "Moral Clarity in a Time of War," *First Things: A Monthly Journal of Religion and Public Life* 129 (January, 2003), 20-28.

64. Ramsey, *Who Speaks for the Church*, 56. In his article on conscientious objection, one finds Ramsey again suggesting that in moral judgments members of a common culture share the "same conscience." Political disagreements arise only in our application of this conscientious commonality. Ramsey, *The Just War*, 130.

65. R. Bruce Douglass, "Paul Ramsey in Review: Who Speaks for the Church?" in *Moral Issues and Christian Response*, ed. Paul T. Jersild and Dale A. Johnson (New York: Holt, Rinehart and Winston, 1971), 61. See also John Bennett, "A Critique of Paul Ramsey," *Christianity and Crisis* 27, no. 18 (October 30, 1967), 247.

66. See Ramsey's explanation of the causes of "deliberate imprudence." Ramsey, *The Just War*, 524.

67. Ramsey, "Some Rejoinders," 207. See also David Little, "The Structure of Justification in the Political Ethics of Paul Ramsey," in *Love and Society*, 139-62

68. See Ramsey's distinction between commensurability and proportionality in *Doing Evil to Achieve Good: Moral Choice in Conflict Situations*, ed. Richard McCormick and Paul Ramsey (Chicago: Loyola University Press, 1978). Also see Joseph Allen's comments on this distinction in "Paul Ramsey and his Respondents since *The Patient as Person*," 92.

69. Ramsey, "Paul Ramsey Replies," 282.

70. See, for instance, Ramsey's comment on the relation between Paul Lehmann and William James. *Deeds and Rules*, 67. The suggested criticism is ironic given Ramsey's own substantial debt to the idealism of Royce and Bosanquet.

71. See for instance Ramsey's suggestion of the particular costs which are obscured by those who argue in favor of withdrawing from Vietnam. Paul Ramsey, *The Just War*, 485.

72. See Ramsey's statements on the March 10, 1967 bombing raid over North Vietnam. Paul Ramsey, *The Just War*, 533.

Part III
War

Chapter 7
War as the Judgment of God

Niebuhr's writings on war have been one of his lasting contributions to theological and political discourse in the United States. However they are often also critiqued for certain perceived relativistic, consequentialist tendencies. James Childress' autobiographical reflection offers a paradigmatic example of Niebuhr's influence.

> . . . only in college did I really begin to appreciate Quaker pacifism. And yet its initial temptation was soon quashed by exposure to Reinhold Niebuhr's devastating critique of the Quaker claim that nonviolence is both right and effective in resisting injustice. Niebuhr's realism itself proved to be problematic because it lacked adequate moral restraints and at times wandered in what Paul Ramsey called "the wastelands of consequentialism." Subsequently I found an intellectual and moral home in the just-war tradition (JWT), which I have tried to interpret and reinterpret, as well as use in reflection on armed conflicts.[1]

Ramsey himself, as the quotation suggests, set the stage for this reading of Niebuhr. All of Niebuhr's work on war and politics, Ramsey tells us, properly fits under the heading of the principle of proportionality.[2] Thus, Ramsey confines Niebuhr's contribution to a corner, and what he saw as a rather untidy corner, in the broader theory that he and later ethicists would develop. With his idealistically inspired critique, Ramsey set much of the context for later readings of Niebuhr. Niebuhr is thus often seen as functioning primarily to clear the way for the development or recovery of more systematic deontological ethic for dealing with war.

There is some truth in portrayals of Niebuhr as a proportionalist or consequentialist. Niebuhr's encounter with pragmatism had inclined him in this direction. Consistent with the pragmatic tradition, Niebuhr was worried about responsibility for foreseeable consequences. It is a mark of fanaticism to understate the costs of one's proposed policy or activity. As such, Niebuhr's work often focused upon the significance of realism in discussing the ends of war. He was also active, especially in his editorials, in the measuring of means against alternate means and against the ends at which they aimed. Like Max Weber's "ethic of responsibility," Niebuhr's ethics is constructed to counter the fanatic tendency to ignore costs incurred in service to purportedly "ultimate ends."[3] Proportionalism and attention to consequences are thus important elements in any statement of Niebuhrian ethics.

But simply to say this suggests too little about the strength of Niebuhr's thought. Niebuhr's encounter with pragmatism had left him with a deep respect for the dangers of narrow ideological justifications of the use of force. It had also suggested the ways in which the virtues of criticalness, responsibility, and humility might be helpful in times of massive conflict. Niebuhr took up these insights and found that there were theological grounds for their articulation. In an era that has rediscovered the significance of narrative, virtues, and theologically grounded perspective, Niebuhr's approach to war deserves a new hearing. When read in the context of the Niebuhr's overarching fight against fanaticism and idolatry, it becomes clear that Niebuhr's conception of war does more than lay out a framework of moral reasoning for assessing particular wars. It provides a moral conception of war that sensitizes one to recurrent fanatic tendencies that often overwhelm actors during massive human conflict. This conception of war, while taking seriously the historical responsibility of humans, reminds those contemplating and participating in war of their own limitations, their own past sins, and the constant state of their own temptation toward sinfulness. Like the pragmatists, Niebuhr recognizes that fanaticism is often at the root of and expressed within war. Unlike the pragmatists, Niebuhr reacts to this fanaticism with a theological conception of war as the judgment of God.[4]

I will begin this chapter by relating an account of war developed by William James, on which Niebuhr drew in his early writings. I will then present Niebuhr's conception of war as the judgment of God, and explore the implications of this conception in relation to pacifism and militarism. Finally, I will explore the project to which Niebuhr saw the Christian prophet called in times of war.

A Jamesean Encounter

In 1910, a few weeks before William James' death, James published an essay on the contemporary problem of peace and war.[5] The problem, James posits, is found in the reductive views of the good held by both the "peace-party and the war-party." Both sides, James writes, "are on imaginative and sentimental ground. It is but one utopia against another, and everything one says must be abstract and hypothetical."[6]

Neither side in this argument wins over the other. In the end, they both offer fanatical accounts of war. The war-party rightly locates the goods manifest in times of war: service, virtue, discipline, and sacrifice for the common good.[7] They also rightly locate the poverty of the peace-party in its individualistic anthropology and reductive view of society as oriented at maximizing pleasure and minimizing self-sacrifice. But the war-party oversteps in making war into "a sort of sacrament."[8] It sees only the goods in war and underestimates the costs of military conflict, and thus seeks to establish war as a permanent feature in human life. The peace-party has made the opposite mistake. It rightly recognizes the costs of war, but does not come to grips with the good of war as a social cause. The peace-party has conceived of life as a banal process of commercialism and pleasure seeking, and thus has failed to see the goods represented in the kind of sacrificial service involved in war.

The only solution, James suggests, is to produce a "moral equivalent to war." Society must undertake quests to change the world that are significant enough to evoke passion, demand discipline and virtue, and require genuine sacrifices. But, if the society is wise, it will find quests that do not break into outright violence. Only thus can a society find a sustainable peace movement that genuinely fulfills the needs of mankind.

Reinhold Niebuhr read James' essay in 1914, and was, apparently, impressed with its argument.[9] Something of James' argument would resonate in all of Niebuhr's later writings on war. The fanaticism of the war-party and the peace-party, Niebuhr finds, did need to be broken. But Niebuhr develops his own argument against militaristic and pacifistic manifestations of fanaticism in different directions from James'. James, in his effort to defend the martial virtues, had not said enough about the ways in which the ideal of service to the community could be twisted in the modern state to serve unjust ends.[10] Further, James, when articulating the positive qualities of war, had limited his treatment to the function of war in providing a moral and social structure for one's own society. He had found that, though some of the effects of war were of enduring value, war was a social practice that could, with relative ease, be eradicated without losing its beneficial effects once the problem of war was understood. In Niebuhr's mature theology, war does not function simply in service to domestic social and moral formation. War is, in an important sense, a practice that properly functions to preserve the historic order of relative justice from the abuses of particularly grievous forms of idolatry. Seeing war as such, Niebuhr could not be as enthusiastic as was James about the promise of a world in which war was eliminated.

These are important differences between Niebuhr's and James' accounts of war. Still, perhaps most important difference in understanding Niebuhr's re-conceptualization of the problem of war fanaticism deals with Niebuhr's grasp of the religious grounding of war and peace fanaticism. James had suggested, with his reference to the war-party's treatment of war as sacrament, that the war debate might have religious overtones. Niebuhr finds that the debate is steeped in religion. Clashes between the war and peace parties are more than a fanatical disagreement about goods; they are a manifestation of competing idolatries. Combating idolatry requires more than a new project for society. It requires a reestablishment of the place of war in relation to the Christian God.

War as the Judgment of God

For Niebuhr, history is, as we have seen, a realm maintained by God's judgment. "God is," Niebuhr writes, "the ultimate source of that indestructible order in the world against which man's pride and self-will beat in vain."[11] This order, and this judgment is to be found in the continual frustration of human telos within history and in the particular occasions within history in which social structures and created and crushed. Through the universally pervasive frustration of telos (God's indiscriminate judgment) the human is reminded that no matter how relatively good she or he finds her or himself, she or he is never free from the guilt of past sins and the temptation to self-deceptive sinfulness in present action. No person and no social unit within sin-stained history lives up to the indiscriminate measure of perfect love. As such, this measure serves to convict each person and each community of its sin.[12] Evil can never be simply externalized, and can only be dealt with adequately if one recognizes the extent to which she or he is culpable for and tempted to evil her or himself. Through the particular occasions of social collapse and destruction in history (God's discriminate judgment) the human is reminded that God has not left history as an area of meaninglessness, but rather has calls upon persons and communities to preserve the possibility of those partial realizations of good available within history against the idolatrous grasping of sinful humanity, so that they may be taken up in God's ultimate action of salvation. As the prophets saw, every conquest, be it one's own or that of one's enemies, contains a lesson about the work of God in the world. Within history thus conceived, war does not offer to the Christian a unique and unfathomable moral problem. On the contrary, Niebuhr writes, "international crisis merely reveals in its most vivid form what human history is like."[13] War is a sign of God's indiscriminate and God's discriminate judgment in history.

There are no wars in the Kingdom of God. The sign of that Kingdom is found in the lion and the lamb that lay down next to one another; partially contradicting their historical relation in the act of fulfilling their ultimate natures in harmonious existence.[14] War constitutes a frustration of ultimate telos in loving relation for all involved. "The struggle for justice and the struggle for peace," Niebuhr writes, "have the same sanction in the commandment of love."[15] No act of or abstention from a justifiable war constitutes perfectly loving action. In war the ultimate good of the warrior and of the civilian is ruptured in the effort to realize a partial historical good. Such is the manifestation of God's indiscriminate judgment. As such, war should be first perceived as a reminder of the common and persistent waywardness of all humanity including the opponent and the self.[16] As Niebuhr writes: "all historic struggles are struggles between sinful men and not between the righteous and sinners" and "the injustice and tyranny against which we contend in the foe is partially the consequence of our own injustice."[17]

But war is not only a reminder of common sinfulness, it is also one of the means by which God quashes those idolatrous centers of human power that threaten the possible realization of relative goods available within history. This destructive use of power, while not simply identifiable with God's saving love, is one part of the divine politics that finds its ultimate end in the perfection of history itself. Like a potter working with a vessel damaged in the process of formation, God unmakes parts of God's creation without discarding the raw material that will be used in a new and more perfect creation. Humans are involved in this discriminate judgment, both as the instruments of and subjects within the order of God's judgment. Indeed, seeking responsible approximations of love within history will lead humanity at its best to function as God's instruments within those areas where human politics and divine politics overlap in the project of maintaining the relative justice of history.[18] "The final victory over man's disorder," Niebuhr writes, "is God's and not ours; but we do have responsibility for proximate victories."[19] But no strain of human politics is ever simply identifiable with God's politics, even that portion of God's politics that falls within history. Every human instrument of God's judgment is also subject to God's judgment. "To declare the omnipotence of God is to insist that the ultimate power which maintains the order of the world is superior to all subordinate powers and majesties which tend to create anarchy by making themselves the premature and inadequate centers of order in the world."[20]

Sinful humanity is, needless to say, not pleased with this arrangement. Responding sinfully to anxiety about their own fulfillment, humans do not wish to accept their position as responsible but sinful creatures in a world ultimately maintained and saved by God. As such they reject God's grace as manifest in God's judgment and gift of salvation and seek either to replicate God's transcendent act of love, or to usurp God's position as the ultimate judge of history. Humans thus continually confuse God's politics with their own. The naming of this idolatry is the starting point for Niebuhr's approach to the morality of war.

> If we cannot believe that God has resources to negate and to wipe out the corruption of egotism that all our actions betray, if we do not know that we are 'justified' not by our own goodness but by the goodness of God, we remain in the awful predicament of either trying to find a vantage point in history from which we can act 'purely,' or persuading ourselves that we have found such a vantage point and declaring a 'holy war' from it.[21]

In their sin, humans thus take up fanatic and idolatrous pacifism or idolatrous militarism. Neither, Niebuhr suggests, offer a viable Christian alternative.

Political Pacifism

It is unfortunate that Niebuhr's position on war has often been summarized using the supposedly Niebuhrian dichotomy between "irrelevant purity" and "guilty responsibility" or between "Christian witness" and "effectiveness."[22] Readings of Niebuhr that have found such a distinction to be central to his own theology have often asked why one would seek sinful responsibility when Christian witness against such sinfulness is a viable alternative. Niebuhr has, some pacifists suggest, found that Christian love is not effective and as such abandoned it in favor of a non-Christian criterion of responsibility.

Niebuhr himself is partially to blame for this misunderstanding of his position. During the run up to World War II one of his colleagues posed to Niebuhr the question: "Why is it that the world is divided between those who wish to be pure and those who wish to be responsible?"[23] Niebuhr promptly started repeating the question for rhetorical effect in public presentations. Niebuhr also often, without further qualification, reminds his reader of the guilt in which all responsible action is involved, and at times makes comments that at least seem to suggest that acts of politics, coercion, or killing *per se* constitute intrinsically sinful acts.[24] Finally, Niebuhr's continued emphasis on the need for justifying grace in order to participate in responsible action may seem to imply that responsible actions *per se* constitute sins which one is allowed to intentionally undertake in light of God's forgiving grace.

The lack of clarity in Niebuhr's statements on these points is an unfortunate impediment in articulating a coherent and viable Niebuhrian position on morality and war. Niebuhr is often insufficiently careful when dealing with these concepts, and no review of his work should understate this fact.[25] Thankfully one is not simply left with such confusion. There are, in Niebuhr's works, moments in which Niebuhr offers a more subtle account of guilt, responsibility, and false purity. In these moments, responsibility is more Christian, the means of maintaining historical justice more clearly suitable for moral justification, and the search for "purity" more corrupt than the simplified statements of Niebuhr's position suggest.

The Moral Quality of Violent Power Per Se

In an earlier chapter I noted that Niebuhr at times wrong-headedly treats all imperfect actions as if they constituted sins and imparted guilt on the person who undertakes them. As I noted, his intent at such times is to remind the actor of her or his past sinfulness and current temptation to sin, and to instill humility in choosing a path in the midst of limited available options. Unfortunately, the upshot is a language game that runs the danger of suggesting that all actions are depraved, and thus threatens the significance of historical moral differences amongst the options. Violent action is the paradigmatic instance of imperfect action for Niebuhr, and thus following the above pattern he at times falls into the error of treating it as a case of sinfulness *per se*. This is, for the reasons suggested above, a problematic position. But it is not the only way that Niebuhr talks about violence. Several comments throughout his writings suggest a more subtle position.

Moral Man and Immoral Society offers one of Niebuhr's most sustained treatments of the morality of violence. This is unfortunate inasmuch as many facets of Niebuhr's thought in this work are left behind in his more mature writings. Still, his reasoning here is suggestive, and some of his later comments suggest that his view of the moral quality of violence in this document is consistent with his later views. Contemporary pacifists, he posits, confuse the moral quality of acts of violence by claiming that such actions are intrinsically evil. This would only be the case, he suggests, if "violence is a natural and inevitable expression of ill will, and non-violence of good will."[26] But, in the world as it stands this is not the case. It is true that violence entails the sacrifice of certain goods which are usually central to social human life and ultimately necessary to the realization of human telos. However, within a world in which the simultaneous realization of all genuine human goods is not a realistic possibility, Niebuhr finds that none of these particular values can be absolutized. As Niebuhr notes elsewhere: "life is in conflict with life in an imperfect world, and therefore no one has the opportunity of supporting the principle of the sanctity of life in an absolute sense."[27] In a history distorted by sin there are times when the good will calls for war while the ill will stands behind the status quo order praying for peace.

Niebuhr returns to this theme in 1955 when he voices criticism of pacifists for whom "violence is regarded as sinful; no matter how just the cause."[28] Some later works make a similar point concerning the moral quality of violence in a theological framework. The order of God's judgment is, Niebuhr suggests, an expression of God's unyielding power. This order includes God's use of power in war. But the Christian does not accept that God's will is corrupt due to involvement in such uses of power.

> [The Christian Faith] does not accept the idea that power is of itself evil; and that the source of all power must therefore be lacking in holiness. One of the attributes of holiness is undoubtedly majesty. The Apostle's Creed begins with the credo: 'I believe in God the Father Almighty, Maker of heaven and earth.' The closing ascription in our Lord's prayer is: 'For thine is the . . . power and the glory forever'[29]

No doubt, the order of God's judgment is not the order God ultimately wishes for the creation, nor is God's grace in maintaining this order to be simply identified with God's ultimate will and loving action in Christ. Still, within the bounds of history "the terrible character of His wrath" is seen by the Christian as "justified judgment upon the various idolatries of history."[30]

Further, in Niebuhr's careful moments, he is clear that responsible action within history is in no way to be *simply* contrasted with the demands of love. Love as an indiscriminate measure ultimately stands over against all preferential acts including acts of war, but this does not mean that preferentially responsible acts are not demanded by love in its function as a discriminate measure within history. God's good creation, though frustrated, still contains the raw materials for the realization of goodness, and God's gracious act in Christ has revealed that the partial realizations of goods within history will ultimately be brought to fulfillment in the eschaton. Within sin-stained history, human social organization and the goods associated with this organization are dependent upon some level of coercive force. As such, the Christian is moved by her or his view of love to use those levels of force necessary to protect and realize those human goods which are available within history. Such is not the abandonment of love, as if love were a simple possibility if one did not use force.[31] The judicious use of force is an act that grows out of one's concern for the neighbor and as such realizes love to that extent possible in a horrible situation. Though historical coercive and preferential justice may always fall short of the pinnacle of perfect love, it is not, Niebuhr writes, "essentially a compromise with evil or simply an approximation of love in an evil world. It expresses the social responsibility which stems from one dimension of love."[32]

Finally, a generous reading of Niebuhr must assume that he does not mean to suggest that responsible actions, especially violent actions, *per se* are intentional acts of sin within history and *as such* only viable under the umbrella of justifying grace. Niebuhr may never have found an adequate formula for dealing with both the universality of sinfulness and the particularity of sins, but one should not on the basis of this gap in his theoretical scheme suggest that he meant to advocate for intentionally evil acts within history. In fact, his treatment of the need for justifying grace may, in most cases, be read as an effort to avoid fanatical corruption of historical morality. Humanity in the grips of sin always seeks ultimate fulfillment under its own power, and in the fanaticism of its own project neglects the real values that it destroys in the process of the project. Justifying grace is that grace which allows one to deal with anxiety about her or his predicament as a creature trapped in a world in which her or his ultimate telos is stymied. To the extent that the self knows itself to be justified and accepts its justification, the self is freed from anxiety to react appropriately to those relative goods available in history. Justification is not, then, to be understood as an excuse for inappropriate actions within history, but rather as the grounding for any proper appraisal of one's responsibility for those historical possibilities of justice that exist.

Responsibility is thus not a non-Christian criterion. Nor is responsibility deployed within a field of simple moral ambiguity which admits of no discriminating judgments.[33] Though war is not a simple act of love it is an act which at its best serves the highest level of justice possible within the order of history. The Christian, to the extent that she or he is freed from illusions about participation in or ability to bring about the Kingdom of God is able to act responsibly within history and avoid pretensions that obscure the discriminating judgments necessary to historical morality.

The Idolatry of Political Pacifism

The putative search for purity does not fare so well in Niebuhr's thought. The practical dimensions of Niebuhr's critique of pacifism are well documented.[34] Unfortunately, the theological underpinnings of his position are at times obscured in treatments of his thought.[35] As such, Niebuhr's argument often appears to be a simple statement that political pacifism is often surreptitiously involved in coercion and in the last resort ineffective in achieving its own aims. These points are important within Niebuhr's criticism, but they are points which grow out of his broader theological understanding of the idolatry of political pacifism.

In his mature writings Niebuhr's primary concern with political pacifism is that it confuses the goodness of the pacifist or the pacifistic movement with the goodness of Christ. The perfect act of love which saves the world is God's act through God's *only* begotten son. It is idolatry to claim ownership of Christ's role in this act. The Christian, Niebuhr suggests, finds her or his ultimate confidence not in her or his own action, but in God's action on her or his behalf. As Niebuhr responds to one pacifist critic:

> The redemption in Christ is . . . the revelation of a divine mercy that alone is able to overcome the contradictions of human history from which even the best of us cannot extricate ourselves. I believe, with the Protestant Reformation, that any claim that we have overcome this contradiction and that Christ has become our possession merely leads to a new form of egoism, namely, pharisaic pride.[36]

Niebuhr's insights into the *de facto* impurity and ineffectiveness of political pacifism grows out of his recognition that positions that confuse the goodness of the self or the self's social movement with the goodness of God will run up against the strictures of God's judgment in history. No human effort to achieve perfection within history can be successful, and any project that aims at such is bound to be frustrated.

Political pacifism can be either paternalistic or sectarian, but either mode is idolatrous from Niebuhr's perspective. The social gospel movement advocated for a form of paternalistic pacifistic idolatry. They reduced Christ's action to a pattern for a non-violent political strategy aimed at the production of perfect justice within history. If only the world would live by the ethic of Jesus, these pacifists claim, justice could be achieved without hostility. For Niebuhr, such claims finally constitute a rejection of the reality of both one's own place as sinner and one's position in need of God's grace.

> All of these beliefs are pathetic alternatives to the Christian faith. They all come finally to the same thing. They do not believe that man re-

> mains a tragic creature who needs the divine mercy as much at the end as at the beginning of his moral endeavors. They believe rather that there is some fairly easy way out of the human situation of 'self-alienation.' In this connection it is significant that Christian pacifists, rationalists like Bertrand Russell, and mystics like Aldous Huxley, believe essentially the same thing. *The Christians make Christ into the symbol of their own faith in man.*[37]

In the end, paternalistic pacifism is not a Christian alternative to worldly politics. In failing to accept its place in the scheme of God's judgment it fails to realize and protect the relative goods of history for which God has provided. The upshot of this project is not the actualization of justice, but rather the allowance of unnecessary evil. The pacifist project "to set up the Kingdom of God on earth ends in a perverse preference for tyranny, simply because the peace of tyranny means, at least, the absence of war."[38]

Surrounded by the widespread and highly influential paternalist pacifism within the United States prior to World War II, Niebuhr was concerned that life in a modern democracy might be conducive to such a moral and theological error.[39] Overly simplistic views of the historical struggle and fragility of relative justice achieved within democratic society made the internal norms of this society seem absolute. The vested interests of capitalistic centers in avoiding conflict led to a reification of peace so as to avoid economic disorder. The success of modern democracies in obscuring the extent to which their order depends upon the viable threat and use of violent force led some to believe that they lived in a society of perpetual peace. Those in the upper and middle classes found it all too easy to ignore coercive economic and social forces within the society, deadly though they may be. Identifying generally non-violent bourgeois life with the ethic of Jesus, they were free to live with the delusion that theirs was the politics of God. This was a pretense embraced at America's greatest peril. "American peace as a symbol of the goodness of man," Niebuhr writes, "can be maintained only at the price of accentuating every vice in American character, particularly the vices of Pharasaism and self-righteousness."[40] World War II was in part a divine judgment against such pretensions.[41]

Niebuhr has often been read as more favorable to sectarian pacifism. These pacifists suggest that participation in Christ's perfect love offers a way of life available to the Christian so long as she or he disavows worldly responsibilities that might lead to an acceptance of overt violence. Niebuhr, as we shall see below, certainly does find a certain kind of ascetic pacifism useful. But it is important to draw a distinction between the prophetic use of pacifism of which he does approve and the sectarian pacifism of which he does not. As with paternalistic pacifism, Niebuhr finds that sectarian pacifism is grounded ultimately in a deflation of Christ's distinctive act of love and a reductive account of the goods available within historical reality.

Sectarian pacifists have confused Christ's perfectly loving act with the historical dimension of that act taken alone. Christ's act could disavow historical partiality while remaining transhistorically oriented toward the good of all.[42] This was possible because of Christ's divine transcendence of history. In contrast, the historically bound pacifist's "disavowal of the natural relationships and responsibilities of ordinary life leads to the destruction of life itself."[43] Far from being an act of Christian witness, the effort to participate fully in Christ's love in history ends in a rejection of the possibilities within history to which Christ calls the Christian.

> Thus, the Christian ideal of love has degenerated into a lovelessness which cuts itself off from a sorrowing and suffering world. Love is made to mean not pity and sympathy or responsibility for the weal and woe of others, it becomes merely the abstract and negative perfection of peace in a warring world.[44]

In the end, Niebuhr's problem with political pacifism is found in the low Christologies upon which political pacifism is based, and the idolatrous pretensions to which these low Christologies give way. Each in its efforts to participate in God's politics cuts Christ's perfect and divine act of love down to a simply humanly realizable measure. Seeking escape from the order of God's judgment the pacifist denies the necessity of Christ's divine transcendence, and pretends to be able to replicate Christ's acts. For Niebuhr, such is not a viable Christian alternative. The idolatry of the peace-party is thus denied on theological grounds.

Power

Thus, Niebuhr was, as Childress' short summary at the beginning of the chapter suggests, an ardent critic of political pacifism. His criticism was so successful that at times his position is presented simply as a critique of those who would flee from the responsibility of power politics. Several contemporary commentators have, in the light of recent events, appealed to Niebuhr's legacy and lamented the waning of Niebuhr's realistic call for responsibility in the world of Christian ethics.[45] Their insights into the burdens of American power in the contemporary world bear many signs of Niebuhr's influence. As Niebuhr would remind us, with power comes responsibility. Though a nation must always strive for greater heights of justice, it cannot wait on its own perfection before wading into responsible action in the world nor can it wait for perfect means to achieve the relative peace available in history. But Niebuhr's realism is not a realism aimed only at the pretensions of those who eschew power politics. It is also a realism that seeks to counter the idolatrous fanaticism that so often accompanies historical human uses of power. Though power *per se* is not intrinsically evil, Niebuhr's confessional position leads him to reject the idea of any simply human use of power that is not involved in a history of sins and the occasion for temptation to further sin. War is an intrinsically imperfect act, falling short of and partially contradicting the ideal of loving relations. As such, the fact that war is at times the best available option in history is a sign of God's judgment against all involved, even those who take themselves to be, and even those who are in fact, fighting for the more just cause.

The Idolatry of Power

Niebuhr's suspicion concerning the human use of power is clear in his treatment of one use of pacifism of which he did approve: prophetic pacifism. In ancient Israel the prophets had undertaken certain acted analogies to relate God's will and action to the people of Israel. Jeremiah bought a field prior to the Babylonian exile, Hosea married a harlot. These prophets did not confuse these actions with God's acts of justice or with political strategies for the people of Israel. Jeremiah was not proposing a real estate scheme. Rather, they understood that these were symbolic acts, using imperfect figural symbols to point to the perfect actions and attributes of God. For Niebuhr, it is in such a function that pacifism can contribute to Christian discourse on war. This pacifism

> seeks to raise *symbols* of the perfect Agape of Christ in history, without making any claims that the character of human history will be changed thereby but rightly insisting that such *symbols* remind Christians of the peril as well as the necessity of using instruments tainted with sin to fight evil.[46]

The acts of such pacifists should not be confused with acts of perfect love, but they should stand as symbols of this love and as such remind humanity of the judgment of God against all of history and the hope that God gives to all of history.

> We who allow ourselves to become engaged in war need this testimony of the absolutist against us, lest we accept the warfare of the world as normative, lest we become callous to the horror of war, and lest we forget the ambiguity of our own actions and motives and the risk we run of achieving no permanent good from this momentary anarchy in which we are involved.[47]

War can never be a simple act of love, and war is always involved in and inevitably the occasion for sin on the part of all involved. Prophetic pacifism is a symbol of God's indiscriminate judgment which shines light upon historical humanity's failures even in the moments of its greatest temptations to self-righteous fanaticism.

War as a human activity is always distinguishable from war as the judgment of God, even while any particular war exists as both simultaneously. "Perfect power and goodness," Niebuhr writes, "can be united only in God, where the contest of life with life is transcended and where the possession of power does not lead to its misuse in the struggle for existence."[48] While some wars within history may be justifiable, humans exist in a world at war due to their own sinfulness and their own sins. God is involved in such struggles not by God's own failure, but by God's wish to maintain and ultimately redeem a history skewed by human failures. Humans wield limited power with imperfect virtue and knowledge. God wields perfect power with perfect virtue and knowledge. At best, humans participate in wars aimed at maintaining a limited part of the relative justice available within history. God's involvement is one part of a broader politics that finds its end in the ultimate salvation of the world. It is, Niebuhr suggests, an idolatrous spirit that collapses such distinctions.

Unfortunately, times of war are conducive to such idolatrous spirits. The Christian must, Niebuhr writes, avoid the temptation "to succumb to the hysteria of war and to become corrupted by the immense spiritual pride and self-righteousness of the nations."[49] Rarely in human life are the stakes, and the concomitant anxieties of humanity, as high as in times of war. How shall war, with its grave costs, be justified? Anxious persons do not like narrow margins of assurance. It is always tempting, in one's anxiety, to flee from the complexity of reality and the frailty of one's position in that reality to a premature and naive sense of clarity in a time of war. In such times, it becomes easy to confuse national myths with divine revelations. It becomes easy to claim one's state as a savior state, spreading divinely imparted values that will provide for the ultimate stability of history. Those arguing for war are tempted to absolutize the values for which the war is fought, to present a homogenized and aggrandized picture of their own society, to present a homogenized and vilified picture of the enemy society, to overestimate the ease of victory, to underestimate the cost of battle, to claim any means are justified in achieving victory, and to prematurely close their position off from contributions and critiques offered by others. These temptations are not themselves sin. Sin is found in the will that indulges such temptations, even if it must deceive itself into believing its own pretensions in the process.

It is an unfortunate fact that with the responsibility that attends great power, the temptations to idolatrous pretense also increase. With massive power to support it, a nation's pretensions become more plausible. History or providence, it seems, has established the nation as an international leader. Politicians and citizens are always prone to confuse growth in power with growth in virtue pertaining to the use of power.[50]

There is always some truth mixed in with such pretensions. Great powers are the instruments of God's order. But like Babylon and Assyria in the Old Testament, none are necessary instruments, and none grows so powerful as to stymie God's judgment when such comes against them.

This was a central idea in Niebuhr's post World War position. As Niebuhr writes to his fellow Americans as citizens in a neophyte great power following World War II:

> We were indeed the executors of God's judgment yesterday. But we might remember the prophetic warnings to the nations of old, that nations which become proud because they were divine instruments must

in turn stand under the divine judgment and be destroyed. . . . If ever a nation needed to be reminded of the perils of vainglory, we are that nation in the pride of our power and our victory.[51]

As some states take positions of international leadership on the basis of their power other international actors come to resent the power vested in those leaders. This resentment is partially due to the pretentious envy of lesser powers themselves, but it is also born of the perspective these lesser powers have upon policies born of exaggerated claims to knowledge, virtue, and power on the part of great power states.[52] In the meantime, great powers tend to idolatrously overestimate their reach and ability to control the world, and as a consequence spread themselves too thin, thus dissipating their power. Slowly the prestige and security of great powers is eroded by their own pretentious foibles. Thus is the stage set for a new divine judgment in history.

The rise and judgment of such pretensions may be ultimately unavoidable within history. Though there have been great empires, none has maintained, and the Niebuhrian suspects none will be able to maintain, permanence within history. But the ultimate unavoidability of judgment does not mean that one should disavow the search for those virtues which will allow relatively more just centers of power to endure within history as long as possible. Nor are nations and their leaders left without resources in this task. History repeatedly offers up the judgments of God which, when properly interpreted by the prophetic spirit, convict all participants in history in their sinfulness.

Repentance and Responsible Action

"It is good to know what to do with an uneasy conscience," writes Niebuhr, for it is the uneasy conscience that, without leading to withdrawal from responsibility, "must bring forth fruits meet for repentance."[53] The language of repentance does not, for Niebuhr, simply offer a way of talking about the need to produce sad warriors in a time of conflict. Repentance is a facet of the faith position from which the Christian should properly view the world. It is a source of virtue, especially in times of conflict.

Beyond all moral distinctions of history we must know ourselves one with our enemies not only in the bonds of a common humanity but also

> in the bonds of a common guilt by which that humanity has become corrupted. The Christian faith must persuade us to be humble rather than self-righteous in carrying out our historic tasks.[54]

The repentant person accepts his or her own position as responsible but sinful creature dependent upon God's unique act for her or his salvation. She or he acknowledges the sins of the self and the self's nation that have contributed to the need for the order of God's judgment in history, recognizes the imperfection of all means and ends available to a person in her or his limited position, and faces squarely the dangers of her or his own self-deceptive tendencies toward idolatry despite her or his apparently best efforts at avoiding such temptations. The penitent disposition shapes one's view of and response to war in many ways.

For instance, as concerns the call to war, repentance leads to a critical view of the tendency toward self aggrandizement and vilification of the enemy in the arguments for war. No person aware of her or his own, and her and his own country's imperfections and failures ought to fall to a naive acceptance of national myths. In a world where all are recognized as sinners there can be no savior nations, delegated with the task of making history come out right.

Recognition of moral complexity in one's own nation's position and one's opponent's is essential, Niebuhr suggests, in keeping violent conflict in its proper place. When one is deluded into believing that historical struggles constitute clashes between simple good and evil, violent conflict comes to seem inevitable, even if there is no immediate threat from the opponent. But "if such a conflict is inevitable there is no good reason for not choosing the moment most propitious to our cause for initiating it." From the doctrine of an inevitable war, Niebuhr writes, "the proposition of a preventive war is quickly derived." Thus, emerges "the curious desire to invite the catastrophe which we ought to avoid."[55] God's judgment comes to remind humanity that the world is not so simple as such a pretentious picture would suggest.

Indeed, the penitent person is chastened from the overuse of violent force. Unburdened by the belief that her or his ideology is simply identifiable with, and thus guaranteed success by God's plan for history the penitent person perceives the fragility and risk of historical action. Violence is, Niebuhr tells us, a negative tool; it limits evil, but does not by itself produce good. One ought not to expect that creativity will follow immediately in the wake of destruction. "The anarchy of war which results from resistance to tyranny is not always creative . . . at given periods of history, civilization may lack the resources to fashion a new and higher form of unity out of momentary anarchy."[56] For this reason violence ought to be deployed only in an instance of last resort,[57] and when violence is necessary, it must be followed quickly by a realistically grounded effort to minimize the damage to the defeated nation and reinstall order.

Nor does the repentant disposition only affect one's perception concerning when war is proper. It also influences how one fights a war. While the self-righteous warrior may fight out of vengeance and hatred, the repentant warrior rejects such motives. If she or he must join in conflict, she or he does so with the recognition that "the evil in the other shall be borne without vindictiveness because the evil in the self is known."[58] Forgiveness and pity, Niebuhr tells us, are, in their human manifestations, born out of a recognition that the enemy and the self are not entirely different from one another. Both stand in need of God's grace. Only one who is truly able to grasp this truth, Niebuhr suggests, is able to recognize the need of the neighbor even in conflict.[59]

For the repentant person, it becomes clear that the purpose for war is not the destruction of the "evil enemy" but rather the reestablishment of relatively just historical concord. Because violence is only licitly used in service to a positive end, and because violence is at best a negative tool, its use should be limited. Conflict and coercion are, Niebuhr writes in an early work, "so fruitful of the very evils from which society must be saved that an intelligent society will not countenance their indiscriminate use."[60] The resources on which the relative concord of history depends, be they material, cultural, or spiritual, must be, to the extent possible, protected from destruction.

The repentant person also becomes aware that the strategic and political goals available within history are not great enough to justify any means. Historical justice is always a relative justice and there are times in which even the more just cause does not warrant the means necessary to defend it.

> . . . even a nation can reach the point where it can purchase its life too dearly. . . . Even nations can reach a point where the words of our Lord, 'Fear not them which are able to kill the body but rather fear them that are able to destroy both soul and body in hell,' become relevant.
>
> The point of moral transcendence over historical destiny is not as high as moral perfectionists imagine. But there is such a point, though

> the cynics and realists do not recognize it. We must discern that point clearly.[61]

Niebuhr himself was largely reticent in delimiting such boundaries. He was worried that during a nuclear standoff articulating the length to which one would not go in protecting one's country could be heard by the opponent as an invitation to go a step beyond. Still, his reticence in this area should not be construed as an indication that he took there to be no immutable boundaries concerning means of international conflict.

Finally, the repentant person recognizes that her or his perspective, and the perspective of her or his neighbor, is limited and potentially tainted by sinful pretense. As such, she or he recognizes the need for critical dialogue in a time of war. If left in the dark, decisions can be easily monopolized by those whose narrowly focused goals lead them to an inadequate consideration of the means they choose in waging war. "The military mind," Niebuhr notes, "is inclined to disregard moral and political factors in strategy and it is therefore unsafe to give it a final moral and political authority in matters of this kind." For this reason, Niebuhr finds that, to that extent possible, "general principles of strategy ought to remain under democratic scrutiny."[62]

There are, no doubt, many other ways in which the repentant disposition affects one's reaction to wars. Some of these are not susceptible to such concise summary as those above. To see war as the judgment of God is to locate oneself in the midst of a story in which all history is seen as meaningful as it is maintained and ultimately saved by God. Within such a story, there is no final security for those who must make decisions while aware of their own past sinfulness and their own tendencies to sin. But they are at least grounded in their own knowledge of their predicament and their knowledge of God's grace. To the extent that they accept their position before God, they are enabled to undertake responsible action within history. Repentant, they avoid the idolatrous fanaticism of the war party.

The Prophet in a Time of War

Before concluding, it is important to say something concerning Niebuhr's "method" for approaching war. He is certainly in no simple sense a practitioner of just war ethics. While Niebuhr does at times use the just war criteria as a set of working principles for justice, his general response to those criteria is rather cool. Niebuhr fears that the virtues of repentance and responsibility cannot be adequately transmuted into a code of conduct. He is also worried that a rationalist war ethic would wrongly be taken to replace the need for the Christian's self-assessment as responsible sinner altogether. Such a shift would, he posits, play into the hands of a yet another form of idolatry.

> If men learn to live with any charity under these conditions of their existence, the charity must obviously be something more than a cool calculation which limits animal passion. For the mind, from which rationalists expect to derive this calculation, is intimately related to our passions, and frequently aggravates them.
>
> Charity can come only from a faith and a repentance which surveys the whole human situation in such a way that we know ourselves to be involved with even our worst enemies in a common human situation, for which there is no final resolution in our own resources.[63]

No set of rules, no matter how carefully crafted, could substitute for those dispositions that Niebuhr sees as growing out of one's recognition of her or his place before God. Without the virtues derived from such a perspective these rules are, as Niebuhr writes, "more likely to confuse than illumine the conscience."[64]

One can see how a rigid just war approach might obscure many of the morally relevant factors in decision making from Niebuhr's perspective. The just war criteria point attention to the immediate causes and conditions for actions in war. They do not seek to place particular wars within a broader narrative of human history and God's judgment in that history. As such, an overly narrow focus upon the criteria can obscure the ironies of history in and by which God's judgment works. From a just war perspective one might approach the Second World War as a war which is simply justifiable on the basis of particular transgressions on the part of the Nazis without being chastened by the lessons from the ways in which the Allied victory in First World War provided the context for the rise of Nazism itself. Without recognizing the judgment of God against itself, a large part of the meaning of the war would be missed, and the United States' temptation to pride would be aggravated.

It is, Niebuhr thinks, the role of the prophetic Christian to interpret history so as to evoke repentance and enable responsibility in the face of a world in crisis.[65] This is no easy task. To accomplish it one must locate particular wars within the narrative of human sin and divine judgment, tracing lines among past sins, ongoing idolatrous tendencies and temptations, and the conflicts in which society is enmeshed. History is, for Niebuhr, never meaningless. It is a process in which the eyes of faith find limited and partial lessons from the divine. But neither is history self interpreting.

The picture produced by the prophet will be complex. The indiscriminate judgment of God serves as a hermeneutical guide, reminding that no historical conflict exists due to sinful contribution from only one side in the dispute. Wars spring from complex interactions in which many, even beyond the immediate conflict, are often implicated. Producing a sufficiently thick description of the place of particular wars within the narrative of history will require in-depth historical and cultural studies to sufficiently fill out the particular past sins and contemporary idolatrous tendencies of all involved. The myths, ideologies, and practices which inform the social movements of history must be sifted and analyzed so as to derive a picture of the contemporary conflict. The earlier passage covering the unique American bourgeois temptation to sentimental pacifism exemplifies one point at which Niebuhr undertook such a task.

The role of the prophet is further complicated by the fact that social myths, ideologies, and practices exist within the flux of time and as such are not immutable. The particular idolatries to which a society is tempted may change in an instant. As Niebuhr writes in one of his first articles following Pearl Harbor:

> It is interesting to note that already the Wheelers and the Tafts and all that ilk, who yesterday insisted that Britain had nothing but national and imperial motives, today make virtue of the fact that it is our duty to 'beat the hell out of' our foes when their militarism challenges our liberties and not those of another nation only. Tomorrow they will be proving that we are fighting, not merely out of the motive of self-interest, but to 'preserve civilization.'[66]

Neither account, he notes, is without its mixture of truth and pretense. But following this event, Niebuhr's own focus shifts away from the critique of sentimental pacifism toward warning against the dangers of vindictive self-righteousness in wartime.

Though the prophet's account may find more overlap with one than the other, it ought not to satisfy either fanatic hawks or doves in a time of war. It will provide shelter for few absolute statements concerning the good or evil of either one's own or one's enemy's ideologies, strategies, causes, or means in war. Further, it will claim no final security from criticism or error.[67] But it will be an account which seeks to understand history in the context of the Christian narrative in which none is free from sin even as it insists that God provides ultimately for the meaningfulness of action even in disputes between sinners, and even when perfection is not a viable alternative.

For the Niebuhrian such an account grounds any adequate approach to particular wars. It is this approach that constitutes the middle way between the idolatries of the war-party and the peace-party. Such may not provide a clear deontological scheme for dealing with war, but it does provide an account of those virtues that allow any moral analysis in war to resist the dangers of fanaticism wherein one's claims to good intention come to justify reductive pictures of the world and one's own place within it.

Conclusion

As we have found in other areas covered in this work, here Niebuhr's perspective is influenced by his early encounter with pragmatism. James' work sensitized Niebuhr to both militant and pacifist fanaticism. But Niebuhr's own work goes far beyond this initial influence. Niebuhr's mature theology produces a moral image of war as the judgment of God. This image grounds a responsible repentant reaction to war, and provides a basis for humble prophetism in a time of war. Needless to say, it is a somewhat different image of war that Ramsey produces. For Ramsey it is not fanaticism, but the collapse of order that poses the most significant moral danger in a time of war. His image of war is calibrated to respond to this somewhat different threat. Before returning to critique Niebuhr's moral conception of war, we must turn to elaborate the alternate vision of war as presented by Ramsey.

Notes

1. James Childress, "Just War Tradition and the Invasion of Iraq," Churches' Center for Theology and Public Policy, <http://www.cctpp.org/archives/childresspaper.htm> (8 July 2006).

2. Ramsey, *The Just War*, 429. Some ethicists after Ramsey would not be even so generous. In caricature, Niebuhr's position has been portrayed as an uncritical apology for American power and as an argument leading to an understanding of war as a "crusade" for the sake of the neighbor. See Richard H. Rovere, *The American Establishment and Other Reports, Opinions and Speculations* (New York: Harcourt, Brace & World, 1962), 13, and D. Stephen Long, *Tragedy, Tradition, and Transformism*, 53. In contrast, see Charles Brown's comments in *Niebuhr and His Age*, 7.

3. See Max Weber, "Politics as a Vocation," in *From Max Weber: Essays in Sociology* (New York: Oxford University Press, 1958), 120. Note that this distinction locates the primary moral problem in terms of moral fanaticism whereas an appeal to deontology is often constructed as a reaction to the dangers of moral relativism. I am thankful to Robin Lovin for pointing out the parallelism between Niebuhr and Weber on this point.

4. "War as the Judgment of God" is the title of an article by H. Richard Niebuhr. While Reinhold's most famous exchange with his brother, H. Richard, concerning war found the two on opposing sides, Niebuhr's mature approach to war in some ways parallels, and no doubt also is indebted to, the treatment of war found in a broad review of his brother's work. Relating these two conceptions of war is, unfortunately, a task that goes beyond the scope of this work. For an analysis of H. Richard's work See Richard B. Miller, *Interpretations of Conflict* (Chicago: University of Chicago Press, 1991), 125-47.

5. William James, "The Moral Equivalent to War," in *The Writings of William James: A Comprehensive Edition*, ed. John H. McDermott (Chicago: The University of Chicago Press, 1977), 660-70.

6. William James, "The Moral Equivalent to War," 663.

7. William James, "The Moral Equivalent to War," 668.

8. William James, "The Moral Equivalent to War," 664.

9. See Richard Fox, *Reinhold Niebuhr: A Biography*, 35-36. At this time, Niebuhr produced a paper that suggested that James' "moral equivalent" would best be found in the concrete practices of the Christian Church. This was a solution to James' problem that would not survive Niebuhr's later realist picture of the Church as a historical institution.

10. For what seems to be a direct answer to James' claims about the romanticism of war, see Reinhold Niebuhr, "The Nation's Crime Against the Individual," *The Atlantic Monthly* (November, 1916), 611, also Richard Fox, *Reinhold Niebuhr: A Biography*, 46-47.

11. Reinhold Niebuhr, *The Essential Reinhold Niebuhr*, 24.

12. See my earlier treatment of love as a principle of discriminate and indiscriminate criticism in Chapter 2.

13. Reinhold Niebuhr, *Love and Justice*, 268.

14. Ronald Stone, "An Interview with Reinhold Niebuhr," *Christianity and Crisis* 29 (March 17, 1969), 52.

15. Reinhold Niebuhr and Angus Dun, "God Wills Both Justice and Peace," *Christianity and Crisis* 15, no. 10 (June 13, 1955), 75. There is, albeit imperfect, a parallel between Niebuhr's and David Hollenbach's approach to the relation between pacifism and just war theory. See *Nuclear Ethics: A Christian Moral Argument* (New York: Paulist Press, 1983), 29-31.

16. See Langdon Gilkey, *On Niebuhr*, 208. See also, Niebuhr, *Faith and History*, 125.

17. Niebuhr, *The Essential Reinhold Niebuhr*, 114, and *Christianity and Power Politics*, 35.

18. See Niebuhr, *The Essential Reinhold Niebuhr*, 25, 29, and *Love and Justice*, 281.
19. Niebuhr, *The Essential Reinhold Niebuhr*, 100.
20. Niebuhr, *The Essential Reinhold Niebuhr*, 25.
21. Niebuhr, *Love and Justice*, 295.
22. See John Howard Yoder, *Christian Attitudes to War, Peace, and Revolution: A Companion to Bainton* (Elkhart, Ind: Co-op Bookstore, 1983), 427, 351. Yoder writes that, for Niebuhr, war "is sin because it is destructive. . . . But it is the right sin to commit." See also Paul Ramsey, *Speak Up for Just War or Pacifism*, 119.
23. Niebuhr, "The Parable of the Wheat and the Tares," Compact disk of a sermon by Reinhold Niebuhr preached in 1952, CD N665 3-4, The Reinhold Niebuhr Audio Collection (Richmond, Va.: Union Presbyterian School of Christian Education).
24. For instance, Niebuhr at one point states that "We will know that we cannot purge ourselves of the sin and guilt in which we are involved by the moral ambiguities of politics without also disavowing responsibility for the creative possibilities of justice." Elsewhere he suggests that a political cause is "tainted" by concomitant guilt to the extent that "it involves itself in the evil of causing suffering to the innocent." See Niebuhr, *The Nature and Destiny of Man*, 2:284, and *Love and Justice*, 222.
25. For a reading of Niebuhr that finds his approach to be finally confused on such issues see Edmund Santurri, *Perplexity in the Moral Life: Philosophical and theological considerations* (Charlottesville, Va.: University Press of Virginia, 1987), 165-81. Santurri's later works, however, have tended to present Niebuhr in a more favorable light. See "Christian Realism and the 'Law of Peoples.'" *Journal of Religious Ethics* 33, No. 4 (December 2005), 783-814.
26. Niebuhr, *Moral Man and Immoral Society*, 172.
27. Niebuhr, *An Interpretation of Christian Ethics*, 175, also *Moral Man and Immoral Society*, 174.
28. Niebuhr and Dun, "God Wills Both Justice and Peace," 75.
29. Niebuhr, *The Essential Reinhold Niebuhr*, 23.
30. Niebuhr, *The Essential Reinhold Niebuhr* 24.
31. In one article written during World War II, Niebuhr states: "We cannot support the war with an easy conscience, but we will resist and refute the delusion that we might have had an easier conscience had we permitted the world to sink into slavery." Reinhold Niebuhr, "Our Responsibilities in 1942," *Christianity and Crisis* 1, no. 24 (January 12, 1942), 1.
32. Niebuhr and Dun, "God Wills Both Justice and Peace," 75. See also Niebuhr's comments on Brunner's mistake in overstating the distinction between justice and *agape*. Reinhold Niebuhr, *The Essential Reinhold Niebuhr*, 154.
33. Niebuhr is not, despite John Courtney Murray's suggestive treatment, to be identified as an "ambiguist." See *We Hold These Truths: Catholic reflections on the American proposition* (New York: Sheed and Ward, 1960), 279-85.
34. See, for instance, Colm McKeogh, *The Political Realism of Reinhold Niebuhr: a pragmatic approach to just war* (New York: St. Martin's Press, 1997), 19-37, James Childress, *Moral Responsibility in Conflicts: Essays on nonviolence, war, and conscience* (Baton Rouge, La.: Louisiana State University Press, 1982), 29-62, and Richard Harries, "Reinhold Niebuhr's Critique of Pacifism and his Pacifist Critics," in *Reinhold Niebuhr and the Issues of Our Time*, ed. Richard Harries (Grand Rapids, Mich.: W.B. Eerdmans, 1986), 105-21.

35. See, for instance, the comments of John Howard Yoder, *Christian Attitudes to War, Peace and Revolution*, 409.

36. Niebuhr, *Love and Justice*, 269.

37. Niebuhr, *The Essential Reinhold Niebuhr*, 105. Italics mine.

38. Niebuhr, *Love and Justice*, 270.

39. See Niebuhr, *Christianity and Power Politics*, 83-93.

40. *Christianity and Power Politics*, 40-41.

41. Niebuhr, *Love and Justice*, 180-83.

42. It is interesting to note that Niebuhr's treatment of ascetic and sectarian pacifism may be indebted to Barth's early treatment of mysticism. The mystic attempts to negate the self in an effort to reach to God, but, Barth writes, "no self-negation to which we may refer them (were it even suicide!) is so great and so profound as the actuality, as the self-negation to which all other negatives can only point, the self-negation which is immediately imbued with the positivity of God." *The Word of God and the Word of Man*, 205.

43. Niebuhr, *An Interpretation of Christian Ethics*, 168; See also Niebuhr's similar comments in "The Christian Witness in a Secular Age," 842.

44. Niebuhr, *Christianity and Power Politics*, 41-42. Niebuhr's comments here are aimed at an isolationist pacifism, but they are no doubt applicable to any pacifism that disavows responsibility to justice.

45. See, for instance, Jean Bethke Elstain, *Just War Against Terror: The Burden of American Power in a Violent World* (New York: Basic Books, 2003), 106-11; also Joseph Loconte "The War Party's Theologian: President Bush carries on the liberal tradition of Reinhold Niebuhr," *Opinion Journal, from The Wall Street Journal Editorial Page* (May 31, 2002). <http://www.opinionjournal.com/taste/ ?id=110001782> (30 April 2006). Compare these accounts to Peter Beinart, "The Rehabilitation of the Cold-War Liberal" *The New York Times Magazine* (April 30, 2006). <http://www.nytimes.com/2006/04/30/magazine/30liberal.html?_r=1&oref=slogin> (1 May 2006).

46. Niebuhr, *Faith and History*, 208. Italics mine. See also *The Nature and Destiny of Man*, 2:72-76, *An Interpretation of Christian Ethics*, 168, and *The Essential Reinhold Niebuhr*, 104, 119.

47. Niebuhr, *The Essential Reinhold Niebuhr*, 119.

48. Niebuhr, *The Essential Reinhold Niebuhr*, 26.

49. Niebuhr, *Essays in Applied Christianity*, 296.

50. See Niebuhr, *Love and Justice*, 183-189.

51. Quoted in Charles Brown, *Niebuhr and His Age*, 123. Similarly, Niebuhr would write during the early years of the cold war that "the pride and self-righteousness of powerful nations are a greater hazard to the success in statecraft than the machination of their foes." Niebuhr, "The Illusion of World Government," in *Christian Realism and Political Problems* (London: Faber and Faber Limited, 1953), 37.

52. See, Reinhold Niebuhr, "Why They Dislike America," *The New Leader* 37, no. 15 (April 12, 1954), 3-5.

53. Niebuhr, *Love and Justice*, 270.

54. Niebuhr, "Our Responsibilities in 1942," 2. See also *An Interpretation of Christian Ethics*, 207; "The Climax of War," *Christianity and Crisis* 4, no. 9 (May 29, 1944), 2; and "Prayer and a Global Civilization," *Christianity and Crisis* 4, no. 15 (September 18, 1944), 1-2. While the primary source for Niebuhr's ethics of repentance in responding to war is doubtless to be found in the prophets of Israel, it is important to note that this emphasis is also to be found in other places in the Christian tradition. As Martin Luther

writes: "You should not march out to war saying, 'Ah, now I have been forced to fight and have good cause for going to war.' You ought not to think that justifies anything you do and plunge headlong into battle. It is indeed true that you have a really good reason to go to war and to defend yourself, but that does not give you God's guarantee that you will win. Indeed, such confidence may result in your defeat—even though you have a just cause for fighting the war—for God cannot endure such pride and confidence except in a man who humbles himself before him and fears him." Martin Luther, "The Soldier and His Conscience," in *War and Christian Ethics*, ed. Arthur F. Holms, 153.

55. Niebuhr, *Essays in Applied Christianity*, 97.

56. Niebuhr, *The Essential Reinhold Niebuhr*, 118, also 29.

57. Niebuhr writes that "We cannot dispense with military power as the ultima ratio of international relations. But we do have to keep it in that position of the ultimate instance and not use a meat ax in situations in which a deft manipulation of loyalties or channeling of aspirations is called for." Niebuhr, *Love and Justice*, 194. Interestingly, Niebuhr notes in his early work, and intimates several times in his later works, that he approves of what he calls "pragmatic pacifism." Niebuhr's description of "pragmatic pacifism" finds some commonality with the contemporary movement of just peacemaking. See the unfortunately subtitled *Just Peacemaking: Ten Practices for Abolishing War*, ed. Glen Stassen (Cleveland, Ohio: The Pilgrim Press, 1998). As Niebuhr writes, the pragmatic pacifist seeks to mitigate "the struggle between contending forces, by insinuating the greatest possible degree of social imagination and intelligence into it and by providing the best possible means of arbitration so that violent conflict may be avoided." Niebuhr, *An Interpretation of Christian Ethics*, 16. Niebuhr would, no doubt, differ with many of the proposals that have been generated by the just peacemaking movement. A necessary initiative in maintaining peace in a sinful world, he would remind, is found in maintaining a viable threat of force. But he certainly seems to recognize the need for such a movement. See Ronald Stone, *Prophetic Realism*, 84-121.

58. Niebuhr, *An Interpretation of Christian Ethics*, 201.

59. Some of Niebuhr's most positive and unqualified use of love language comes exactly in his treatment of the need to overcome self-righteous hatred of the enemy in war. See, for instance, Niebuhr, *Love and Justice*, 218-21.

60. Niebuhr, *Moral Man and Immoral Society*, 238.

61. Niebuhr, *Love and Justice*, 237. Such a position should be expected inasmuch as Niebuhr was an Augustinian. As Rowan Williams writes, for Augustine, "There can be no crusades, no victory at any price: [the Christian ruler] has the alarming task of discerning the point at which what he is defending has ceased to be defensible because the means of defense beyond this point undermine the real justice in the state by implicitly treating it as an absolute, to be preserved at all cost. No particular *ordo* is identical with the order of God's city . . ." Williams, "Politics and the Soul: A Reading of *The City of God*," 66.

62. Niebuhr, "Is the bombing necessary," *Christianity and Crisis* 4, no. 5 (April 3, 1944), 1. See also his comments in *Love and Justice*, 237.

63. Niebuhr, "The Climax of the War," 2.

64. Niebuhr and Dun, "God Wills Both Justice and Peace," 77; See also Niebuhr, "The Problem of a Protestant Social Ethic," 8.

65. Ronald Stone writes that "A theology that followed Reinhold Niebuhr would probably trace out the many historical causes that led from injustice to war while proclaiming the just God as the meaning and the fulfillment of history." Stone, *Christian*

Realism and Peacemaking: Issues in U.S. Foreign Policy (Nashville, Tenn.: Abingdon Press, 1988), 29. My account goes somewhat further than this suggests. The Niebuhrian would be interested in providing accounts of present temptations to idolatry as well as historical injustice. Still, I take his comment to be suggestive of the position I develop here.

66. Niebuhr, *Love and Justice*, 294. See also *Christianity and Power Politics*, 61.

67. Niebuhr and Dun, "God Wills Both Justice and Peace," 77.

Chapter 8
War as an Act of Covenant Love

Paul Ramsey's approach to war at first appears to be an aberration in twentieth century Protestant ethics. In the mid-twentieth century, Protestants often viewed just war thought with suspicion. It was, these Protestants thought, a form of traditionally Catholic rationalism that had grown out of a natural law abandonment of the gospel. Ramsey challenged this conception of just war and laid the groundwork for an ecumenical renaissance of just war thought that continues on even today. The just war idea is not, Ramsey taught, a product of secular natural law. It is an application of love to the realm of history. Contemporary theorists had mistakenly abandoned the unfolding of loving reason in concrete history, and had come to the wrongheaded conclusion that war was intrinsically evil. This left modern thought on war bereft of moral structure. War came to be conceived as an area of human activity outside the bounds of morality. What is needed in order to reclaim war as a morally ordered space is an account of both the duty and limitation of war. Ramsey sets out to recover the just war notion of a good war, a war waged out of love. Only thus, he thought, could one hold the moral center against the chaos that threatens to overwhelm the system of morality in times of human conflict.

This was not a completely novel idea at the time. Some Catholic theologians and ethicists of the period were expressing similar sentiments about the need for order in war.[1] But how is it that Paul Ramsey comes to appreciate this line of thought? I have shown in earlier chapters the ways in which Ramsey's encounter with absolute idealism had allowed him to find common cause with certain trends in Catholic natural law thought generally. Here, I will suggest that Ramsey's encounter with idealism also shapes his openness to and interpretation of the just war tradition in his mature works. Both Ramsey's distinctive interest in particular areas in just war theory and his conclusions when dealing with these areas suggest that his thoughts were shaped in relation to the idealistic account of war.

The upshot of Ramsey's development is a conception of war as a morally positive, delimited act of covenant love. In explicating this development I will first provide a short review of idealistic thought on war, focusing on Hegel's work out of which later idealistic accounts develop. I will then move on to discuss Ramsey's conception of the problem of the modern conception of war, his development of an account of war as an act of good politics in international relations, and his work in illuminating the structure of particular moral relationships in the midst of war. Finally, I will shortly recount the role that Ramsey thought the Christian and moralist ought to fulfill in relation to war. This will provide us with a view of Ramsey's moral conception of war that can be profitably compared and contrasted with Niebuhr's.

A Hegelian Encounter

By the time Ramsey offers his own mature moral conception of war he has left behind the practice of explicitly citing idealistic philosophers. Yet, it is clear that during his early immersion in idealistic writings he came into contact with the distinctive arguments about war taking place in idealism. While the idealists do not produce any one set of uniform conclusions on the subject, their perspectives on war do develop in relation to a common origin in the work of G.W.F. Hegel.

Much of modern thought on war has been aimed at arguing for, and finding means to achieve, the eradication of war as a human practice. As Immanuel Kant argues, rational participants in international affairs would seek the realization of a world in which the rights of states are mutually recognized and perpetual peace reigns.[2] Hegel reacts against this trend. Kant, Hegel believes, offers only an abstraction of morality and society that denies and thus threatens the true moral structure of history as embodied in the concrete existences of set of particular, partially antithetically related sovereign states. Kant's transcendent ideal of perpetual peace contributes to a false dichotomy between morality and the concrete policies and interests of particular states, and thus challenges the true structure of ethical life in loyalty to one's community with the false promise of disembodied righteousness.

> The substantial welfare of the state is its welfare as a particular state in its specific interest and situation and its no less special foreign affairs . . . its principle for justifying wars and treaties is not a universal thought (the thought of philanthropy) but its actually injured or threatened welfare as something specific and peculiar to itself.
>
> At one time the opposition between morals and politics, and the demand that the latter should conform to the former, were much canvassed. On this point only a general remark is required here. The welfare of the state has claims to recognition totally different from those of the welfare of the individual. The ethical substance, the state, has its determinate being, i.e. its right directly embodied in something existent, something not abstract but concrete, and the principles of its conduct and behavior can only be this concrete existence and not one of many universal thoughts supposed to be moral commands. When politics is alleged to clash with morals and so to be always wrong, the doctrine propounded rests on superficial ideas about morality, the nature of the state, and the state's relation to the moral point of view.[3]

If one is to correct for this error one needs to correct the Kantian conception of the state. The state, as a particular expression of the Absolute, Hegel believes, is the source of moral identity. As Ramsey writes in his notes during graduate school, Hegel rejects "individual, private, diverse values and interests as the basis for the state." The state binds members of concrete societies together in spite of these values, not because of them. Again as Ramsey writes, for Hegel "the State is '*ethical substance*,' the mask of God in the world."[4] But, no particular state simply *is* God in the world. As a particular rational expression of the Absolute, each state must also exist over against other antithetical states. Ongoing tension and occasional violence in these antithetical relations is to be expected.

Nor is the necessity of war morally problematic. It only seems to be so from the confused perspective of atomistic philosophy. Contemporary social contract theories wrongly construe the state as the means to realizing individual interests. War demands individuals to sacrifice some of their interests individualistically conceived. The purported evil of war thus follows from an analysis of the state from the individual's atomistic perspective.[5] But this account of the evil of war is, Hegel believes, grounded in a misconception of both the individual and the state.

Only in service to the state are individuals drawn out of moral turpitude and attachment to evanescent individual goods. As such, war offers an "ethical moment" in the life of the citizenry. "War," Hegel writes, "is not to be regarded as an absolute evil and as a purely external accident, which itself has some accidental cause, be it injustice, the passions of nations or the holders of power &c., or in short, something or other which ought not to be."[6] War is exactly that practice that best manifests true morality. In war citizens of the state act upon their duties to the state, which transcend all individualistic attachments that might impede true morality in everyday life. War is a moral moment exactly because it demands sacrifice in service to the ultimate good known to humanity.

Locating true morality in the context of the immediate political community may seem to leave one without any moral claims to appeal to when these communities come into conflict. Unlike conflicts within the state, which can be solved by appeal to the sovereign will of the community, conflicts between states are conflicts between independent sovereign entities. Each state is a particular will. There are no abstract rules for governing the conflict of these wills. "Since states are related to one another as autonomous entities and so as particular wills on which the very validity of treaties depends, and since the particular will of the whole is in content a will for its own welfare pure and simple, it follows that welfare is the highest law governing the relation of one state to another."[7] As one commentator notes, this conception of morality leads Hegel to reject the possibility of substantive abstract criteria governing the resort to war.

> According to Hegel the concept of a 'ius ad bellum' is . . . necessarily void, because such a concept presupposes some criterion of justice by which the claims of two belligerent parties can be assessed. In one of his early writings, Hegel is clear about this: war is a clash between two concepts of right. In the absence of a third party, which might assess the claims of the belligerent parties, the question is not, 'which of the rights alleged by the two parties is the genuine right,' but—since both parties have a genuine right—'which of the two rights is to give way' ('welches Recht dem anderen weichen soll'). In war there is a conflict

> between two concepts of right. . . . The same judgment might be considered unjust or immoral from one perspective and at the same time just or moral from the other perspective.[8]

Ramsey's graduate notes again parallel this reading of Hegel. For Hegel, Ramsey writes, every "state must insist upon its right to survive and *be*: when a political issue is joined between two states, *power* decides the one which will lead the historical movement."[9]

Still, it would be wrong to assume that Hegel's approach has foreclosed upon any possibility of ethics within war. Even while Hegel throws into question the viability of abstract *ad bellum* standards, his confidence that all relations are in some sense ordered within the mind of the Absolute brings him to assert a new level of moral *in bello* relations.[10] Even the "state of nature" among states, it turns out, is held within the structured moral order of the Absolute.

> The fact that states reciprocally recognize each other as states remains, even in war—the state of affairs when rights disappear and force and chance hold sway—a bond wherein each counts to the rest as something absolute. Hence in war, war itself is characterized as something which ought to pass away. It implies therefore the proviso of the *jus gentium* that the possibility of peace be retained . . .[11]

From this rather inauspicious point Hegel produces a surprisingly robust account of the moral strictures that obtain within war. Objectively, mutual recognition among states prohibits any form of warfare aimed at the complete destruction of the enemy. Further, the envoys and noncombatants of the opposing state ought to be protected from attack. War, Hegel writes, ought not to be "waged against domestic institutions, against the peace of family and private life, or against persons in their private capacity."[12] This protection even extends to military personnel as soon as they are removed from participation in their military functions. Once they have surrendered or become incapacitated they are to be treated as noncombatants.[13] Nor does Hegel's *in bello* ethic only treat the objective dimension of war. Hegel also develops an account of the dispositional requirements of morality in combat. Courage, Hegel writes, is only given its "significance" by "its end and content."[14] A courageous act is only moral to the extent that its author is properly oriented toward service to her or his state. Acts of war are properly oriented toward this end, and ought not to be grounded in enmity toward the opposing soldier. Killing in war is properly an impersonal act. One does not seek to kill this or that person, but seeks only to repel the force that threatens her or his state. "Modern wars," Hegel writes, "are therefore humanely waged, and person is not set over against person in hatred. At most, personal enmities appear in the vanguard, but in the main body of the army hostility is something vague and gives place to each side's respect for the duty of the other."[15]

Such is the starting point for idealism's discussion of the moral issues of war. It also seems, in many ways, to lay behind Ramsey's approach to war. Selections from Hegel's *Philosophy of the Right* were assigned reading in Hendel's graduate courses, and Hendel specifically touched upon Hegel's approach to war in his lectures.[16] Ramsey was familiar with these readings and with later idealistic arguments on war put forward by figures like T.H. Green and Bernard Bosanquet. Whatever Ramsey's immediate impression of the idealistic account of war during his graduate work, the shape of his own mature approach to war suggests that he is deeply indebted to this tradition for the framework of his own thought.

This is not to say that Ramsey simply adopts the idealistic account of war. He could not do so. The Christian needs some different account of the enduring nature of historical international conflicts from that provided in idealism. The intransigence of historical conflict could not, for the Christian, arise from the need for offsetting absolute states. Further, a Christian could not take the state to be an ultimate source of value, nor could she or he accept service to the state to be the proper ultimate end of life. Finally, the Christian could not rest mutual recognition in war on an idealistic account of the relations of persons in the Absolute. Ramsey would eventually address the first two issues by drawing on the Augustinian tradition and upon his own conception of Christian love as channeled through the structure of the nation. He would address the last with his development of a casuistic account of faithful covenant relations among persons in times of war. In the end Ramsey would find that one could, drawing upon the Christian tradition, develop accounts of the errors of contemporary perspectives on war, of the interrelation of nation states, and of the delimited shape of actions in war. These accounts would reflect the idealistic position without depending on all of its premises.

To lay out how Ramsey provided for these shifts and how he eventually articulated what he took to be a distinctively Christian war ethic, it is necessary to start with a statement of what he took to be the problem in conceiving of and reacting to war in the contemporary world. After this problem is set forward I will continue on to trace two major themes of Augustinianism and agapism in his *ad bellum* ethics, and to develop his casuistic approach to proper intent in covenant relations during war.

Modernity and the Problem of War

In the early 1960s Ramsey presents an account of the distinctive problems modernity has in conceptualizing war. For Niebuhr, it will be recalled, the main problem in war time is to avoid the extremes of fanatic idolatry as represented by the war-party and the peace-party. Ramsey sees the problem somewhat differently. If war is licit, Ramsey thinks, it must maintain the enduring essential relationships that love unfolds in history. As such, it must have some recognizable and stable moral structure.

> If non-pacifism is correct, it is correct not first of all because we can foreknow that there can be no greater evil that the consequences supposed to follow from non-resistance to tyranny and aggression, but because there is a perennial truth in the just-war doctrine which in every epoch of our human history Christian love, of its own inner logic, will be impelled to affirm and renew as proper Christian action, even in the face of a great deal of ignorance of what the actual consequences will be.[17]

If war is moral, it will be locatable as part of the conceptual structure of the mind of God expressed in history. As James Turner Johnson writes, Ramsey "understood himself as a theologian drawing on *immutable ideas* to explicate Christian just war doctrine." Ramsey, Johnson tells us, used major figures in the traditions as "windows on the absolute" in his own "effort to think through the requirements of a *core idea*, the absolute moral norm of Christian love for the special case of contemporary war."[18]

The western world has in the past, Ramsey tells his reader, been caught up in the unfolding of loving reason and focused upon the form of war as an act of love.[19] The problem in contemporary ethics, Ramsey posits, is to be found in the modern flight from participation in the unfolding of divine reason and the correlative erosion of the sense that war has a moral form that should guide reasoning within this practice and prevent it from collapsing into the search for abstract and impossible final historical success.

Ramsey locates this flight from reason as an upshot of the rise of "pragmatic politics," especially as embodied in contemporary contextualist theological ethics.[20]

> For decades we have undertaken only to administer a not-very-wet baptism to modern man's notions about the use of armed force. This view may be described as a tame version of limited war. According to this view, killing in war is intrinsically wrong, but this immorality may nevertheless be done if the acts of war are calculated to lead to a lesser available evil among the consequences. Such 'lesser evil' pragmatic warrants for possible Christian participation in war locate decisions to resort to armed force among the 'situational ambiguities.' This is to justify the doing of evil that good may come of it . . .[21]

The effect is parallel to that which Hegel saw produced by Kant's conception of the world of perpetual peace. Morality has been abstracted and presented as extrinsic to the practice of politics. The so called absolute good of life and the purported moral imperative to eradicate war from history have been set against the concrete need for force in the pursuit of justice in historical society so as to set "raw power against weak and abstract morality and sets truth and goodness against power."[22]

With war so conceived, Ramsey posits, the participants in this conceptual world are left with only inadequate options. When war becomes apparently *unthinkable*, one has recourse only to either pseudo-thoughtful irresponsibility or irrational participation in international conflict. Pacifism is clearly wrong in its irresponsibility, but once one accepts the alternative, that the best option available is constituted by a moral evil, limits upon actions become tenuous at best. With the abstract good of peace placed as an absolute, the only recourse is to total war so as to impose peace on the world. Conceived as a field of action outside the boundaries of the ethical, war quickly becomes a slippery slope in which any action can be justified. Moral relativism becomes the rule of the day.

With the problem so described, it becomes apparent that what is needed is a clear statement about the necessity for and the moral appropriateness of war in history. "Were we once," Ramsey writes, "to concede that armed conflict is an unavoidable feature of the life of nations, or that there are any circumstances that warrant the first use of violence, then the banishment of force would in the first instance be impossible and in the second undesirable."[23] What is needed is a conception of the good war. The light of loving reason must be shed upon the ambiguities of war so as to sort out the positive obligations and inherent limitations in this action. If war is an evil it should, henceforth, not be undertaken at all. But if it is found to be a righteous human undertaking, then it should not be left in the shadows of moral ambiguity where calls for concurrent murder and remorse are found to be sufficiently offsetting to count as ethical demands.[24]

Thankfully, Ramsey posits, God does not leave us alone in our search for the defining characteristics of a good war. Though divine reason may have been repressed, it is never fully defeated, and always maintains itself somewhere within historical community. It must be possible to find this community and recover the rational Christian ethos that has been occluded by the rise of pragmatic relativism.

> The chief problem facing us is not *what* are the moral limits upon the just conduct of war, but *where* are these principles, i.e., *where* are the men in whose minds and *where* is the community of men in whose very *ethos* the propelling reason for ever engaging in war also itself lays down intrinsic moral limits upon how the defense of civilized life should proceed?[25]

Though modern Protestantism has largely taken the wrong road, Ramsey finds fellow conceptual travelers such as Robert Osgood, John Courtney Murray, Thomas Murray, and John C. Ford whom he believes to representatives of divine reason still calling out to contemporary society. Ramsey's own project is to reclaim the moral form of the good war in his own community and carry this conception to the heart of protestant ethics.

Augustinianism, Agapism, and Good Politics

Ramsey's treatment of the resort to war is not always systematic. It is, however, built around a set of relatively stable themes. The following treatment of Ramsey's *ad bellum* ethics will focus on two themes in his writing. Ramsey's "Augustinianism" allowed him to articulate a picture of history in which sovereign nations battle over the realization of limited policy goals. Ramsey's agapism allowed him to articulate a clear moral permission, and indeed obligation, for recourse to war inasmuch as war came to represent a concrete expression of love in history. I shall argue that these two themes are best held together in Ramsey's essay "The Uses of Power" in which he lays out his understanding of war as a manifestation of good politics. The upshot is a system in which recourse to war is recognized as a morally positive act.

Augustinianism, Babel, and the Anarchy of States

The idealists had presented a picture of the world composed of numerous sovereign nations standing in tension with one another in the thought of the Absolute. In this world, conflict among nations was a permanent fixture of history. This gave the idealists a metaphysical grounding for their rejection of the abstract and transcendent ideal of perpetual peace proposed by Kant. Accepting the indelibility of the current ordered state of tension allows one to avoid flight from the moral order represented in this order. Ramsey, in his own work as a Christian theologian, would produce another account of why it is that history finds itself as a realm of ordered conflict, and why it is that Christians ought not seek perpetual peace. The answer was to be found in the reality of sin and the effects of sin within history.

Early on in Ramsey's work, Ramsey found that the story of the Tower of Babel ought to be one of the guiding narratives in Christian politics. As Ramsey writes in 1947, this story tells of how, because of sin, the nations are handed over to a "confusion of tongues" that prevents the nations from understanding one another. This condition leads to both "irrepressible conflict" and "the disintegration of civilization."[26] Each nation learns its own language, and misunderstands the other's. Each nation is marked by sin and thrown into a world in which wars are part of the process of history. In this way, Ramsey writes, this myth tells of "the origins of a world of countervailing constellations of political power, which we can the multi-national system."[27] Nor is there any escape from this system. All of history is lived "on the underside of that verdict at Babel."[28]

This picture of the multi-national system reappears in a slightly different form in Ramsey's exploration of Augustine's conception of the just war. Here Ramsey sought to answer a problematic question. If sin had corroded the languages of the nations and given them partial and skewed views of the good, how ought a Christian to relate to these nations and how ought one to relate to the moral claims of nations in times of war?

Augustine, Ramsey notes, famously critiqued the classical notion that the state embodied absolute justice. The historical society can provide no finally enduring moral source. Augustine admits that historical community at its best may have the form of justice, but he challenges "the common assumption of the Graeco-Roman political theory that justice is the *ethical substance* of a commonwealth."[29] This assumption must be challenged in light of the true ethical substance represented by charity as practiced in the City of God. "Given man's citizenship in the City of God," Ramsey writes, "his citizenship elsewhere is not merely relatively inferior; it must be seen as radically deprived of the ethical substance formerly attributed to it before that which is new had come."[30] There can be no ultimate value in the historical community; the "classical" *identity* of the historical society and absolute value has been broken. Augustine's conclusions, it seems, parallel those to which Ramsey came in his dissertation.

But Augustine does not leave history without any form of order. Instead he returns to provide a new definition of the commonwealth. Rejecting the idea that a community is held together by its grasp of abstract conceptions of justice, Augustine, according to Ramsey, believes "people to be bound together by agreement in their will and purpose."[31] This produces a new understanding of historical justice.

> Justice is the form of man's loves; in the State it is the form of that love or agreement to pursue in common the objects which a 'people' desire. Moreover, social justice 'arises from' a common agreement as to the objects of their love (will); and, since the agreement would break down and the people become a mere multitude without minimum or greater degrees of participation in the life of a nation, accepted schemes of justice serve to strengthen that common will, or love which constitutes the *res publica*.[32]

Though history offers no final form of justice, this general will of the society takes on a kind of moral status of its own. Though it is not to be confused with the absolute good, it is an expression of the will common to the self and the other in the society. The City of God may stand over against this will to the extent necessary to break its idolatry, but it does not challenge its basic status as the highest norm available to a participant within history. The Christian is called to contribute to and defend this socially embodied claim to justice as a member of historical society "because of the alliance of his will with the will (and love) that constitutes him with the rest of the multitude a people."[33]

One might note at this point that, inasmuch as Ramsey was planning to develop an *ad bellum* ethic on this Augustinianism, he seems to have a problem. Since, according to this unique reading of Augustine,[34] Augustine held that each nation has its own sovereign common will, it appears that there is no common moral claim to appeal to when these communities come into conflict. Like Hegel, it seems, Augustine on this reading has produced a multi-national system so pluralistic that common norms for resorting to war are impossible to produce.

For Augustine, Ramsey claims, the conflict between these concrete social wills can not be resolved by appeal to some abstract standard of justice purported to stand over all participants. As Ramsey writes, later just war thought would

> shift from voluntarism to rationalism in understanding the nature of political community, and therefore an increasing emphasis upon the natural-law concept of justice in analysis of the cause that justifies participation in war. . . . Augustine was more correct and realistic in believing people to be bound together more by agreement of will and purpose than by agreement in their general conceptions of justice.[35]

Each side in a war may fight justly in accord with its own will, which is the only substantive moral measure available to it. Ideally, Ramsey writes, one will seek to

> preserve but also to enlarge . . . agreements of will and the scope of peaceful orders on this earth. But is it not likely that there will be occasions on which love or will in-forming secular justice cannot be extended into greater combinations, that appeal must then be made the *ultima ratio* of war, and that the existing justice Augustine has in mind when speaking of the 'just' war may tragically be on both sides?[36]

In a sinful history in which conflicting communal wills represent the highest source of moral appeal, war is indeed a tragic reality.

This by itself is not the whole story. Like Hegel's picture of the anarchic state system, Augustine's picture also entails certain limitations. War cannot, on this Augustinian account, be a defense of absolute value, as absolute value does not present itself in history. The goal of war must not be to establish perpetual peace or ultimate justice. Once one has accepted that she or he lives in an ordered state of tension, there is no need to flee from this world with projects that would challenge this order in favor of some transcendent goal. As such, war cannot be total war, but must be war in service to a limited "national policy."[37]

War as an Act of Love: the Positive Moral Status of War

Ramsey's "Augustinianism" allowed him to present a picture of history as a realm in which sovereign national wills find themselves in perpetual tension with one another. But the Augustinian theme could not form the whole of Ramsey's treatment of war. By replacing the absolute sanction of the national will with a relative sanction, Augustine had broken the idolatry of the state. But Augustine, by concentrating so much on the absolute justice in the City of God, had also highlighted the ambiguity of war rather than the moral permission for war. Augustine's statements on the justification of force are, Ramsey concludes, "incidental to his stress upon the mental pain this misery should cause every man to feel."[38] It is not even clear that, for Augustine, war can properly be said to be an act of love within the bounds of history. "Inordinate self-love," Ramsey notes, "may be *absent* when the public good is in question; but whether it is love that is *present*, governing the Christian in what concerns the public good, and leading him to suffer no injustice to be done, may be questioned."[39]

Without some correction, Ramsey thought, this Augustinian focus on the perfect peace of heaven could all too quickly be transformed into a project to deny altogether the moral obligation to serve one's neighbor through the structures of history. Ramsey's war ethic could not be so focused on the ambiguity of war. As Hegel's approach to war suggests, in order to avoid the mistake of dichotomizing historical power and morality, one must have something more positive to say about the historical use of force. Ramsey comes to a similar conclusion. As such, in tracing out the second theme in his work, Ramsey finds more commonality with contemporary Roman Catholic theology that went beyond Augustine's emphasis to develop an account of the rationality of war within the limits of a postlapsarian history. For these theologians "emotional distaste for devastation or even regret over increased violence" is not a governing experience. "Let the capacity to make war be whatever it may be," Ramsey writes, "Catholic thought seeks to make its way between the immorality of abandoning the public good to defenselessness and the immorality of an improper defense."[40] Historical ambiguity must be corralled within the structure of morality so as not to allow a collapse of the whole structure into chaos. An adequate approach to war must reach beneath phenomenal tragedy to find the "moral permission" for war.[41]

Ramsey himself had been, for some time, developing a more robust Christian account of the permission for war. For Ramsey, even if not for Augustine, war was to be conceived as an act of love. In *Basic Christian Ethics*, as we have seen, Ramsey had developed his account of Christian love as an other-oriented motive that had to be filled out with a natural law account of right action to be put into practice. In order to protect one's neighbor from attack, it is, in the mix of history, at times necessary to resort to force. Even Jesus' actions in clearing the temple reveal that an ethic of non-resistance is not always a proper way to defend the interests of God and one's neighbors in the world. Unjust circumstances "may not only permit but even on occasion require Christian love to adopt physical methods of resistance."[42]

Ramsey would later develop this theme in relation to his reading of Niebuhr's own ethics. Niebuhr, as we have seen, focuses on the ambiguity of national interests in times of war so as to combat morally fanatic and idolatrous rejections of penitent responsibility. Ramsey, in his effort to reclaim a clear moral permission for war stresses the extent to which service to and defense of national interest can be an expression of love. While Niebuhr stresses that all nations fall short of the perfecting sacrifice given by Christ, Ramsey retorts that in history love does not require sacrifice of nations. Under the guidance of "self-giving love . . . are not nations, in the light of their total task in behalf of their own people and all the future generations and their possible contribution to the community of mankind, duty-bound to 'sacrifice the sacrifice'" when it comes to national interests and defense?[43] Thus is the relative justice of the social organism strengthened beyond what Ramsey's reading of Augustine's relativizing scheme allows.

This emphasis is also often found in Ramsey's works on war. In *War and the Christian Conscience* Ramsey could describe war as a viable

Christian act, "lest many more of God's little ones should be irresponsibly forsaken and suffer more harm than need be." The move to allow for war is not, he writes, really an exception to the prohibition of killing, it is "a determinate expression of justice and mercy."[44]

Some of Ramsey's later writings even seem to go further in stressing the Christian obligation to rescue one's neighbor by the use of violent force.

> No authority on earth can withdraw from 'social charity' and 'social justice' their intrinsic and justifiable tendencies to rescue from dereliction and oppression all whom it is possible to rescue. This is why the traditional just war theory did not hesitate to justify 'aggressive war,' that is, initiative in the charitable extension of an ordered justice. This justification can never be withdrawn; it can only be limited, supplanted, or put in abeyance. This happens when political prudence is tragically compelled to judge that more harm than good will be done in the attempt.[45]

Indeed, in Ramsey's later writings, he would seek to articulate a grounding of just war thought in what he calls a "*presumption against injustice*" or a presumption "*to restrain evil and protect the innocent.*"[46] With the grounding of just war thought so conceived, it is clear that war is, properly conceived, clearly within the realm of morality. It is, in fact, a Christian obligation.

War as an Act of Good Politics

By deploying his "Augustinian" and agapist themes when treating war, Ramsey reproduces much of the effect of the idealistic approach to war on Christian grounds. Ramsey's "Augustinianism" and his use of the myth of Babel allows him to explain why history is composed of a relatively stable, but tense, anarchic state system in which each state represents a general will of its own. Ramsey's emphasis upon war as a manifestation of love in history allows him, like the idealists, to locate war as a form of service to the greatest common good known in history and thus to shore up the status of war as a morally licit activity. These two themes, grounded as they are in slightly different readings of the Christian tradition, at times find themselves in tension with one another. Augustine's emphasis on the limited ends of war within history do not always sit well with Ramsey's conception of war as an act of love which on occasion is inhibited by the prudential concerns of history. Still, there is no necessary conflict between the two themes, and, in my judgment, Ramsey was able to successfully hold these themes together to great effect in his article "The Uses of Power."

In this essay, while continuing to eschew abstract standards for justifying recourse to war, Ramsey develops a delimited, positive view of the decision to go to war by elaborating the concrete requirements any war must fulfill in order to be a proper act of rational politics. In this article, war is located in terms of its moral permission as an act of politics, normatively conceived. Politics proper exists as an intrinsically moral and rational practice.[47] As a moral and rational practice, politics is aimed at the common good of the parties in relation to which it exists. This means that politics is aimed primarily at the common good of the community in which the politics is immediately practiced, and secondarily at the common good of all other communities in relation to which the immediate community finds itself. The *bene esse* of politics—the "*proper act of being politics*"—in the context of a national existence is constituted by the acts being oriented at the common good of the nation, and at the overlap between the national good and the common good of the international community.

This by itself, however, tells us little about what it means specifically to be politics. All rational practices are aimed at the common good of the persons or groups in relation to which they exist. So what is it that makes politics distinctive? The *esse* of politics—the "*act of being politics*"—is found in "the use of power, and possibly the use of armed force."[48] Within politics "*post lapsum* and this side of the resurrection" there can be no effective search for the common good of the political community that lacks such a use of power.

Within this conceptual world, war is properly an act of politics. It is the use of armed force in service to neighbors in the national community and, when feasible, in service to neighbors in the international community. Conceived as such it becomes clear that war is an act with morally positive content. It is an act that finds itself in service to, and as such structured by, the common good of the communities at which it aims.

Unfortunately, as Ramsey maintains with Augustine, within history it is impossible to bring perfect justice to *all* parties in the world. Nations are limited in power and thus limited in their proper sphere of activity.[49] The overlap between three areas of tension demarcates the area in which the licit resort to force ought to be located.[50] First is the tension between the *esse* and the *bene esse* of politics itself. The procurement and maintenance of power is a necessary condition for the enactment of the purpose of political action. As such, rational political action will not undertake actions that erode the power of the actor so as to disproportionately reduce its ability to serve the common good in the future. Second is the tension between the national and the international common good. There is no guarantee in a sinfully skewed world that these will perfectly overlap, and often they will at least partially conflict. While aiming primarily at the good of one's own nation, seeking the greatest overlap and balance between this good and the international good is essential to maintaining moral foreign policy. Third, there will be a constant tension within history between the *de facto* order of power in the world, the order of international law, and the ideal arrangement of humanitarian good. All of these tensions ought to be considered in the decision to have recourse to violent force.

In this way, Ramsey locates war as a positive moral act within the limitations of history. Ramsey's thought is continuous with earlier reading of Augustine inasmuch as he maintains that all political conflict is conflict undertaken in service to less than an ultimate value. Ramsey also maintains his "Augustinian" position inasmuch as his conception of politics avoids proposing abstract standards of justice that exist independent of the particular wills of concrete states. Standards of international law, and abstract humanitarian good, are never simply identified with the moral duty of the state, and each state must make its own determination about the shape of its own common good, and about the proper balance of this common good against other standards of action. The *causa belli* is not articulated in terms of the absolute rights and duties of states, but rather in relation to the calculations of welfare in which all concrete politics are embroiled. But, unlike in Augustine's treatment, this conception of war is more consistent in viewing war as a proper act of loving politics. War is always aimed at an imperfect good, but it should always be aimed at the greatest good possible from the perspective of the participant state. In this light, it is clear, from Ramsey's perspective, that war can be understood as an act aimed at the best service to the neighbor possible within history. War, properly conceived, is an act of love in a sinful world.

Love of the Enemy and of the Noncombatant

At the same time that Ramsey is developing this positive account of recourse to war as an act of historical politics normatively conceived, he is also working through another problem in which his interests overlap with the idealists. How ought one to conceive of proper intent in war, and what concrete limitations bear upon right actions within the relations that exist within war? Hegel suggests that acts of war should be impersonal; oriented toward repelling the force of the enemy rather than at killing particular persons. Proper recognition of the other in war demands that combatants directly target members of the opposing community only if these members function as a part of a threatening force. Ramsey in his own time finds a similar argument brewing in contemporary Catholic theology, and, in the end, argues for a position that finds some similarity with Hegel's own. Maintaining covenant with the enemy demands that, in at least one ethically important sense, acts of war should never intend to kill any person.

From Pacifism to Love Motivated Combat

In a pacifistic argument that Ramsey developed during his graduate work, Ramsey at one point explicitly rejects "the 'major' Christian tradition, which says that in a just war, one motivated by love for *all* national entities involved, one may look down the sights of a gun and with love though regret, towards the individual soldier, pull the trigger. Whether or not this is possible *psychologically* it seems to be plain that *objectively* such is not the case."[51] If this early Ramseyan position were true, a covenant account of loving relations in war would be impossible. If it is impossible to shoot at a person while standing in structured loving relation with her or him, it will be impossible to have a war in which the Christian could participate.

By *Basic Christian Ethics*, Ramsey has, as we have seen, rejected this early position in favor of a position which, in a sinful world, allows that an inner orientation of love might require one to defend society as a means of service to the neighbor.[52] "Violence and bloodshed are no doubt horrifying, especially in destructive, total war, but the word 'unlovely' has in Christian ethics a mainly spiritual not a mainly physical meaning."[53] In comparison to his early pacifist position, the "psychological" dimension of love in acts of war has come to seem more possible, while the "objective" dimension has come to appear less morally significant.[54] As Ramsey writes here, "the 'mournful Christian warrior' does not blubber over his gunpowder."[55] The ambiguity of war, if war is an acceptable moral act, must be trumped by its moral propriety as an act of love.

Agapic Casuistry: Defense and Noncombatancy

Unfortunately, within a decade Ramsey would conclude that his framework in *Basic Christian Ethics* was underdeveloped. As he shifts from his reliance upon an extrinsic natural law to a purely love grounded war ethic, it becomes clear that love must demand something more in terms of the delimitation of action in war. His earlier ethic could depend upon the secular natural law to fill out the structure of the act to which the "spirit" of love would drive the Christian. But as a comprehensive position, a solely "spiritual" focus suggests too much about what might be allowed in war and says too little about the shape of an act of war as a moral act. If war is to be an act of covenant love, the covenant relations within it must be delimited. Claims about intentionality taken alone could not achieve this. "Intentions alone," Ramsey writes, "are always open to suspicion, unless they are also controlled by some more objective determination of right *action*."[56] One must, by an analysis of relevantly similar and dissimilar cases, prove the intentionality of the act and determine the proper description of the act.[57] Only if the act is morally acceptable under this description ought one to continue on to consider other facets of the act.

Ramsey finds this kind of contextualized principled reasoning represented in the history of the Christian tradition. From Augustine to Thomas Aquinas, Ramsey concludes, the Christian tradition has allowed violence only if it is grounded in love, rather than "reciprocity or the standards of an equal justice alone."[58] Such can be shown through an analysis of the cases considered by Augustine and Thomas Aquinas. Both saints allow for the direct targeting of combatants in war inasmuch as these combatants function as a threat to the public good,[59] but Augustine's and Thomas' analyses of the case of self-defense reveal that their arguments for the moral acceptability of war are not simultaneously arguments for the moral acceptability of retributive motives.

In the case of self-defense, where there is no neighbor to defend, Augustine denies the Christian recourse to mortal combat. As such, one can see that Augustine does not accept the use of violence because of the guilt of the aggressor. In either case (that of the unjust attack on the public good, or that of the unjust attack on the self) the aggressor is equally guilty. The only significant difference between the two cases has to do with that which is defended. In the case of the public good, one is defending one's neighbors while in the case of self-defense there are no neighbors to defend. Augustine's different reactions show his own way of drawing the line between two forms of intentionality in relations to particular objective cases. The Christian, as a sinner for whom Christ died, does not kill an attacker for their moral failings. The Christian is only allowed to kill inasmuch as the attacker *functions* as a material threat to the security of a neighbor.

Thomas Aquinas takes this analysis another step by proposing that one could undertake an act of self-defense so long as one does not in this act intend the death of the attacker. The death of the attacker might be one of the effects of the act of self-defense, but it is not the effect at which the action aims. Famously, Thomas argues that the act has two effects: both saving the self and killing the attacker.[60] One is the intended effect of the action while the other is foreseen, but not intended. So long as one only aims at the continued survival of the self, the act remains, at least in virtue of its intended object, morally licit. Only after such a determination of the object of the act ought one to continue on to calculate the proportional good and evil involved in the effects of the action.

Unfortunately, Ramsey concludes, Thomas' casuistry fails. Aquinas in this argument has overstepped in allowing intentionality too free a rein in moral analysis. How could one, from Aquinas' perspective, provide a case grounded distinction between righteous intention in self-defense and unloving intention in killing the unjust aggressor? At least at this point, Ramsey believes Aquinas could not. As later Catholic casuists clarify, one properly intends both the end of one's action and the means that *in fact* bring about that end. If one wished to deploy the doctrine of double effect, the act that brings about the two effects must be objectively separable from the ill effect. One could not, on this later Catholic account, by an act of sheer will, avoid intending the death of the attacker that brings about the continued survival of the self in an act of self-defense.

The upshot of this analysis is that double effect apparently could not in any plausible account be applied to the case of combatants in war.

Combatants must be conceived as being directly targeted by the Christian in light of their objective standing as a threat to the public good. Attacks upon them must be governed by measurements of proportionality to the threat they pose to the public good. But so long as one is acting within the framework of war, combatants must be conceived as licit targets for direct and intentional attack. Noncombatants, however, do fall under the protections afforded by double effect reasoning. These are persons who do not stand as a material threat to the public good. By definition they are not functional combatants. Thus, one who acts out of love cannot find any grounds to directly target these individuals. Acts bringing about their foreseeable deaths are only allowed inasmuch as their deaths might be the proportional and unintended effect of some other action, such as an act of violence directly targeting licit military targets.

War Without Intent to Kill: Incapacitating Gases

Still, Ramsey was not entirely happy with concluding at this point. One continuing problem nagged at him. Hegel, as we have seen, argues that in war the dignity of the particular opposing combatant ought to be recognized by means of avoiding the intention to kill her or him as an individual. Ramsey, through his analysis of the Christian traditional arguments has reproduced much of Hegel's concern about the function of persons in war and has protected noncombatants from direct targeting, but he has no sufficient means of articulating substantive moral relations among opposing combatants in war. While one's relation to the materially unjust aggressor does establish some limits on act of war, namely the limits of proportionality, war still seems to entail that one intend to destroy the opposing combatant during war. If such is true, does not this constitute some level of break in covenant relations at least among those who were active combatants in ongoing lethal combat? Ramsey recognizes that even Thomas Aquinas is willing to make combatants licit targets, but Ramsey never seems to have settled his own disquiet with the idea. At one point in *War and the Christian Conscience*, he poses the apparent dilemma: "Shall we say that in this instance it is right to do evil that good may come of it? Or that, in this instance alone as an exception, the means used—the direct killing of the unjust aggressor—should be judged to be right in itself?"[61]

To solve this final dilemma, Ramsey needs a new case, a new thought experiment. He does not get the casuistry involved straightened out until 1966, when he comes across the new case presented by the possible use of incapacitating gases. If, Ramsey thought, incapacitating gases could be a licit tool of war, something Ramsey doubted on grounds of proportionality, it would be possible to incapacitate opponents in war, and thus win the war, without killing them. Through the prism of this case, it becomes clear that the *killing* of the enemy is not essential to the act of war *per se*. It is an accidental factor. As such, acts of war can be contrasted, Ramsey surmises, with cases of protest by self immolation, in which the death of the protester is an essential to the act. Self-immolation uses killing as a means to the end that the protester seeks in a way that acts of war do not use killing as a means to the end that the good warrior seeks. This distinction allows a breakthrough in conceiving of the relations between competing soldiers in war.

> When one thinks about it, a soldier who kills an enemy combatant need not want his death as a means, he need not *in a certain morally relevant sense* directly do his death. He rightly wants (and this is one way to express the meaning of direct violence upon forces) and he directly does the enemy's *incapacitation* as a combatant; and so far, at least, in the tragic evil of war, killing is the only way to incapacitate him.[62]

Thus, war, if fought properly, is fought without ever intending the death of any particular person in the war. "The objective of combat is the incapacitation of a combatant from doing what he is doing because he is this particular combatant in this particular war; it is not the killing of a man because he is this particular man."[63]

Ramsey is careful to note that he does not take this argument to "remove altogether the charge that all such killings 'treat humanity whether in oneself or in another as a means only'—when that is the only means of incapacitating oneself or another."[64] Nor does Ramsey take this use of the doctrine of double effect as related to opposing combatants to be the dominant usage of that doctrine. Double effect continues primarily to function in protecting the noncombatant from direct targeting in the broader sense he had outlined before.[65]

What he believes he has produced is a proper moral description of the definitive act of war. By this description, the rightness of the act of war is clearly distinguished from the immorality of other ostensibly similar acts. The ambiguity of war, in which liberals and pragmatists ground their lesser evil analysis, is contained by the proper conception of the acts involved. War remains "a tragedy and a physical evil; but this is not in question."[66] The question is whether war has a place and a shape in the given moral order. The answer to this question is now shown to be an unequivocal yes. To shore up the perception of the moral order, it is necessary to have a language that draws clean distinctions between moral and immoral acts. Ramsey's description uses casuistry to dig into and reveal the intent of the agent in relevant cases to show that war can be, not merely the lesser evil, but a right action in itself. War does not fall outside the sphere of delimited covenant relations or morality, it is an inherently morally structured activity. War is undertaken as a means of neighbor service, defending against some threat to, or promoting the safety and spread of the common good of one's community. In service to this goal one intentionally seeks to incapacitate material enemy combatants by proportional means while avoiding any direct targeting of noncombatants and accepting their deaths only as the proportional unintended effects of legitimate acts of war.

From Deferred Repentance to Licit Deterrence

Since Ramsey played so large a part in arguments over deterrence in the United States, it is worthwhile to shortly show how his arguments here follow a similar line to that found in his arguments about the avoidance of directly targeting enemies in war. His early work on the topic presents a set of tensions with his Hegelian/Christian emphasis on immediate moral order which is resolved only through a long period of the deployment of contextual reasoning.

Ramsey's first major engagement with deterrence policy came in his book *War and the Christian Conscience.* There he argues that nuclear weapons are, by their nature, indiscriminate. The morality of warfare depends upon discrimination between combatants and noncombatants. Thus, the deployment of nuclear weapons is inherently immoral. Further, drawing on the work of Herman Khan, Ramsey concludes that in order to be effective, a deterrent policy must include the intent to deploy the weapons under some circumstances. Khan, in fact, went so far as to argue that nuclear weapons should be set up so as to automatically launch in the event of an attack that destroyed a sufficient percentage of the United States. Deterrence, on this account, provided no rational end for the use of nuclear arms that was intended. Deterrence settled for mutual destruction if either side launched an attack. For Ramsey, this was a morally unacceptable position. A scheme that entailed force deployed without a rational end under some circumstances was morally unacceptable.[67]

The implication was that participation in a deterrent strategy was morally repugnant, and thus ought not to be allowed. In *War and the Christian Conscience*, however Ramsey crafted an exception to this rule that would allow American leaders to continue their participation in politics, even while deterrent strategy continued. There was, Ramsey posited, only one significant difference between political and personal ethics. In political ethics, since one was dealing with the momentum of a corporate entity, at times one must accept an immoral policy for the present in order to remain in power so as to create a context in which the policy could be changed. The nation must repent of the immoral policy, but there are times when this repentance can be deferred.[68] For Ramsey, the policy of nuclear deterrence appeared to be such a policy.

This was an awkwardly Kierkegaardian moment for Ramsey. His only justification for the continued participation in politics was a kind of teleological suspension of the ethical in order to allow a return to the ethical.[69] While Ramsey never withdrew his claims concerning deferred repentance, this was the only point at which he deployed the idea as the only moral justification for participating in a deterrent regime.[70] As it became clear that some strategy of nuclear deterrence was necessary in superpower relations, he came to believe that it must be possible to think through the problem of nuclear deterrence. His later work on nuclear deterrence can be read as an effort to solve the problem without such an exception to the ruling moral order. As in his treatment of the apparently direct targeting of combatants, Ramsey was interested in finding a way in which the use of nuclear arms for deterrence could be cleanly fit within the moral order of political life.

Ramsey attempted to fit deterrence into a morally orderly politics in his later writings via three arguments. First, Ramsey held that nuclear weapons targeted at legitimate military targets may have a deterrent effect due to the collateral damage which would accompany any nuclear strike. Second, he argued that the possession of nuclear weapons, without the threat of a nuclear strike, constituted a deterrent force due to the mere potential use of these arms. Finally, Ramsey argued, against Khan's claim above, that it may be possible to achieve deterrence by appearing ready to use nuclear arms without actually intending to use nuclear arms (the bluff).

Under the pressure of academic debate, Ramsey eventually withdrew his arguments in favor of the bluff. His other two arguments, however, continue to stand as representative of some of the most subtle moral reasoning of Ramsey's career. Ramsey recognized that a deterrent derived from potential collateral damage would only be effective if the collateral damage involved were disproportionate to the ends aimed at in the nuclear volley. This appears to reproduce the original problem. Can one morally *threaten* to do something one knows to go beyond the bounds of moral reason? Ramsey famously responded that this dilemma could be sidestepped inasmuch as "the threat of something disproportionate is not always a disproportionate threat."[71] Exactly how to interpret Ramsey here is a subject of debate.[72] It appears that Ramsey is suggesting that the act of launching nuclear weapons must be measured against the value of some particular military objective, while the act of threatening such use must be measured against the value of maintaining the peace established by deterrence strategy.

Ramsey's appeal to the morally licit deterrent effect of the possession of nuclear weapons hangs on similarly subtle distinctions. When pressed on whether an opponent would be convinced of a deterrent threat by the mere possession of nuclear weapons, Ramsey notes that there is a "distinction between the *appearance* and the *actuality* of being partially or totally committed to go to city exchanges."[73] It may be, he notes that the nation should manifest the "*apparent* resolution to wage war irrationally." Again, the meaning of the claim here is open to multiple interpretations. It seems possible, on this account that a nation may be licit in taking measures to provide a show of being willing to target civilian centers. But it should never embrace an actual resolution to do so. This brings Ramsey quite close to the bluff strategy he had abandoned elsewhere.

Such subtle analysis was necessary, Ramsey was convinced, in order to bring contemporary policy into line with the structure of reason in history. He was confident that this could be achieved inasmuch as he was convinced that within the play of historical occurrence reason was always working itself out. A society may be able to skirt the cunning of historical, providential reason for a time, but in the end, all things must either conform to reason or float away into an amoral abyss. By working out the justification of deterrent strategy, Ramsey was simply thinking through a problem which, on his account, must have a solution if it was an enduring facet of human life.

There are differences between Hegel's account of war and Ramsey's. The limitations of conduct in war in Ramsey's account are couched in terms of covenant relations rather than mutual recognition in the context of the Absolute. Further, the end of battle in service to the state is not so ultimate as Hegel took it to be. Military service to one's country is a form of love in history as enacted through service to one's state, but it is not service directly to an ultimate good. Still, the similarities between the two accounts are certainly striking. Though Ramsey develops his arguments in conversation with contemporary Catholic casuists, both the topics he takes up and the conclusions he reaches suggest that he was sensitized by the idealistic account of war.

The Christian and Moralist in a Time of War

Before concluding this chapter it is useful to say a bit about Ramsey's view of the duty of the moralist and the Christian in a time of war. Since there is a large amount of overlap between this and his general account of Christian responsibility in public dialogue, we need not spend much time on the subject. But, given the contrast between Ramsey's construal of the role of the Christian and moralist in a time of war and Niebuhr's conception of the humble prophet in a time of war, Ramsey's treatment of this subject is significant. Niebuhr, it will be recalled, locates the primary problem of war in the temptation to idolatrous militarism and pacifism, and as such sees the Christian in a time of war as a humble prophet interpreting the events of history so as to illumine the order of God's judgment in history which should chasten all parties involved. Ramsey suggests a different vocation for the Christian. According to Ramsey, the largest problem facing the modern world when it comes to war is found in a lack of appreciation for war as a good act of politics and a delimited act of Christian love. As such, it is not surprising that Ramsey finds that the main role of the Christian and the moralist in a time of war is to argue for this conception of war, and to lay out what this conception requires in terms of right action in war situations.

The moralist and the Christian in a time of war are thus to function as casuists. The goal is not to tell what to do in specific instances, but to provide an account of what *kinds* of acts are licit and illicit within proper politics. The moralist "anatomizes" the political decision making process; revealing its own inherent moral structure. Moralists "do not tell the statesman what to think, but they *anatomize* how we will think in considering the alternatives of intervention or non-intervention in particular situations."[74] It falls outside of the sphere of expertise of these figures to comment upon particular applications of the principles that they have laid out. The applications of principles of the just war tradition must be left to persons functioning as magistrates, soldiers, etc.

Thus, Ramsey and Niebuhr produce tasks for the Christian at a time of war that reflect their own deepest concerns. Niebuhr sees the Christian combating the danger of morally fanatic idolatry. Ramsey sees the Christian, in the midst of an especially chaotic time of political decision, providing a stabilizing influence on moral discourse by presenting an account of the standards of what any good war ought to look like.

Conclusion

Ramsey's development of the just war ethic suggests that his thought was influenced by the idealistic tradition. His concern about the creep of abstract morality and correlative relativism in "modern" approaches to war, his work in providing a positive statement of the place of war in the moral order without suggesting any abstract standards for governing the *jus ad bellum*, and his ongoing concern about the avoidance of intentional killing in war and the protection of noncombatants all suggest ways in which Ramsey was influenced by the work of earlier idealists. This did not leave Ramsey alone in his quest. His work on war ethics found common cause with many contemporary Catholic theologians and ethicists, and set off an ecumenical rebirth of just war thought. No matter his sources, his articulation of the moral conception of war as an act of covenant love shifted much of the discussion of war in contemporary ethics.

The two conceptions of war produced by Niebuhr and Ramsey, combined with their differing perspectives on authority and public dialogue, respectively guide Niebuhr and Ramsey as they approach particular wars. As they simultaneously approached the Vietnam War then they were led by perspectives that were informed by divergent traditions in American culture. Before concluding it is worthwhile to say something about the relations between these perspectives and the strengths and weaknesses they left to those that work from them.

Notes

1. See, for instance, John Courtney Murray's treatment of war in *We Hold These Truths*.

2. See Immanuel Kant, "Perpetual Peace: A Philosophical Sketch," in *Kant: Political Writings*, trans. H.B. Nesbit, ed. Hans Reiss (New York: Cambridge University Press, 1991), 93-130.

3. G.W.F. Hegel, *Hegel's Philosophy of Right*, trans. T.M. Knox (Oxford: Clarendon Press, 1967), 214-15.

4. See Paul Ramsey's class notes on The Philosophy of History, Box 43, The Paul Ramsey Papers, Duke University Library. See also G.W.F. Hegel, *Hegel's Philosophy of Right*, 209-210. Italics mine.

5. Kant writes that "If . . . the consent of the citizens is required to decide whether or not war is to be declared, it is very natural that they will have great hesitation in embarking on so dangerous an enterprise. For this would mean calling down on themselves all the miseries of war, such as doing the fighting themselves, supplying the costs of the war from their own resources, painfully making good the ensuing devastation, and as the crowning evil, having to take upon themselves a burden of debt which will embitter peace itself and which can never be paid off on account of the constant threat of new Wars." Kant, "Perpetual Peace: A Philosophical Sketch," 100.

6. Hegel, *Hegel's Philosophy of Right*, 209.

7. Hegel, *Hegel's Philosophy of Right*, 214.

8. Thomas Merten, "Hegel's Homage to Kant's Perpetual Peace: an Analysis of Hegel's *Philosophy of Right* §§ 321-340," *The Review of Politics* 57, no. 4 (Fall, 1995), 679. The "early writing" referred to is Hegel's *Die Verfassung Deutschlands*. For an English translation, see G.W.F. Hegel, "The Constitution of Germany," in *Hegel's Political Writings*, trans. T.M. Knox (Oxford: Clarendon Press, 1998), 210.

9. See Ramsey's class notes on The Philosophy of History, Box 43, The Paul Ramsey Papers, Duke University Library.

10. How exactly to interpret Hegel's grounding of *in bello* ethics is contested. Some scholars point to Hegel's belief that, at least in Europe, neighboring countries came to form a "family in accordance with the universal principles underlying their legal codes." See Hegel, *Hegel's Philosophy of Right*, 297. This would suggest a kind of secondary community among nations from which moral standards of war might arise. Other scholars find Hegel to be inconsistent on the point, and suggest that his move here is truly a sign of the failure of his moral perspective. See Thomas Merten, "Hegel's Homage to Kant's Perpetual Peace," 685-91. It is also possible, as I suggest above, that Hegel's *in bello* standards follow from his metaphysics. If states are ideas that must exist in relation to other states, then any war in which one state fails in a substantial way to recognize the dignity and enduring value of the existence of the other state as a fellow distinct idea in the mind of the Absolute would constitute an act of self-alienation at some level. As Hegel writes, even in war, states "reciprocally recognize each other . . . as something absolute." G.W.F. Hegel, *Hegel's Philosophy of Right*, 215. Regardless of the reason, it is indisputable that Hegel does produce a robust account of *in bello* restrictions on war.

11. G.W.F. Hegel, *Hegel's Philosophy of Right*, 215.

12. Hegel, *Hegel's Philosophy of Right*, 215.

13. Thomas Merten, "Hegel's Homage to Kant's Perpetual Peace," 684.

14. Hegel, *Hegel's Philosophy of Right*, 211-12

15. Hegel, *Hegel's Philosophy of Right*, 297.

16. On a list of "subjects for special study" from Hendel's course Social and Political Philosophy, he includes "Hegel's view of War and its Significance." See handout in Box 43, The Paul Ramsey Papers, Duke University Library.

17. Ramsey, *War and the Christian Conscience*, 10. Elsewhere, he writes: "The just war theory cannot be repealed; it can only be violated. It states the limit beyond which war as such becomes itself a wholly non-human and non-political activity, and the point beyond which military force becomes senseless violence, and our weapons no longer weapons of *war*. This is not because war has an 'essence' or 'nature' but because man has; and because political society has a nature to which military means must be kept subordinate." Ramsey, *The Just War*, 164.

18. James Turner Johnson, "Just War in the Thought of Paul Ramsey," *The Journal of Religious Ethics* 19, no. 2 (1991), 185. Italics mine.

19. See Ramsey, "The Just War Theory on Trial," 489. Hendel, perhaps with a bit too much nostalgia, had taught Ramsey in his graduate work of the time when Grotius had "demonstrated the universality of a system of Natural Right, or 'laws of perpetual obligation,' which obtained among men everywhere, whether in or out of political societies, or at war or peace, and he wrote about them as one confident that such laws of right had a force to restrain princes and peoples in their strife, if only these rules were well expounded in the plain language of reason." See C.W. Hendel, "The Meaning of Obligation," 241-42.

20. On pragmatic politics, see Ramsey, *War and the Christian Conscience*, xxii. Notably, Ramsey includes the "increasing pragmatism of the Niebuhrians" in his general critique. (pp. 3). See also Ramsey's comments on the American ethos in *The Just War*, xix, and 42. On contextual ethics, see Ramsey's treatment of Paul Lehmann in *Deeds and Rules in Christian Ethics*, esp. 92-93.

21. Ramsey, "Politics as Science Not Prophecy," 20.

22. Ramsey, "Force and Political Responsibility," 52.

23. Ramsey, *The Just War*, 50.

24. In a rare occurrence, Ramsey favorably quotes Joseph Fletcher's statement that "tragic situations are a cause for regret, but not for remorse." Ramsey, *Deeds and Rules in Christian Ethics*, 188.

25. Ramsey, *War and the Christian Conscience*, xxii.

26. Paul Ramsey, "Beyond the Confusion of Tongues," *Theology Today* 3, no. 4 (January, 1947), 447.

27. Ramsey, *Speak Up for Just War or Pacifism*, 184.

28. Ramsey, *The Just War*, 179.

29. *War and the Christian Conscience*, 24. Italics mine. Ramsey's language here is suggestive of the idealistic treatment of "ethical substance." As Ramsey notes, "The word 'form' is Augustine's own, but not the word 'substance.'" Ramsey, *War and the Christian Conscience*, 17.

30. Ramsey, *War and the Christian Conscience*, 20.

31. Ramsey, *War and the Christian Conscience*, 32. The "rationalist" option, Ramsey finds, was "to embrace a definition of a commonwealth which was so idealistic as to be a logical class without any members." Ramsey, *War and the Christian Conscience*, 25.

32. Ramsey, *War and the Christian Conscience*, 28.

33. Ramsey, *War and the Christian Conscience*, 39.

34. Most scholars agree that Ramsey's is a rather selective reading of Augustine. While Augustine had no systematic just war theory, he did offer a more substantive account of the *jus ad bellum* than Ramsey's interpretation admits. See Charles Curran, *Politics, Medicine, and Christian Ethics*, 73-74, and James Turner Johnson, "Paul Ramsey and the Recovery of the Just War Idea," *Journal of Military Ethics* 1, No. 2 (July, 2002), 142.

35. Ramsey, *War and the Christian Conscience*, 32. Interestingly, Augustine is not the only person Ramsey would describe as grounding society in will rather than abstract rationality. As Ramsey writes in his dissertation, Bosanquet makes "the will rather than reason the substance of the state." But, in the case of Bosanquet, Ramsey goes on to make explicit that Bosanquet did not mean to abandon contextual rationality. "Since he means the reasonable will, [he] does not depart from the Hegelian tradition." Ramsey, "The Nature of Man," 128.

36. Ramsey, *War and the Christian Conscience*, 29. Ramsey's reading of Augustine is profitably compared with his later treatment of the "tribunal" and "arbitrament" models of war. The tribunal model, which is reflective of Ramsey's "rationalist" option above, portrays war as the execution of a judicial sentence. This model begins with an abstract account of the morality of war and "seems to require that the justice or injustice of the cause be sun-clear to all observers." This, Ramsey asserts, is not an acceptable model for dealing with war today. The arbitrament model on the other hand "more correctly exhibits mankind's struggles for justice in the nation-state system with *its politically embodied justices on which men do not always agree*." In this model, war, again, appears as a struggle between national wills that seek to implement their own understanding of justice. See Ramsey, *The Just War*, 130-31. Italics mine. See also Ramsey's use of the metaphor of the "state of nature" amongst anarchic states in Ramsey, "The Just War Theory on Trial," 484.

37. *War and the Christian Conscience*, 29.

38. Ramsey, *War and the Christian Conscience*, 27. Ramsey's own mental anguish is, due to his method, rarely visible, but one should not doubt its presence. It is impossible to read his treatment of the promise and tragic illicitness of incapacitating gases without recognizing that Ramsey appreciated the horrors of war. See Ramsey, *The Just War*, 477.

39. Ramsey, *War and the Christian Conscience*, 38.

40. Ramsey, *War and the Christian Conscience*, 75.

41. "He who cannot grasp the nettle of the fact that there are *moral permissions* in regard to war—indeed responsibilities to be discharged in this regard—should retire from offering advice to Princes (which means all citizens and their political leaders in a democratic state)." Ramsey, "Politics as Science Not Prophecy," 21.

42. Ramsey, *Basic Christian Ethics*, 169.

43. Paul Ramsey, "Love and Law," in *Reinhold Niebuhr: His Religious, Social, and Political Thought*, 112. Also Ramsey, *Nine Modern Moralists*, 138. For a more detailed treatment of Ramsey's early concept of love in relation to war see William Werperhouski, "Christian Love and Covenant Faithfulness," 104-13.

44. Ramsey, *War and the Christian Conscience*, 305-6.

45. Ramsey, *The Just War*, 36.

46. Ramsey, *Speak Up for Just War or Pacifism*, 54, 83.

47. One might ask what the relation is between love and "rational politics." As James Turner Johnson has often pointed out, Ramsey's language when approaching the

normative conception of politics has both Christian and secular modes. In the Christian mode, Ramsey speaks of justice in historical practice as springing from the transformation brought about by love. In the secular mode, Ramsey speaks of justice as arising from attention to the reason intrinsic within certain political practices. These two modes of speaking make sense together if, as I have suggested in earlier chapters, Ramsey is holding on to a worldview in which the unfolding of "divine charity" and the unfolding of "Absolute reason" are largely identified with one another. See James T. Johnson, "Paul Ramsey and the Recovery of the Just War Idea," 136-140; "Just War in the Thought of Paul Ramsey," 191-97.

The ideas Ramsey is deploying here trace back to his graduate work with Hendel. For instance, take Ramsey's notes on Hendel's construal of the ideal of Greek society. "The Greek view of the *ethical-political* is a basic category for any theory of society. It is indispensable to conceiving *men living in community without losing individuality and living on in continuous* relationships—the whole being a good, and the individual acting for good, without *detracting* from the other. This is *the* conception, *the category*, of *human* community. This [is the] only way to get true community of real individuals." See Ramsey's notes on Social and Political Philosophy, Box 43, The Paul Ramsey Papers, Duke University Library.

48. Ramsey, *The Just War*, 7. Unfortunately, Ramsey never clarifies exactly what constitutes "power." Pinning this content down proves troubling for his definition. If power is conceived broadly, so as to include the "power" of moral suasion, it would seem that his definition of politics covers most of human life. This was certainly not Ramsey's intent. At times Ramsey writes that the state holds a monopoly of power within its own borders, and seems to interchange "decisive physical power," "armed force," "coercion," and "violence" with power in general. See David Little, "The Structure of Justification in the Political Ethics of Paul Ramsey," in *Love and Society*, 141-42. This suggests a more narrow definition of power as the (potential) use of coercive (or violent, or lethal) force. Unfortunately, at best this definition offers an oversimplified and misleading ideal. No state in history, and certainly no state in a contemporary globalized world, ever actually has a monopoly on coercive force. In the world that obtains, force is always more pluralistically distributed. At worst this definition offers a reductive view of which acts constitute politics proper. Political acts need not draw immediately upon those forms of violent force which the state could plausibly be said to have a monopoly upon.

49. Ramsey at one point favorably quotes Robert Osgood: "nations might better renounce the use of war as an instrument of *anything but* national policy." Ramsey, *War and the Christian Conscience*, 29.

50. I draw here upon Ramsey *The Just War*, 9-14. In another article, Ramsey draws out a different set of criteria for the *jus ad bellum*, listing "just cause," official declaration of war, and "last reasonable resort." He categorizes all of these as "teleological" criteria. Ramsey, *The Just War*, 131.

51. Paul Ramsey, "Destructive Force is Never Justifiable," (1940-1942?), 7-8, Box 35, Paul Ramsey Papers, Duke University Library. For a discussion of this work see D. Stephen Long, *Tragedy, Tradition, and Transformism*, 10-20. I suspect that this work was written in late 1941 or 1942, since in it Ramsey has already adopted some of his idealistically influenced Christian linguistic framework. He contends that war could only be justified if it were "compatible with all the neighbor-relationships in which we stand." It is probable that Ramsey was influenced here by T.H. Green's arguments against the Hege-

lian view of war as impersonal. See T.H. Green, "The Right of the State Over the Individual in War," in *The British Idealists*, ed. David Boucher, 217-36.

52. Ramsey, *Basic Christian Ethics*, 166-84.

53. Ramsey, *Basic Christian Ethics*, 182.

54. "If such a one is forced for the sake of his neighbors *visibly* to step over a corpse, he can, I maintain, find within himself, in his Christian conscience, a sanction which depends on a proper reading of his actual situation, and the needs of neighbors determining his vocation." Ramsey, *Basic Christian Ethics*, 180.

55. Ramsey, *Basic Christian Ethics*, 188. See also "The Manger, The Cross and The Resurrection" *Christianity and Crisis* 3, no. 6 (April 16, 1943), 3-4.

56. Ramsey, *War and the Christian Conscience*, 50-51. As he writes in 1976, "While agent-morality is not settled by the physical structure of the agent's action, still the rectitude of that agency does arise from regarding physical events and connections (in the moral landscape of others) as achieving decisive moral significance in determining the actions by which one intervenes into the world of lives in conflict." See Ramsey, "Some Rejoinders," 195.

57. See chapter 3.

58. Ramsey, *War and the Christian Conscience*, 43.

59. Ramsey, *War and the Christian Conscience*, 38, 40-41.

60. As Ramsey notes, the end of continued self survival is, in Aquinas' work, deemed proper on the basis of natural law reasoning. See Ramsey, *War and the Christian Conscience*, 44. Ramsey himself had, in his earlier work, suggested a scheme in which the end of an act of self-defense was found in continued service to one's neighbor, and thus not grounded in the same way. See Ramsey, *Basic Christian Ethics*, 175-80.

61. Ramsey, *War and the Christian Conscience*, 41.

62. Ramsey, *The Just War*, 471. For a useful and slightly broader treatment of Ramsey's development and treatment of the doctrine of double-effect, see David Attwood, *Paul Ramsey's Political Ethics*, 75-90.

63. Ramsey, T*he Just War*, 502.

64. Ramsey, *The Just War* 472.

65. See Ramsey, *Speak Up for Just War or Pacifism*, 102.

66. Ramsey, *The Just War*, 414.

67. Ramsey, *War and the Christian Conscience*, 263-72

68. Ramsey, *War and the Christian Conscience*, 11-13, 163, 311.

69. This is the same point at which Ramsey was contemplating a related suspension of the ethical in the treatment of some cases of abortion—a position he would later reject as he developed distinctions to better think through such cases. See *War and the Christian Conscience*, 179.

70. To some extent Ramsey himself continues to participate in discussions about deterrence in a spirit of deferred repentance, as the United States never adopted his schemes for manufacturing a justifiable system of nuclear deterrence. See Ramsey, "Some Rejoinders," 209-211.

71. Ramsey, *The Just War*, 303.

72. For an extremely generous reading that treats several possible interpretations of the claim see David Attwood, *Paul Ramsey's Political Ethics*, 183-197.

73. Ramsey, *The Just War*, 254.

74. Ramsey, *The Just War*, 27.

Chapter 9
Two Moral Conceptions of War in Dialogue

Recasting the insights of two different philosophical traditions on Christian grounds, Niebuhr and Ramsey have obviously developed quite different moral conceptions of war. For Niebuhr perfect love is defined by Christ's perfect action. Love stands over every practice in a time of war convicting the participant of her or his past sin and reminding her or him of the need for repentant responsibility. In this moral conception the complexity and moral ambiguity of war are stressed so as to chasten the fanatic idolater in a time of war. For Ramsey, who identifies love with the morally structured relations possible in history, war, if it is licit, must be an expression of love in history. War is tragic, but an adequate ethic of war will not focus upon this tragedy, but rather upon the moral structure that obtains even in the midst of tragedy, guiding lovingly rational participation in war. The focus of this moral conception must be upon the accessible moral structure of the good war so as to combat the moral relativism that reigns when war is conceived outside the bounds of morality.

These two moral conceptions of war ought not to be conflated. But, neither should they be construed as simply contradictory. Niebuhr has constructed a moral conception of war that highlights the danger of moral fanaticism in a time of war while Ramsey has developed a conception that highlights the danger of moral relativism. These are, predictably, overlapping but divergent conceptions. This chapter will begin by pointing out the convergence of these two moral conceptions in terms of their theological understandings of the limitations of history. After exploring this convergence, I will continue on to suggest some of the strengths and weaknesses of the two moral conceptions as these emerge from a dialogue between the two positions.

War and Historical Limitation, A point of Contact

The overlap between the conceptions of war deployed by Ramsey and Niebuhr is significant; so much so that Ramsey was able to present his war ethic at one point as "an extension within the Christian realism of Reinhold Niebuhr—an added note within his 'responsibilistic' ethics."[1] Given the divergent conceptions of war I have shown in Ramsey's and Niebuhr's writings, this claim ought to be seen as an oversimplification. Ramsey leaves much of Niebuhr's scheme behind in his "extension," even if he did not recognize the emphasis he was abandoning. But this claim should not be treated lightly.

Niebuhr articulated a theological account of the state of history that recognized the need for both force and the limitation of force in international relations. Ramsey, especially in his Augustinian mood, drew upon this theological grounding even as he developed it in his own distinctive ways.[2] As Ramsey writes, Niebuhr's theology prevents the "already-not yet" tension of the Biblical worldview from collapsing into the "already-some day" utopianism that has so misled contemporary social gospel theologians.[3]

Ramsey's use of Niebuhrian theology also runs deeper. As I have pointed out in earlier sections, Ramsey, in his effort to stress the strictness of Christian morality, at times suggests that Christ's love is not essentially different from the love that is demanded of every Christian within history. This establishes a certain tension between his conception of love and Niebuhr's conception of Christ's love as an impossible ideal. Still, when reacting to pacifistic critiques, Ramsey finds the "impossible" heights of Niebuhr's Christology to be useful tool. In reaction to those who call for an imitation of Christ's avoidance of violence, Ramsey deploys a Niebuhrian argument concerning the impossibility of perfectly imitating Christ. It is, he writes, a naive optimism that transforms "the cross of Christ directly into a political alternative." "Our political responsibility," Ramsey continues, "must be examined in the light of Christ, but also in the shadows revealed and cast by that light. For this reason, Christian vocation in politics cannot be reduced to 'suffering as an alternative opponent of injustice.'"[4] It is no mistake that this passage is found in the paragraph preceding Ramsey's statement locating his own project within Niebuhrian realism.

Ramsey returns to this theme in his last book when responding to Christologically framed criticisms posed by John Howard Yoder. It is, Ramsey indicates, impossible for other humans within history to imitate Christ's particular actions.

> His incarnation, his life as the God-man among us, his suffering, his death, his resurrection were unique, never to be repeated. Certainly not by us. He was THE Pattern, so as at any moment to assume an accusative role of Judge. He is the Pattern, yet also Savior. We are neither co-Creators nor co-Saviors. Hence, as the Reformers knew, we are to follow him—*from a distance*.[5]

Suggestively, Ramsey follows this passage with a "footnote" in which he defends the centrality of Christology in Reinhold Niebuhr's thought. "The life, teachings, and crucifixion of Jesus were," Ramsey had written earlier, "decisive for [Niebuhr's] elucidation of the *relevance* of an *impossible* ideal."[6] Ramsey now continues on:

> Without [taking seriously the incarnation, life, teachings, crucifixion, and resurrection] Reinhold Niebuhr would have had no appeal beyond the 'social gospel.' He would have had no hold by which to recover for American Christianity 'the strange new world within the Bible.' . . . the figure of Jesus as he is there in the text was undeniably in the center of his attention. To avoid acknowledging this, many people today say that Niebuhr's 'theological source' was anthropology and politics. This is manifestly false.[7]

It is, Ramsey recognizes, Niebuhr's recovery of the height of Christology that provides for his perspective upon the limitations of history.

Ramsey and Niebuhr both, then, agree that the morality of war must be worked out within the limitations of history revealed by Christ's act. It is from this common point that the two positions, while still overlapping, begin to diverge. Niebuhr is primarily concerned with the avoidance of both fanatic militarism and fanatic pacifism. As such he relies upon the *impossibility* of the ideal of just peace to chasten responsible participants in history from overreaching, but maintains the *relevance* of the ideal so as to guide persons to seek approximations of the ideal within the limitations of history. Ramsey is primarily concerned with the relativism that he sees arising from an ethic aimed at the realization of abstract transcendent outcomes of perfect peace. Thus, he produces an argument for the primacy of attention to right conduct rather than good outcomes.

This leads to differences in the ways that Niebuhr and Ramsey deploy the idea of relative justice in relation to the resort to war is quite different. Niebuhr uses the fact of the relativity of justice available to emphasize the sin of humanity, and thus to prompt penitence and attention to the costs of one's own position. Here the imperfections of history stand as a sign of God's judgment and a reminder of the danger of idolatry. War arises from past immorality and is often, Niebuhr stresses, immoral on all sides. Ramsey uses the relativity of justice in history to stress the clear moral permission for war. In an imperfect world, pursuit of national interest, even at times at the regrettable expense of others, become an expression of love. Ramsey also uses the relativity of history to underline the unique and disparate general wills of nation states. Since there is no clear agreement on international measures of justice, states must define and defend their own national interest to the best of their abilities. War, Ramsey suggests, may often be morally undertaken by all sides.

A similar overlap and divergence can be found in Niebuhr's and Ramsey's treatments of just war conduct. Both recognize that within history the ends of conflict only justify limited means. God is ultimately in control of history, and God's action is the only hope for the perfection of the world. Humanity ought not to seek ever more effective means under the delusion that by the use of these means it might be able eventually to bring about the perfection of history. But, again the ways in which Niebuhr and Ramsey describe and deploy this insight take them in different directions.

Niebuhr, as I have cited, suggests, but does not pursue in detail, the possibility that some means of war reach heights of destruction that can never be justified. But Niebuhr's limitations on the means of war are always couched in terms of the need for virtuous judgment and prudential and realistic analysis of the values to be protected or produced and the costs to be sustained. He does not develop any analysis of *kinds* of acts in war or any clear distinctions between kinds of targets. Thus he does not produce a deontological ethic. The moral warrior penitently and realistically assesses the costs of war in the light of the relative ends available in history. Morality is found primarily in setting aside uncritical adherence to purportedly ultimate ends and duties, and in taking responsibility for the realistically foreseeable costs of political and military decisions.

Ramsey takes a different route. He stresses the primacy of determinations of right in a world where the outcomes of actions are construed as beyond one's control. The perfection promised in Christian eschatology, he posits, frees the Christian from undue concern about outcomes. "This means, in ethics, that calculating the consequences, predicting either benefits or disaster to come, is not the paramount way to distinguish right and wrong actions. We tend the garden of the future we see, but we do not *depend on* outcomes or take charge of God's ruling and overruling providence."[8] While Ramsey can speak of limitation of conduct in war in terms of a means/end calculus wherein some means are never proportional,[9] he more frequently speaks in terms of kinds of acts that ought never to be undertaken no matter the end at which one is aiming.[10]

Thus, both Niebuhr and Ramsey were concerned about humans sinfully overstepping their bounds, both recognize the danger that over inflated ends may erode the proper limits of means in warfare, and both seek to articulate moral conceptions of war that allow for responsibility within history. These are significant overlaps in their often contrasted perspectives on human conflict. But Niebuhr and Ramsey describe, and react to these tendencies in typically different ways. For Ramsey, utopian projects are understood as moral abstractions that function to erode the moral structure of history. In the light of abstract hopes for peace, war comes to be seen as a practice in which all acts are sinful, and the distinction between moral acts of war and war crimes are left behind. Ramsey reacts with a conception of war as an expression of covenant love within history. For Niebuhr, utopian projects are properly seen as morally fanatic. Nationalistic militarism and naive pacifism offer temptations to idolatry that undermine the virtues of penitent responsibility. These idolatries must be quashed by recognition of humanity's place in the order of God's judgment, acting not in perfection, but in recognition of the relevant impossible ideal of divine peace and justice revealed in Christ's unique act on the cross. Needless to say, these conceptions of war provide both insights and blind spots to the moralists who deploy them.

War as an Act of Covenant Love: Critical Assessment

In the aftermath of the horrors of World War II, Ramsey was a major contributor to the recovery of just war reasoning in general and the distinctions between combatants and noncombatants in specific. Without his influence, it is doubtful that such reasoning would have made inroads so quickly and significantly into contemporary Protestant thought. In the decades between his work and the present, deontic reasoning concerning the licit use of force has made a major impression on both religious and secular institutions and on the public debate about the use of force. His continuing influence in this discussion is indicative of the importance of Ramsey's refusal to accept the idea that the moral ambiguities of war are resistant to moral analysis. War, if it is to be licit, must be dragged into the light and revealed as a potentially moral activity so as to distinguish it clearly from those immoral activities that may seem superficially similar.

At the same time, one must acknowledge several problematic tendencies in his analysis of war which appear when viewed from a Niebuhrian perspective. Ramsey tends to understate the moral significance of responsible and realistic calculations of proportionality and consequence in times of war, and fails to develop an ethic that supports sufficient criticism of claims that the resort to force is justified. Although they overlap, it is helpful here to treat his approach to the *in bello* and *ad bellum* just war criteria separately. I will begin with a short treatment of his *in bello* ethic.

The In Bello Ethic

First, in Ramsey's effort to recover the moral permission for force, Ramsey's focus on right intention may be seen at times as leading to an understatement of the significance of the costs of war and the importance of calculations of proportionality in just war thought. John Bennett recognized this danger. As he writes to Ramsey

> My one fear is that you write with so much gusto about just targeting that you may too easily find reasons to shoot if you are sure that the

> targeting will be just. What you say about prudence covers the issues here in general terms, but I still have my anxieties.[11]

Such an under-emphasis on proportionality was not Ramsey's intent. As he responds:

> I am certainly not opening the door to any degree of violence so long as the principle of discrimination is satisfied. That, which itself is by no means a matter of mere motivational intention, then does shift our judgment to questions of proportion. The latter too is a moral matter, though it is a question of prudence assaying the relative goods and evils in consequences.[12]

Still, it is hard, given Ramsey's emphasis, not to conclude that there is a tendency in Ramsey's position to make proportionality into a second-rate moral requirement.

This valuation is suggested in Ramsey's treatment of nuclear deterrence. When arguing that potential collateral damage could have a deterrent effect, Ramsey was forced to acknowledge that this effect depended on the disproportionate collateral damage that would follow. This is acceptable inasmuch as "the threat of something disproportionate is not always a disproportionate threat." As Michael Walzer concludes:

> Perhaps that argument is right, but I should stress that its result is to void the proportionality rule. Now there is no limit on the number of people whose deaths we can threaten, so long as those deaths are to be caused 'collaterally' and not by taking direct aim. As we have seen before, the idea of proportionality, once it is worked on a bit, tends to fade away. And then the entire burden of Ramsey's argument falls on the idea of death by indiscrimination.[13]

There is some justification for an emphasis upon discrimination in Ramsey's writings. When Ramsey started writing, Protestant ethics had largely lost track of the moral relevance of the distinction between combatants and noncombatants in war. Without the distinction, moral thought about war was impoverished. In this climate, Ramsey was right to emphasize the difference between acts targeting noncombatants and acts targeting combatants. He was also right that no other measure can erode the import of the distinction itself. No matter how proportional by some other standard, an indiscriminate act is always an indiscriminate act.

But Ramsey's emphasis often seems to take him somewhat further than this. In an early article protesting the dominance of prudential reasoning in guiding acts of war, Ramsey writes that calculations of proportionality are, by themselves, like requirements in animal ethics that prevent "wanton cruelty." As he writes, "the teleologically suspended ethics of the code of the S.P.C.A. is quite capable of ruling that it is 'immoral' to use methods that cause laboratory rats more pain and maiming without commensurate medical or scientific decisiveness. This outlook has not yet come upon any *crucial moral consideration*."[14] Here Ramsey's rhetoric suggests that proportionality has not only failed inasmuch as it has wrongly taken a sole role at the center stage of ethics, it also seems to have been wrongly taken to be a "crucial moral consideration."

The distinction between these two kinds of judgment involved in determinations of discrimination and proportionality also comes to the fore in Ramsey's suggestion that the principle of discrimination deals with the "inherent" morality of an act of war while proportionality deals with some other facet of the act. There are at least two distinguishable bases for this distinction in Ramsey's thought.

In the first it appears that this is a distinction between the moral grounding of the judgments involved. In one article, Ramsey contrasts the "tests of *inherent wrongfulness* (the deontological tests)" grounded in the common reason of the *jus gentium*, with the "political" and "individualistic" measure of consequence and proportion which are grounded in judgments concerning the "stupidity" of the policy.[15] Given this distinction, Ramsey suggests that decisions regarding proportionality and consequence "may be tragically wrong" but not "inherently wicked."[16]

This distinction does not withstand scrutiny. If discrimination is a measure embedded in the *jus gentium*, it seems that proportionality would also qualify as such. Surely, proportionality is, if anything, a much more widely accepted standard than discrimination in historical consensus. Admittedly, how to apply this principle is debatable, but this is true of applications of the principle of discrimination as well. As Ramsey recognizes in calmer moments, determinations of who counts as a functional combatant depend upon accurate observations of the conditions of the particular war. One could undertake an "objectively" indiscriminate act while, because of misinformation, ignorant of the fact that the targets truly constitute functional noncombatants. Indeed, Michael Walzer has critiqued Ramsey's treatment of nuclear deterrence for deploying reason to over-think the moral issues at hand, bending deontic conclusions against their proper course.[17] Thus, these judgments, like prudential judgments, must deal with issues of "stupidity," issues of prudence, and issues of willingness to do the right. Ramsey has failed here to produce a plausible absolute distinction between the two kinds of judgment.

The second grounding for Ramsey's distinction between the inherent moral quality of discrimination and non-inherent moral quality of proportionality and consequential concerns is a different matter.

> Under the first test, 'doing evil' means doing evil directly, having in view some good end or consequence to come from it; and that is inherently wrong. . . . Under the second test, however, 'doing evil' means doing the *lesser* evil among manifold consequences of a *not indiscriminate* act. In this sense and when one comes to count the costs 'doing evil' is not always wrong.[18]

Exactly what Ramsey means here may be clarified by a statement a few paragraphs after this initial statement.

> Yet proportion or prudence or judgments concerning the lesser evil among the ends of action have nothing to do with whether something is the direct object of the action's impact and something else the collateral or side-effect unavoidably also produced by the action. That depends on the verdict under the first test, the principle of discrimination. This test can and should be independently applied, and an assessment of any proposed action should first be made in terms of discrimination, in order to determine the actions that are ever permissible. Then one has to choose, from among actions that are morally tolerable because they are not indiscriminate, those actions that should actually be done because of an apt proportion between their good and evil consequences.[19]

Here Ramsey is not, at least not necessarily, claiming that deontic judgments are more firmly morally grounded, or that they are necessarily more epistemically secure. He is claiming that deontic concerns are overriding when they come to conflict with concerns of proportionality or consequence. In these passages, he is laying out the grammatical rules for the moral language game he believes everyone approaching the conflict of these types of concern should obey. Since discrimination is an overriding concern, determinations of discrimination ought to be made first so as to establish the set of morally acceptable options on which one ought to calculate proportionality.

Ramsey's logic here cannot be questioned. That is because it is a logic that he is constructing in the process of his argument. If one plays the language game he sets forth, no other conclusion is valid. However, one might ask if this is the right language game to be playing. There are alternatives. For instance, one might propose a comprehensive account of *in bello* moral logic in terms of proportionality. This proportionalist language game would not require a rejection of the moral importance of noncombatant status. The value of noncombatant immunity could be included within the analysis of proportionality.[20] This language game could also incorporate the value of kinds of moral acts into the calculation of proportionality.

One deploying this alternate language game could hold with Ramsey that targeting noncombatants is always wrong. The disvalue of targeting noncombatants may be so great as to make this an overriding value in all calculations. There would, however, be no grammatical necessity to this judgment. Participants in the discussion could continue to argue about the particular values involved. In some rare cases, it may be that targeting noncombatants is justified by some other overriding value. Joseph Allen, for instance, has argued that such cases may exist. While Allen admits the principle of discrimination under normal conditions of war he pushes Ramsey's position on extreme cases.

> What if one must choose between the right to immunity of a handful of persons, on the one hand, and the destruction of countless millions of people, with all of whom we are in covenant under God, on the other? How morally justified would one be in saying that although, tragically, he unintentionally allowed the deaths of millions upon millions as collateral damage, at least he did not commit murder by direct and intentional attacks upon the innocent? In such an extreme case it is not as clear what one should do as Ramsey may assume. . . . He has a preliminary answer: such cases do not occur. But that reply will not hold up.[21]

Allen's challenge is interesting because it makes clear that one can articulate on the basis of love, and even in the language of covenant love, some basis for exceptions to an absolute rule of noncombatant immunity. Despite Ramsey's claims, as I have suggested earlier, Ramsey does not simply draw out the implications of love in his just war ethic. He grounds his account of what love requires in his own understanding of what constitute real and enduring goods within history. As such, debate about the relative value of noncombatant targeting cannot be resolved by a simple appeal to love, or even covenant love *per se*.

It is beyond the scope of this treatment to develop an alternative to Ramsey's language game in any detail.[22] What is important here is to establish that there is nothing in either abstract logical or Christian standards that necessitates Ramsey's choice of language game. What language game is preferable must be determined in the process of history. Over time different language games may reveal distinctive flaws, temptations, or dangers that afflict them. Ramsey's language game may understate the importance of calculations of proportion and consequence. The proportionalist language game may have the tendency of collapsing diverse goods too easily into commensurability. It may even end up that neither one offers a perfect language game for dealing with all of the moral concerns present in times of war. None of these languages, Niebuhr would remind us, are handed down from heaven, and none should be held outside of criticism.

The Ad Bellum Ethic

Ramsey faces problems in his *ad bellum* ethic that are similar to those posed by his *in bello* ethic, but here, because of his stress on the lack of deontic standards over the resort to war, these problems are magnified. While tracing out his Augustinian theme, Ramsey reminds his reader that wars ought only to be fought for political, and thus limited, goals.[23] Even the "just war" is, as Ramsey states, relatively "justified" in history rather than "just" in an absolute sense. This Augustinianism might have taken Ramsey, as it did Niebuhr, down a road toward developing a critical ethic aimed at rooting out the dangers of overstating the ends of war. Unfortunately, several facets of Ramsey's approach militate against his development of such a critical *ad bellum* ethics.

First, Ramsey's use of the Augustinian theme tends to erode rather than bolster criticism of the ends of war inasmuch as it posits that the ends of states are not to be measured against any external standard of righteousness. "Since at least everyone seeks peace and desires justice," Ramsey writes, "the *ends* for which wars may legitimately be fought are not nearly so important in the theory of the just war as the moral and political wisdom contained in its reflection upon the *conduct* or means of warfare."[24] No scholar who is focused on the dangers of moral fanaticism could say the same. Without a more secure grounding for criticism of nationalistic pretension, Ramsey's ethic is open to Niebuhrian criticism.

Ramsey's use of Augustine also, unfortunately, stops Ramsey from developing a deontic account of the limitations of resort to war. In his wish to avoid placing abstract judgments over against the wills of particular communities, it seems that Ramsey ends up depriving his own analysis of the only standards he believed to be of ultimate moral substance. Although Niebuhr avoided such accounts, later Niebuhrians, as I shall argue below, ought to have a keen interest in deontic standards inasmuch as they have shown themselves to be significant elements in limiting immoral resort to war in the period since Ramsey wrote. Later scholars, at times Ramsey's own students, have acknowledged this lack in Ramsey's system and have sought to fix the problem with a recovery of a more robust account of deontic *ad bellum* standards.[25]

Unfortunately, the weakness of Ramsey's Augustinian theme is aggravated by Ramsey's use of his agapic theme. In his zeal to quash those who construe war as an intrinsic evil, Ramsey at times oversteps in suggesting that the primary moral duty in times of war is a duty to rescue one's neighbor by means of force. Concern for the duty of avoiding harm of one's neighbor all too often is treated like a regrettable, but at times overriding, concern.

In his later writings, when he speaks of the grounding of Christian just war ethics in a "*presumption against injustice*," he even goes a step further.[26] Here it seems that the duty to aid one's neighbor and spread justice becomes a prima facie duty. Properly, Ramsey concludes, the "moral anguish" that confronts those in the just war tradition arises from wars that cannot be fought due to "clashes between '*justice*-reasons' for going to war and '*disproportion*-reasons' for prohibiting it."[27] The Christian, Ramsey writes, ought to feel a "mortal sorrow" when "resort to violence in a palpably just cause cries to high heaven for us to rescue the perishing and *we cannot do so* because in the attempt greater evil would be caused than prevented or corrected."[28] The moral obligation to wage war for the sake of justice seems to linger even when the phenomenal limitations of history preclude its enactment.[29]

This tendency in Ramsey's thought is problematic for several reasons. First, as Ramsey recognizes in his Augustinian mood, history is from this Christian point of view a realm where social structures at their best offer a modicum of relative justice. In such a context an overemphasis upon the "presumption against injustice" may lead to a world in which violence is *always* presumptively justified. An emphasis on the duty to do good by means of force says too little about the war time temptation to ignore the costs of actions in service to one's proposed end. Some greater weight placed on the ideal of peace or the moral obligation to avoid harm seems necessary to correct for this tendency.[30]

Second, Ramsey's treatment of the "moral anguish" about the war that cannot be fought is theologically problematic, as Niebuhr's analysis points out. Certainly, Niebuhr agrees, war is a place for moral anguish, and this anguish ought properly to be felt about the justice that is not done in history. This moral anguish ought to lead to a self-critical stance that leads one to question how she or he has or is contributing to this injustice. But this moral anguish ought not, lest the anguished fall to idolatry, be conceived as moral anguish over the fact that she or he, or that her or his nation, is not able to bring about justice. One can only live a humble and responsible life to that extent that she or he realizes that bringing such justice is beyond her or his ability. It is Christ, and not the self or the self's nation that ought to save the world. By treating only the moral anguish felt when one is prohibited from going to war, Ramsey has come dangerously close to this theological error.

This brings us to the third problem in Ramsey's statement of the moral obligation for war. It dichotomizes justice and prudence and treats them as, at best, tangentially related. For Ramsey, it seems, justice here deals with one's obligation to actively "rescue" the other. Thus, a war might be just and yet imprudent. The "justice reasons" for going to war still bear their moral status enough to give rise to "moral anguish" when they are frustrated by the dictates of prudence. This suggests that the prudential concerns that limit recourse to war are somehow less morally significant than the justice concerns that call one to arms. The virtue of prudence appears to become a second class virtue in relation to justice. As James Turner Johnson notes, Ramsey categorizes all of his *ad bellum* measures as "teleological tests." This, Johnson concludes, "indicates the secondary place he gave them in moral priority: they are tests only of political prudence."[31] This seems an untenable position. If it is love that motivates one to go to war in defense of one's neighbor, it is also love that prevents one from being willing to do disproportionate damage to one's neighbor. Both are full moral requirements for the Christian, and the two ought not to be played off against each other so as to establish one as representative of "covenant" in a way that the other is not.

Finally, the development of a truly critical *ad bellum* ethic in Ramsey's work is limited due to his stance on the proper role of the moralist and Christian in public discourse and moral discernment. After developing those prudential standards by which resort to a good use of force ought to be measured, Ramsey stops to make clear that even if he as a moralist and a Christian can lay out the theoretical standards, he cannot in that capacity be called upon to comment upon the application of these standards. "Nothing," Ramsey writes, "can remove from among the awesome responsibilities of the magistrates the determination of where to draw these lines."[32]

Many of these factors came together in Ramsey's treatment of the Vietnam War. Ramsey's agapism led him to advocate for an aggressive American foreign policy that stressed the obligation to spread conditions of justice and maintain a system of antithetically related nation-states. "Broadly speaking," Ramsey would write in 1964, "the overriding goal of our foreign policy is to create and sustain a system of free and independent nations. We are in the business of nation-building."[33] With the *benne esse* of American foreign policy so defined, military activities against Communism in Vietnam appeared to have a presumptive justification.

While Ramsey's own rules prevented him from articulating any final judgment on the morality of the war, he did find himself able to conclude that there could be no viable moral argument against the war. All such arguments, he argued, would be on prudential grounds, concerning the proportionality of continued American military action. These determinations fell outside the scope of the moralist's judgment. The United State's decisions in Vietnam may have been mistaken, Ramsey notes, but "the outrageous excesses of our public debate over Vietnam, and particularly the charge that these decisions were 'immoral,' demonstrates an astonishing failure to understand *the nature of political decisions*—and on the part of adults and intellectuals who should know better, a reprehensible failure."[34] Prudential political decisions are, by their nature, impenetrably ambiguous, and thus, Ramsey suggests here, not proper subjects for moral judgment.

These were the subjects for political decision, and political decisions were to be made by political authorities. Ramsey's preferential tendencies toward these authorities emerged in his defense of their judgment. "It is hard to see," Ramsey writes, "how any moderately sophisticated statesman in the international system could have an arrogance of power;

he is no builder of a project that he can control or complete; he cannot very clearly count the costs because he cannot—he simply cannot—predestinate the benefits he seeks."[35] He was infuriated by the continual challenges to the prudential judgments made by America's government. By 1969 he would lament the day when it had "become fashionable, as a first move, to disbelieve the moral credibility of one's own government."[36]

Thus, Ramsey's position produced a prima facie duty for military action in Vietnam and ruled out any definitive argument against this duty. By selecting in and out which questions could be answered Ramsey had not succeeded in avoiding a final moral conclusion. He had, as James T. Johnson writes, produced "a forceful argument for intervention on behalf of the South Vietnamese."[37] What is more, he had framed his argument in a way that made it appear that his conclusion was uncontestable on moral grounds.

Exactly when Ramsey decided that military action in Vietnam was no longer justified is not clear. In the fall of 1972 he continued to contend that ecclesial and moral pronouncements declaring continued American intervention unjust stepped beyond the sphere of proper moral and ecclesial judgment.[38] By October of 1973, however, several months after President Nixon had agreed to end direct American military intervention in Vietnam, Ramsey felt comfortable enough to proclaim his own judgment as a moral theologian that the war was in fact not morally sustainable. While continuing to lament the chaos of the debate over Vietnam, he would at this point grant that "certain necessities of advocacy compelled us for an interlude" from the work of elaborating the shape of moral order. "Even confused moral discourse did, after all, help us turn the country from our Vietnam involvement."[39] In the end, he allowed himself the judgment he had so long denied to others: "the Vietnam war was disproportionate and *therefore morally* unjustified."[40]

Ramsey was, as I have noted earlier, right to be concerned about the hubris that often accompanies political arguments in which religious warrant is claimed by one side against the other. He was also right that there is an especially great temptation to this kind of pride in arguments over issues so important as the resort to force. Neither the proponents nor the opponents of particular wars ought to naively or lightly deploy religious rhetoric in these arguments. Still, Ramsey's ethics say too little about the need for prophetic criticism that, while maintaining the virtue of humility, finds itself required to investigate particular military and political conclusions.

In the end, Ramsey's war ethics militate against the development of a sufficiently critical stance for the Christian in a time of war. Ramsey provided the groundwork for an ongoing tradition of just war ethics that seeks to recover and articulate the moral permissions and limitations of war in deontic standards. But, he at times seems to fail in exactly the area where Niebuhr suggests that an overly narrow just war ethics will. Ramsey focuses so much upon the rules of war that he fails to emphasize the grounding for the Christian virtues of humility, responsibility and criticalness. Without such a grounding, it seems that no just war theory will be able to adequately address the problems of moral fanaticism which are so crucial in times of war.

War as God's Judgment: Critical Assessment

Niebuhr's strengths and weaknesses, it is not surprising, provide a mirror image of Ramsey's. Just as Ramsey seems at times to fall into those dangers that Niebuhr's program highlights, Niebuhr at points falls into those mistakes against which Ramsey's system is most vigilant. We can see this both in Niebuhr's occasional tendencies to speak as if war were inherently immoral and in his failure to develop a moral language adequate to support substantive rules for war.

Niebuhr was never a relativist as concerns war, but his emphasis upon the sins that lead to and tempt persons in war and his emphasis upon the costs of war at times lead him to overstate the moral ambiguity of a war *per se*. After World War I, Niebuhr, under the influence of Marxist philosophy and in the light of his disappointment concerning the Versailles treaty, came to see war as caused by the greed and imperialism of national forces.[41] He became a pacifist at this time, and his pacifism was grounded in this conception of war. Even as his later thought shifted to allow for war, he carried much of this view along with him.

By the time Niebuhr wrote *Moral Man and Immoral Society*, he had, as I have noted, been able to recognize that violence could be the means of a good will in a broken world. But at the same time, he maintained a largely cynical view of international conflict and posited a "frank dualism" between individual and social morality.[42] While the self might act out of selfless motives, the state would always be fundamentally selfish.

Still, participation in this form of selfishness seemed justified insofar as this selfishness could be qualified by a push to find the overlap between selfishness and the common good of the international society. This cynicism about national motives, when it later mellowed into a more healthy skepticism, served Niebuhr well while writing on the often duplicitous rhetoric and policy of nation states. But without qualification, it says too little about the need for the call for morality within politics.

In *An Interpretation of Christian Ethics*, Niebuhr could write that "The actions to which men are 'driven' by necessities of the natural order are yet charged with guilt."[43] War, Niebuhr posits, is one of these necessities. This is at best a confused account. In common discourse, guilt can only be incurred in acts that one is free to avoid. To the extent that humans are "driven" to actions by "necessities" it hardly seems that they can be guilty for these actions. Niebuhr's point is not primarily about guilt in this sense. Niebuhr is focused here upon reminding his readers that they are responsible for the costs of their actions, and ought not to be misled by a fanaticism that underestimates or ignores these costs in the light of some perfectionist project. Unfortunately the framework he puts forward at this point is untenable, and runs the danger of unintentionally falling into the trap of relativism Ramsey recognizes in so much of modern discourse on war. By construing all acts of war as entailing guilt, one runs a great risk of sliding down a slippery slope toward relativism when war is declared.

As I have argued in the previous chapter, one can find, especially in Niebuhr's later writings, a more subtle account of guilt and war.[44] War, while never perfect, can be the best approximation of love at times. The existence of war reveals guilt for past sin and the constant temptation to sin in the present. The shift from his earlier scheme to this later more subtle account is not a straightforward matter. In some senses, as I have noted, the more subtle account was present even in *Moral Man and Immoral Society*. Unfortunately, the earlier less subtle account also lived on in some of Niebuhr's writings till the end of his work. Even in his later writings, his tendency to stress the ambiguity of war at times leads him to underemphasize the structures necessary for guiding judgment in a time of war. This tendency is aggravated by his occasional suggestions that guilt is directly linked to killing *per se* and his misguided efforts to interpret guilt in terms of concrete outcomes of one's actions. But the two accounts are separable, and Niebuhr's more subtle account provides a scheme which maintains much of the emphasis of his earlier account while avoiding many of its problems.

The second weakness in Niebuhr's scheme is his inability to sufficiently articulate or support substantive rules of war. This weakness is manifest in Niebuhr's failure to articulate the distinction between targeting combatants and noncombatants. We can see this failure in Niebuhr's reaction to the first use of nuclear weapons. Niebuhr did not find that the use of nuclear weapons against Japan at the end of World War II was morally acceptable. In fact, he laments the fact that his own nation "reached the level of Nazi morality in justifying the use of the bomb on the ground that it shortened the war."[45] Niebuhr had previously challenged the U.S. policy of obliteration bombing in Germany in the latter stages of the war.[46] He now concludes that the use of the atomic bomb against Japan "was merely the culmination of our own strategy of total war, involving the use of ever more powerful obliteration bombing and incendiarism."[47]

Still, despite Niebuhr's intuitive moral repulsion concerning the use of the atomic bomb, the arguments he is able to provide to ground his criticism are weak.

> We can criticize the statesman . . . for lack of imagination in impressing the enemy with the power of the bomb without the wholesale loss of life that attended our demonstration of its power. Suppose we had announced the perfection of the bomb to the enemy, threatened its ultimate use, and given some vivid demonstration of its power in places where the loss of life would have been minimal. The moral advantage of such imagination would have been tremendous. As matters stand now, we have completely lost our moral position, particularly in the Orient.[48]

Niebuhr is not wrong. Imaginative statesmanship was lacking from the decision to drop the bomb, even if the imaginative solutions Niebuhr suggested were not viable.[49] As Michael Walzer has argued, the use of nuclear weapons was not justified so long as other options, such as accepting a negotiated peace with Japan, were still on the table.[50]

What is missing from Niebuhr's account is any sense that there is a moral difference between the loss of life that follows from the nuclear attack against a civilian center and the loss of life entailed by committing soldiers to combat.[51] In an exchange with James Conant, Niebuhr argued that "failing in achieving a Japanese surrender, the bomb would have had to be used to save the lives of thousands of American soldiers who would otherwise have perished on the beaches of Japan."[52] Such a comment reveals an underdeveloped sense of the moral issues involved in this case. It suggests that it may be morally acceptable to directly target foreign noncombatants so as to protect United States combatants. Niebuhr's comment suggests that he did not have access to the distinctions necessary to sort out the moral status of varying targets in this case.

Niebuhr's failure here is not just a sign of his lack of sufficient attention to distinctions between kinds of targets in war. Niebuhr's arguments against the just war theory as a whole tend to underestimate the usefulness of the standards represented in the tradition. Niebuhr was right to suggest that no framework of rules is sufficient if not deployed by a person with the moral virtues and perspective to deploy it appropriately. But this emphasis ought not to distract one from the usefulness of these systems of rules altogether. As James Childress writes

> Even as [Niebuhr] became more sympathetic to Roman Catholic moral theology later in his life, and as several Protestants, particularly Paul Ramsey, began to appropriate the tradition of just war, there is no evidence that Niebuhr significantly modified his criticisms, some of which fail to appreciate the tradition's flexibility in the interpretation of absolute standards.[53]

The critical, responsible, and penitent Christian cannot treat the just war standards as self applying and absolute norms, and she or he ought to resist any reduction of the moral account of war into an overly narrow construal of issues like just cause simply in terms of the immediate occasion for current outbreak of arms. Wars in order to be fully understood must, as Niebuhr rightly recognized, be understood in terms of a broader narrative wherein the sins of all involved ought to be critically assessed. Still, the Christian also ought to use the just war standards as guides to a set of particularly important goods that have been recognized by various human societies through history. Virtue ought not to be replaced by rules, but neither ought one to avoid the use of rules when they serve the ends of shaping consciences and making warfare more humane. It has become clear in the time since Niebuhr's work that explicit rules of war, like the doctrine of noncombatant immunity, can be a factor in directly limiting the conduct of war. Further, the rules of war have become a standard to which most, although not all, international actors appeal even when they are in practice avoiding living up to the spirit of these rules. In their subterfuge, those who do not wish to obey the rules must make a show of their pretense to obey them. Even such subterfuge demands some limitation in the process. This, a Niebuhrian ought to appreciate, is the sign of a highly successful set of human ideals. Unfortunately, Niebuhr's perspective never prompted him to develop an appreciation for the power of these standards.

In the above ways, Niebuhr allows his own emphasis at times to obscure his moral perspective. Ramsey was the first in a line of critics who have pointed out these failings. But an adequate appraisal of Niebuhr's contribution to war ethics ought also to pay attention to what was too often left behind in the transition from Niebuhr's thought to a more deontologically grounded just war approach. Niebuhr's effort to locate particular wars within a broader theological and historical narrative, his attention to the need for penitence in times of war, his critical edge toward the claims of both pacifists and militarists, his focus on issues of prudence, and his emphasis on the dangers of national messianism are points that too often become obscured or lost in the search for a list of criteria for judging war.

The strength of Niebuhr's framework was highlighted in Niebuhr's approach to the Vietnam War. After World War II Niebuhr perceived the rise of a new form of idolatry in the United States. "One has the uneasy feeling," Niebuhr would write, "that our own country is greatly tempted in this critical age to that pride, in which the prophets of old recognized the portent of Babylon's doom."[54] As the United States emerged as a superpower, a popular narrative developed that located the United States as a savior nation, providentially ordained to defend and spread democracy. The forces of good had defeated the evil of Nazism, and now faced the demonic power of Communism. This narrative oversimplified the complex and muddy reality of international politics, and led the United States to fail to take seriously the ways it was resented in other parts of the world. This was, Niebuhr recognized, especially the case in Asia.[55] In 1954 when the French were defeated at Dien Bien Phu Niebuhr hoped that the United States might see the judgment of God in the defeat of this western power and be chastened from entering conflict in the region.[56] He hoped that this would break the "illusion of American Omnipotence" that saw the United States carried on a providential tide of democratic history.[57] While he attempted to suspend his public judgment as the United States entered more intrusively into Vietnam, his continuing frustration at the deceptive presentations of the conflict by the American government led to his becoming one of the first public intellectuals to criticize the war in the mid 1960s.[58] The U.S. government, blinded by its own self-deceptive pretensions, was unable to see the costs of its actions. "American responsibility for the world order is," Niebuhr at one point noted, "a danger if it is taken to mean, as some have interpreted it, a responsibility to impose an American order on the world."[59] In this war, Niebuhr wrote, God must have been laughing at the absurdity of American pretense.[60] Thus the same framework that allowed him to recognize the irresponsibility of isolationism in World War Two also underwrote his criticism of American pretension and self-deception in Southeast Asia.[61]

At a public presentation at the American Academy of Religion in 2005 John Kelsay spoke on what he took to be the advances of just war theory in the recent past, and what he took to be the present challenge for just war theorists. The recent past, he said, had seen a recovery of the content of the just war criteria of legitimate authority and just cause. As we have seen, these developments filled gaps in Ramsey's work on the *in bello* criteria. But Kelsay located the contemporary challenge for just war theorists in a direction that Ramsey did not stress. In the light of contemporary international politics, we need, Kelsay said, a recovery of Reinhold Niebuhr's criticism of all brands of perfectionism in foreign policy, and a correlative new attentiveness to the measures of proportionality.[62] This, I would suggest, is a wise call to action.

Conclusion

During Vietnam, Ramsey and Niebuhr had clashed with one another. Their responses to this clash reflect their different approaches to public discourse. When Niebuhr was asked what he made of other "realists" who disagreed with his conclusions his response was irenic. Facts on the ground are not self interpreting, he said, and realists can certainly come to different conclusions when making sense of these facts.[63] Ramsey however, reacted more polemically. Unable to conceive of disagreement with his deontically secure analysis, he concluded that Niebuhr's "simplicist analysis" amounted to a form of "support for the liberal consensus."[64] Niebuhr's deployment of concepts of "pride" and "pretension" in the end revealed that these concepts were "capable of dissolving any and all categories of analysis and are helpful in none."[65] Perhaps worst,

Ramsey perceived Niebuhr's position as a betrayal of the realism that had always united himself and his sometimes mentor. "The situation at the moment is, I should say, that even Reinhold Niebuhr signs petitions or editorials as if Reinhold Niebuhr never existed!"[66] The best metaphor Ramsey could conjure to account for Niebuhr's current line of argument was one of drunkenness. Now that Niebuhr had imbibed too freely, theologians and politicians would have to appeal to his earlier sober writings.[67]

Ramsey later regretted such statements. In 1981, he acknowledged that during Vietnam "earlier than I, Reinhold Niebuhr was wiser than I."[68] Echoing Niebuhr's words from over a decade before, Ramsey would ask: "Who ever said that those who share a controlling political 'realism' will agree on their *specific* conclusions? Indeed, the contrary is the case."

Both Niebuhr and Ramsey were in the end right. There was no necessity for agreement in the application of moral argument to the case of Vietnam. But there was more than an interpretation of facts that separated Niebuhr and Ramsey at this point. They were not simply applying the same moral concepts. They were not, as it were, of the same mind. From their periods in graduate school on through their development as theologians, the two had been representatives in an ongoing debate in the life of American moral theology that transcended their particular conclusions. Like James and Royce before them they had become personal friends and intellectual and political sparing partners. Their conceptions of love, sin, providence, society, and war all reflect the concerns and tools they had been sensitized to in the infancy of their scholarship. Thus, their disagreement during Vietnam was a manifestation of a much deeper division between the two. Pragmatic and idealistic visions had been reconceptualized in Christian terms, but they had not simply passed away.

Notes

1. Ramsey, *The Just War*, 260.

2. Against those who would charge Niebuhr with Constantinianism or situationism, Ramsey argues, in continuity with the interpretation I have presented above, that Niebuhr is interested primarily in articulating the demands of responsibility within the historical limitations established by God in history. Compare John Howard Yoder, *Christian Attitudes to War, Peace, and Revolution*, 350 and Paul Ramsey's comments in *Reinhold Niebuhr Today*, ed. Richard John Neuhaus, 114.

3. Ramsey, *Speak Up For Just War or Pacifism*, 44.

4. Ramsey, *The Just War*, 260. Ramsey's recognition of Niebuhr's high Christology and the moral implications of this Christology can be found at least as far back in his writings as *Basic Christian Ethics*. See *Basic Christian Ethics*, 291-92.

5. Ramsey, *Speak Up for Just War or Pacifism*, 113.

6. Ramsey, *Speak Up for Just War or Pacifism*, 38.

7. Ramsey, *Speak Up for Just War or Pacifism*, 114. In the spirit of full disclosure, my ellipsis covers Ramsey's indication here that Barth had recovered more of the Biblical worldview than did Niebuhr. As I have suggested in earlier chapters, I take Niebuhr's critical account of Barthian Christology to be part of Niebuhr's recovery of the Christian tradition.

8. Ramsey, *Speak Up For Just War or Pacifism*, 22.

9. Ramsey, "The Church and the Magistrate," *Christianity and Crisis* 25, no. 11 (June 28, 1965), 136. Within the world of limited history, Ramsey writes, the statesman ought to know "something about the means that no end—and about the ends that no means—can warrant."

10. See Paul Ramsey, "Right and Wrong Calculation," 6-9

11. John Bennett to Paul Ramsey, 22 July 1965, Box 2, Paul Ramsey Papers, Duke University Library.

12. Paul Ramsey to John Bennett, 15 February 1966, Box 2, Paul Ramsey Papers, Duke University Library.

13. *Just and Unjust Wars* (New York: Basic Books, 1992), 280. For another critique that locates the problem with Ramsey's reasoning in his construal of intention, see Richard B. Miller, *Interpretations of Conflict*, 147-167.

14. Paul Ramsey, "Right and Wrong Calculation," 7. Italics mine. For Ramsey's consistency on this point compare the above with his comments in *The Patient as Person*, 5. Ramsey's comments in these two locations are profitably compared with Bosanquet's distinction between the moral standards applied to "a dog or a tree" as instruments of the good life and persons as "subjects of rights." See Bernard Bosanquet, *The Philosophical Theory of the State* (London: Macmillan and Company, 1920), 196.

15. Ramsey, *The Just War*, 129.

16. Ramsey, *The Just War*, 444, *f.*

17. Walzer writes that in treating deterrence, Ramsey "multiplies distinctions like a Ptolemaic astronomer with his epicycles and comes very close at the end to what G.E.M. Anscombe has called 'double-think about double effect.'" *Just and Unjust Wars*, 279.

18. Ramsey, *The Just War*, 429-30.

19. Ramsey, *The Just War*, 431.

20. When reviewing this manuscript, one reader suggested that I needed to think more deeply here about the costs of reducing moral language to consequentialism. I find it unfortunate that the post-Kantian moral imagination has become so limited as to equate proportionality with consequentialism. There is no necessity in this linking, and I am certainly not, in this section, discussing a consequentialist option.

21. Joseph Allen, "The Discriminating Realism of Paul Ramsey," *Worldview* 12 (December, 1969), 16. See also Joseph Allen, "'Necessities of State' and the Bellum Justum," *Worldview* 12 (January 1969), 18.

22. The arguments between proportionalists and deontologists have, especially in Catholic circles, been a topic of hot debate. Nor was Ramsey silent in these arguments. While Ramsey was never satisfied with them, Ramsey's exchanges with Richard

McCormick are an important part of this debate. See *Doing Evil to Achieve Good: moral choice in conflict situations*, ed. Richard A. McCormick and Paul Ramsey. For a more recent review of these arguments, see Paulinus Odozor "Proportionalists and the Principle of Double Effect: A Review Discussion" *Christian Bioethics* 3 (August, 1997), 115-31.

23. The magistrate "must determine what he *ought to do* from out of the total humanitarian good that *ought to be*. He is not even responsible for all of the *ought to be* that *ought to be politically done*, since there are other nations and other political actors in the world. He must locate his political obligation, and that of his nation, within an area of incidence between the national and the international common good." Ramsey, *The Just War*, 10.

24. Ramsey, *The Just War*, 152.

25. James Turner Johnson has been a leader in this movement. For his particular criticisms of Ramsey see "Just War in the Thought of Paul Ramsey," 203-5.

26. Ramsey, *Speak Up for Just War or Pacifism*, 54, 83.

27. Ramsey, *Speak Up for Just War or Pacifism*, 72, see also pp. 89.

28. Ramsey, *Speak Up for Just War or Pacifism*, 72.

29. At one point Ramsey writes of the two sides of the "coin" of love as regards war. Love first requires one to "deliver as many as possible of God's children from tyranny, and to protect from oppression." Secondly, love limits war's conduct. Ramsey, *The Just War*, 143. In such a description, it seems that those concerns that limit recourse to war are somehow extrinsic to love.

30. I am not suggesting that a Niebuhrian would favor a prima facie duty against war, as suggested by James Childress and others. Niebuhr's moral conception of war is different from Ramsey's and Childress' positions, and would challenge both to the extent that their claims to prima facie duties might obscure the reality and weight of the goods they do not stress. I am doubtful Niebuhr would find such "prima facie" generalizations useful in thinking about the particularities on which the justness of each war depends.

31. James Turner Johnson, "Paul Ramsey and the Recovery of the Just War Idea," 142.

32. Ramsey, *The Just War*, 10.

33. Ramsey, *The Just War*, 8.

34. Ramsey, *The Just War*, 455, see also 510. Italics mine.

35. Ramsey, *The Just War*, 526.

36. Ramsey, *The Just War*, 99.

37. James T. Johnson, *The War to Oust Saddam Hussein: Just War and the New Face of Conflict* (Lanham, Md.: Rowman & Littlefield Publishers, Inc., 2005), 25.

38. See, Ramsey, "Does the Church Have Any Political Wisdom for the 70's?" *Perkins Journal* 26, no.1 (Fall, 1972), 35-36.

39. Ramsey, "The Just Revolution," *Worldview*16, no. 10 (October, 1973), 40.

40. Ramsey, "Some Rejoinders," *Journal of Religious Ethics* 4, no.2 (Fall, 1976), 206.

41. See Howard Mickel, "Reinhold Niebuhr's Thought on War and Peace: An Analysis of the Development of His Views, 1916-1966." Unpublished PhD dissertation, Claremont Graduate School, 1969.

42. Niebuhr, *Moral Man and Immoral Society*, 271.

43. Niebuhr, *An Interpretation of Christian Ethics*, 75.

44. On Niebuhr's move away from his earlier "frank dualism" see Howard Mickel, "Reinhold Niebuhr's Thought on War and Peace," esp. 61.

45. Reinhold Niebuhr, *Love and Justice*, 233.

46. Reinhold Niebuhr, "Is the Bombing Necessary," 1-2. See also Niebuhr, "Soberness in Victory," *Christianity and Crisis* 5, no. 9 (May28, 1945), 1.

47. Niebuhr, *Love and Justice*, 233.

48. Niebuhr, *Love and Justice*, 233.

49. It is arguable whether a 'demonstration' of the bomb would have been effective. A government committee headed by the Secretary of War had cursorily reviewed and rejected the idea. See Jonathan Glover, *Humanity: A Moral History of the Twentieth Century* (New Haven, Conn.: Yale University Press, 2001), 95. See also Charles Brown, *Niebuhr and His Age*, 123.

50. See Walzer, *Just and Unjust Wars*, 263-268. It is notable that Niebuhr does not seem to have given a negotiated settlement much thought.

51. Niebuhr's suggestion that the statesmen involved in choosing the bombing by "historic forces more powerful than any human decision" should also be criticized. I have already commented on Niebuhr's overly pessimistic account of the forces of history. See Chapter 3.

52. Quoted in Richard Fox, *Reinhold Niebuhr: A Biography*, 224-25.

53. James Childress, "Niebuhr's Realistic-Pragmatic Approach to War and 'the Nuclear Dilemma'" in *Reinhold Niebuhr and the Issues of Our Time*, ed. Richard Harries, 132.

54. Reinhold Niebuhr, "Editorials," *Christianity and Society* 16, no. 2 (Spring, 1951), 4.

55. Niebuhr, "Editorials," *Christianity and Society* 16, no. 2 (Spring, 1951), 5.

56. Reinhold Niebuhr, "The Developments in Indo-China" *Christianity and Society* 19, no. 4 (1954), 4.

57. Reinhold Niebuhr, "America and the Asians," *The New Leader* 37, no. 22 (May 31, 1954), 4. See also Reinhold Niebuhr, "Frustration of American Power," *The New Leader* 37, no. 28 (November 29, 1954), 7-8.

58. Reinhold Niebuhr, "Foreign Policy in a New Context," in *Faith and Politics*, 256, "Vietnam and the Imperial Conflict," *The New Leader*, 49, n. 12 (June 6, 1966), 16-17, "Vietnam: The Tide begins to Turn," *Christianity and Crisis*, 16 (October 17, 1966), 221, and "Without Advice and Consent," *The New Leader* 50, no. 17 (August 28, 1967), 6.

59. Stone, "An Interview with Reinhold Niebuhr," 48.

60. Reinhold Niebuhr, "Vietnam Elections," *Christianity and Crisis* 27 (September 18, 1967), 200.

61. For a more detailed treatment of Niebuhr and Ramsey's works during Vietnam see chapters 11-13 in Kevin Carnahan "Sin, Guilt, Justice and War".

62. John Kelsay, "Issues in just war and jihad traditions with respect to U.S./Iraq conflicts, 1989-2005," (lecture, American Academy of Religion National Meeting, Philadelphia, Pa., November 19, 2005).

63. Stone, "An Interview with Reinhold Niebuhr," 50.

64. Ramsey, *The Just War*, 487.

65. Ramsey, "War and Peace as a Religious Issue," 17-18. Unpublished manuscript, Box 39, The Paul Ramsey Papers, Duke University Library.

66. Ramsey, *The Just War*, 458.

67. As Ramsey writes: "In this we must appeal from Niebuhr drunk to Niebuhr sober." Ramsey "War and Peace as a Religious Issue," 23-24. See also Ramsey, *The Just War*, 488.

68. Ramsey, "Lefever Testimony," 6. Box 15, The Paul Ramsey Papers, Duke University Library.

Conclusion

The debate is not over. Today in America some theologians focus upon the dangerous growth of individualism, abstract rationalism, and facile instrumental reason in contemporary society. Modernity, they lament, is marked by a loss of respect for moral, communal, and institutional authority and structure. In this climate morality is reduced to individual style and preference. To avoid a dilution of our moral identities, they argue, we must reclaim continuity with established traditions, narratives, and structured communities. Reason, knowledge, morality, and meaning, these theologians aver, do not exist apart from the ethos embodied in lives lived within our social institutions. Some of these theologians push for a return to earlier traditional natural law categories of moral analysis. Others claim natural law itself is problematic and advocate for a more pure communally grounded Christian ethic.

Other theologians find solace in the rich diversity of contemporary church and society. They stress the activity of God in breaking down paternalistic systems of the past and allowing for a common search for the good where the voices from many perspectives are allowed greater possibilities of meaningful expression and contribution. God is seen at work in the tensions of social interaction, restraining sin by holding groups responsible to each other and liberating people to greater participation in the creation of political community. Standing against temptations to tribalism, nationalism, or sectarianism, these theologians emphasize the need to remain open to God's judgment against these structures. Even the institutional Church needs to remain open to criticism, pointing out its own failings and partiality within history.

The tensions between these two groups of theologians can be tied to a variety of sources, but the influence of pragmatism and idealism are certainly important factors in creating the current landscape of debate. The arguments amongst these theologians find their place in a debate with important links to an earlier epoch in American intellectual culture.

In the end, Niebuhr and Ramsey occupy a small part in the broader story of the ongoing debate between pragmatists and idealists. Ramsey's work mixes with the thought of other idealistically influenced scholars like Alasdair MacIntyre.[1] The pragmatism that informed Niebuhr's work can still be found informing the works of Cornel West and others. From James and Royce to contemporary debate there is a continuity of shape that ought not to be denied.

It also does not take long to find evidence of the shift in theological argument in which Ramsey and Niebuhr took part. Often theologians, especially those more influenced by idealism, question the faithfulness of their opponent's theology. Pointing to the corrosive individualism and decadence of "modern" philosophy, they associate their opponent with pragmatism or some other branch of modernity, and thus are able to set aside the content of her or his thought. The opponent, it is contended is merely doing secular philosophy under the cover of theological language. This, of course, hides the ways in which all of the participants are indebted to *modern* modes of thinking, whether they be idealist or pragmatist.[2]

Many participating in these arguments are ignorant of their own oversimplifications. In the middle of the century most theologians followed Ramsey and Niebuhr in shifting to more explicitly theological grounding for their arguments. Theologians today may not even be aware of the extent to which their own work is reflective of the ongoing debate between idealism and pragmatism in American intellectual culture. What is needed then is a new, more honest analysis that takes seriously the ways in which all contemporary theologies are related to their modern predecessors. Adherence to the Christian tradition is important, but the multivalence of this tradition has admitted influence from many historical sources and has produced multiple moral languages for coping with a sin stained world. It is to be hoped that full disclosure in this ongoing theological debate might lead to more profitable avenues of dialogue, and shortcut some of the oversimplification that takes place in the contemporary debate.

There is reason to be optimistic about the future of dialogue between idealism and pragmatism. Jeffrey Stout's recent work in relating the two schools is promising. He has located a pragmatic movement embedded in a broader American democratic tradition.[3] His work has allowed for understandings of pragmatism and idealism that bridge some of the gap between James' at times overly thin empiricism and Hegel's at times overly closed notion of traditional reason. I have drawn on this analysis in my own rendering of pragmatism as a tradition in this work. It remains to be seen, however, how much impact these philosophical moves will have on contemporary theology. There are hurdles to applying Stout's work to theology. Theologians influenced by pragmatism may wonder about whether the general framework Stout has provided allows sufficient space to speak of the transcendence of God above all human institutions and traditions. Theologians influenced by idealism may still wonder about the fruitfulness of dialogue among the varieties of democratic and religious traditions. Yet, this is at least reason for hope. Given the affinities of these philosophical schools and their theological counterparts, a new period of creative interaction between philosophy and theology may be at hand.

Niebuhr and Ramsey after the Cold War

In the midst of this dialogue the distinctive contributions of Reinhold Niebuhr and Paul Ramsey ought not to be forgotten. Since their passing the world has changed, and the world has remained the same. Nation states are no longer the dominant powers they once were. Globalization of religion, industry, technology, and weaponry has transformed power relations among people and communities. New political movements have shaken American public life and challenged settled assumptions about social stability that reigned in Niebuhr's and Ramsey's day. Niebuhr's and Ramsey's world was in many ways a very different one from the world we know. Yet just as the pragmatic and idealistic traditions remain relevant, so do the perspectives espoused by Niebuhr and Ramsey. In recent decades American culture has continued to exhibit modes of fanaticism and individualistic relativism that are ripe for critiques from both positions.

The collapse of the global bipolar power structure of the Cold War has created a new context for the use of military force. In the power vacuum left after the collapse of the superpower system modes of local authoritarianism, tribalism, and tyranny have led to massive abuses of human rights around the globe. At the same time the collapse of clear spheres of superpower control has both opened the possibilities for military humanitarian intervention around the globe and made it unclear who is responsible for undertaking such intervention. As recent and ongoing catastrophes in Africa have illustrated, nations have been reticent in taking up this responsibility. Without the narrative of superpower spheres of responsibilities, it has been difficult to motivate nations to take significant action in foreign lands. America has often found itself an irresponsible steward of the power it has in international relations. This was especially the case after the events in Somalia. Ramsey's understanding of the ways in which military activity can be a manifestation of covenantal responsibility has a place in establishing new frameworks for conceiving of the proper use of American military action in the present world. His analysis of the weakness of American liberalism says a great deal about why the United States and other western powers are at times absent at moments when their power is most needed.

But this is not the only analysis that is needed. Even as America withdrew from some of its international responsibilities during the 1990s, another more aggressive narrative was being constructed within American culture. After the collapse of the Cold War the United States emerged as the preeminent national power in the world, and it appeared to those steeped in modern state theory that a new pax Americana might be at hand. Oversimplified visions of a global wave of democracy led to great hopes, and temptations to abuses of power. The second Bush administration came into office with such hopes, and the attacks of September 11th provided a political opportunity to act upon them. An ill planned, disproportionate war in Iraq was soon added to the reasonable military reaction in Afghanistan. Overreach in military policy has now led to a diminishment of effective American power around the globe. New nuclear powers flaunt their disagreements with Washington while reveling in Americas gaffes. No doubt, Niebuhr would have appreciated the irony of the situation into which America has placed itself. He would also, without diminishing America's realistic responsibilities, have spoken out against the pretensions of a nation that thought itself the bearer of democracy and the guarantor of a new order for the world. Calls for a new Reinhold Niebuhr in American political life are now increasingly heard from editorialists and political pundits who long for a realistic critique of contemporary excesses. No doubt the culture would be aided by such a figure.

Nor should Niebuhr's and Ramsey's critiques be limited to international affairs. American social life continues to change, and moral dangers are exhibited in the shifting of domestic political and cultural trends. Ramsey's and Niebuhr's positions still have important points to make when dealing with the social arrangements in the United States.

In recent decades sociologists have noted a decline in American social institutions.[4] At the same time the scope of individual rights demanded by the populace continues to grow. Many Americans would rather enjoy privatized entertainment than participate in social interaction with their peers. At the same time, globalization and the development of new technologies have led to an increase in the number or people we interact with at a distance, while decreasing the intimacy and meaningfulness of these interactions. As a result, the substance of our moral relations often seems frayed. The balance between individual and society, these sociologists fear, has tipped dangerously toward individualistic chaos. No doubt Ramsey would have much to say about the need to combat this erosion of the sense of a common good within society. New thought needs to be given to how our society can recapture the covenantal core of relationships both by rolling back some new developments and by learning how to deepen existing relationships in an ever more technological world.

The paradox of globalization, however, has also led to the rise of a new communitarianism in American politics. While globalization has broken down many traditional barriers, it has also given rise to discomfort among many who wish to hold onto what they perceive as traditional values. Adopting a siege mentality, many groups have adopted modes of identity politics structured to protect their own sectarian projects or to proselytize by means of coercive political power. Some Christian groups have emerged into public dialogue claiming to carry divine mandates to which civil law should be adjusted. Political parties have recognized the influence of these groups and have begun shaping their messages and platforms to sustain their support. Political parties themselves have also found the power in appealing to extreme tendencies in the American populace and focusing on their "base" at the cost of reasonable compromise. Each party advances by stirring up the most fanatic of its constituents, thus bringing about stalemate in domestic politics and garnering extreme frustration from all political participants. Niebuhr would remind us of the need for humility and realism in these debates. No constituency should expect the government to solve all of the world's problems (much less to solve all of its problems overnight), and no political party should become so enamored of its own platform that it refuses to do what is necessary to achieve the partial progress that history affords. Those who confuse their own political projects with God's bring judgment upon themselves and their societies. Without a genuine respect for the God that transcends all our political parties, it may be impossible to live with one another in a sinful world.

These are only the beginnings of points that ought to be more fully explored in the ongoing debate in American moral theology. We live in a complex culture and perceiving and reacting appropriately to the social dangers we face requires appeal to a wide range of different perspectives. Idealist and pragmatic Christians are needed in the ongoing debate about and search for the relatively good life in a sin stained world. Niebuhr's and Ramsey's theologies provide building blocks for further development and fruitful application.

In the end, we can find some comfort in the ongoing debates within American culture generally, and within American moral theology in particular. They are not in all cases evidence of faithlessness on the part of one party or the other. Rather, as Niebuhr and Ramsey did, many in the contemporary situation approach a common point from different perspectives. These perspectives enrich our vision of the good, and provide us a fuller view of the goodness of God that in the end transcends all human expression. With fear and trembling we continue the discussion.

Notes

1. On MacIntyre and Hegel, see Stout, *Democracy and Tradition*, 137-38.

2. One can draw parallels here with MacIntyre's arguments in philosophy. See *Democracy and Tradition*, 137-39.

3. See Stout, *Democracy and Tradition*.

4. See, for instance, Robert Bellah, et al. *Habits of the Heart: Individualism and commitment in American life* (Berkeley, Calif.: University of California Press, 1985), and Robert Putnam, *Bowling alone: The collapse and revival of American community* (New York: Simon & Schuster, 2000).

Bibliography

Allen, Joseph L. *Love and Conflict: A Covenantal Model of Christian Ethics*. Lanham, Md.: University Press of America, 1995.

———. "'Necessities of State' and Bellum Justum," *Worldview* 12 (January 1969): 16-18.

———. "Paul Ramsey and his Respondents since *The Patient as Person*," *Religious Studies Review* 5, no. 2 (April, 1979), 89-95.

———. "The Discriminating Realism of Paul Ramsey," *Worldview* 12 (December, 1969): 13-17.

Attwood, David. *Paul Ramsey's Political Ethics*. Lanham, Md.: Rowman & Littlefield Publishers, Inc., 1992.

Augustine. *Concerning the City of God Against the Pagans*, trans. Henry Bettenson. New York: Penguin Books, 1972.

Barth, Karl. *The Epistle to the Romans*, trans. Edwyn C. Hoskyns. New York: Oxford University Press, 1933.

———. *The Word of God and the Word of Man*, trans. Douglas Horton. Chicago: Pilgrim Press, 1928.

Beinart, Peter. "The Rehabilitation of the Cold-War Liberal" *The New York Times Magazine* (April 30, 2006). http://www.nytimes.com/2006/4/30/magazine/0liberal.html?_r=1&oref=slogin (accessed May 1, 2006).

Bellah, Robert, et al. *Habits of the Heart :Individualism and commitment in American life*. Berkeley, Calif.: University of California Press, 1985.

Bennett, John. "A Critique of Paul Ramsey," *Christianity and Crisis* 27, no. 18 (October 30, 1967), 247.

Bethge, Eberhard. "The Challenge of Dietrich Bonhoeffer's Life and Theology," in *World Come of Age*, ed. Ronald Gregor Smith. Philadelphia, Pa.: Fortress Press, 1967.

Bobbit, Phillip. *The Shield of Achilles: War, Peace, and the Course of History*. New York: Alfred A. Knopf, 2002.

Bosanquet, Bernard. *Science and Philosophy, and Other Essays*. Freeport, N.Y.: Books for Libraries Press, 1927.

———. *Social and International Ideals: Being Studies in Patriotism*. London: Macmillan and Company, 1917.

———. *The Philosophical Theory of the State*. London: Macmillan and Company, 1920.

Boucher, David, ed. *The British Idealists*. New York: Cambridge University Press, 1997.

Brown, Charles C. *Niebuhr and His Age: Reinhold Niebuhr's Prophetic Role and Legacy*. Harrisburg, Pa.: Trinity Press International, 2002.

Brunner, Emil. *Justice and the Social Order*, trans. Mary Hottinger. New York: Harper and Brothers, 1945.

Busch, Eberhard. *Karl Barth: His Life from Letters and Autobiographical Texts*, trans. John Bowden. Grand Rapids, Mich.: William B. Eerdmans Publishing Co., 1976.

Cahill, Lisa Sowle. *Love Your Enemies: Discipleship, Pacifism, and Just War Theory*. Minneapolis: Fortress Press, 1994.

Calvin, John. *Institutes of the Christian Religion*, ed. John T. McNeill, trans. Ford Lewis Battles. Louisville, Ky.: Westminster John Knox Press, 1960.

Carnahan, Kevin. "Sin, guilt, justice and war: Paul Ramsey and Reinhold Niebuhr on the moral framework for just war thought." Unpublished Ph.D. Dissertation, Southern Methodist University, 2007.

Childress, James. "Just War Tradition and the Invasion of Iraq," Churches' Center for Theology and Public Policy, http://www.cctpp.org/archives/childresspaper.htm. (accessed July 8, 2006).

———. *Moral Responsibility in Conflicts: Essays on Nonviolence, War, and Conscience*. Baton Rouge, La.: Louisiana State University Press, 1982.

Cranz, F. Edward. *An Essay on the Development of Luther's Thought on Justice, Law, and Society*. London: Oxford University Press, 1959.

Curran, Charles. *Politics, Medicine, and Christian Ethics: A Dialogue with Paul Ramsey*. Philadelphia, Pa.: Fortress Press, 1973.

Douglass, R. Bruce. "Paul Ramsey in Review: Who Speaks for the Church?" 55-62 in *Moral Issues and Christian Response*, ed. Paul T. Jersild and Dale A. Johnson. New York: Holt, Rinehart and Winston, 1971.

Elstain, Jean Bethke. *Just War Against Terror: The Burden of American Power in a Violent World*. New York: Basic Books, 2003.

Fox, Richard. *Reinhold Niebuhr: A Biography*. Ithaca, N.Y.: Cornell University Press, 1996.

Gilkey, Langdon. *On Niebuhr: A Theological Study*. Chicago: University of Chicago Press, 2001.

Glover, Jonathan. *Humanity: A Moral History of the Twentieth Century*. New Haven, Conn.: Yale University Press, 2001.

Green, T.H. *Lectures on the Principles of Political Obligation*. London: Longmans, 1941.

Halliwell, Martin. *The Constant Dialogue*. Lanham, Md.: Rowman & Littlefield, 2005.

Harries, Richard, ed. *Reinhold Niebuhr and the Issues of Our Time*. Grand Rapids, Mich.: W.B. Eerdmans, 1986.

Harris, Charles. "Love as the Basic Moral Principle in Paul Ramsey's Ethics," *Journal of Religious Ethics* 4 (Fall, 1976): 239-258.

Hauerwas, Stanley. *With the Grain of the Universe: The Church's Witness and Natural Theology*. Grand Rapids, Mich: Brazos Press, 2001.

Hegel, G.W.F. "The Constitution of Germany," in *Hegel's Political Writings*, trans. T.M. Knox. Oxford: Clarendon Press, 1998.

———. *Hegel's Philosophy of Right*, trans. T.M. Knox. Oxford: Clarendon Press, 1967.

Hendel, Charles W. "The Meaning of Obligation," in *Contemporary Idealism in America*, ed. Clifford Barret. New York: The Macmillan Company, 1932.

Hollenbach, David. *Nuclear Ethics: A Christian Moral Argument*. New York: Paulist Press, 1983.

———. *The Common Good and Christian Ethics*. New York: Cambridge University Press, 2002.

Holms, Arthur F., ed., *War and Christian Ethics: Classic and Contemporary Readings on the Morality of War*. Grand Rapids, Mich.: Baker Academic, 2005.

Hoover, Arlie. *The Gospel of Nationalism: German Patriotic Preaching from Napoleon to Versailles*. Stuttgart: F. Steiner Wiesbaden, 1986.

Hunsinger, George. *How to Read Karl Barth: The Shape of his Theology*. New York: Oxford University Press, 1993.

James, William. *Essays on Faith and Morals*, ed. Ralph Perry. New York: Meridian Books, 1962.

———. *Pragmatism*. Buffalo, N.Y.: Prometheus Books, 1991.

———. "The Moral Equivalent to War" in *The Writings of William James: A Comprehensive Edition*, ed. John H. McDermott. Chicago: The University of Chicago Press, 1977.

Johnson, James T. *Ideology, Reason, and The Limitation of War: Religious and Secular Concepts, 1200-1740* Princeton, N.J.: Princeton University Press, 1975.

———. "Just War in the Thought of Paul Ramsey," *The Journal of Religious Ethics* 19, no. 2 (1991) 183-207.

———. *The Just War Tradition and the Restraint of War: A Moral and Historical Inquiry*. Princeton, N.J.: Princeton University Press, 1981.

———. "Paul Ramsey and the Recovery of the Just War Idea," *Journal of Military Ethics* 1, No. 2 (July, 2002): 136-144.

———. *The War to Oust Saddam Hussein: Just War and the New Face of Conflict*. Lanham, Md.: Rowman & Littlefield Publishers, Inc., 2005.

Johnson, James T. and David H. Smith, eds. *Love and Society: Essays in the Ethics of Paul Ramsey*. Missoula, Mont.: Scholars Press, 1974.

Kant, Immanuel. "Perpetual Peace: A Philosophical Sketch" in *Kant: Political Writings*, trans. H.B. Nesbit, ed. Hans Reiss. New York: Cambridge University Press, 1991.

Kegley, C.W. and R.W. Bretall, eds. *Reinhold Niebuhr: His Religious, Social, and Political Thought*. New York: The Macmillan Company, 1956.

Kelsay, John. "Issues in just war and jihad traditions with respect to U.S./Iraq conflicts, 1989-2005," lecture, American Academy of Religion National Meeting, Philadelphia, Pa., November 19, 2005.

Kierkegaard, Søren. *Concluding Unscientific Postscript to "Philosophical Fragments."* trans. Howard V. Hong and Edna H. Hong. Princeton, N.J.: Princeton University Press, 1992.

Kuklick, Bruce. *A History of Philosophy in America, 1720-2000*. Oxford: Clarendon Press, 2001.

Loconte, Joseph. "The War Party's Theologian: President Bush carries on the liberal tradition of Reinhold Niebuhr," *Opinion Journal, from The Wall Street Journal Editorial Page* (May 31, 2002). http://www.opinionjournal.com/taste/?id=110001782 (accessed April 30, 2006).

Long, D. Stephen. *Tragedy, Tradition, Transformism: The Ethics of Paul Ramsey*. Boulder, Colo.: Westview Press, 1993.

Lovin, Robin. *Christian Faith and Public Choices*. Philadelphia, Pa.: Fortress Press, 1984.

———. *Reinhold Niebuhr and Christian Realism*. New York: Cambridge University Press, 1995.

Luther, Martin. *A Commentary on St. Paul's Epistle to the Galatians*, ed. Philip S. Watson. Westwood, N.J.: Fleming H. Revell Company, 1953.

———. *Martin Luther: Selections From his Writings*, ed. John Dillenberger. New York: Doubleday, 1962.

———. *Martin Luther's Basic Theological Writings*, ed. Timothy F. Lull. Minneapolis: Fortress Press, 1989.

Macintosh, D.C. *The Pilgrimage of Faith in the World of Modern Thought*. Calcutta: The University of Calcutta, 1931.

MacIntyre, Alasdair. *A Short History of Ethics: A History of Moral Philosophy from the Homeric Age to the Twentieth Century*. Notre Dame: University of Notre Dame Press, 1997.

Markus, R. A. *Saeculum: History and Society in the Theology of St. Augustine*. New York: Cambridge University Press, 1988.

McCormick, Richard and Paul Ramsey, eds. *Doing Evil to Achieve Good: Moral Choice in Conflict Situations*, Chicago: Loyola University Press, 1978.

McKenzie, Michael C. *Paul Ramsey's Ethics: The power of 'Agape' in a Post-modern World*. Westport, Conn.: Praeger, 2001.

McKeogh, Colm. *The Political Realism of Reinhold Niebuhr: A Pragmatic Approach to Just War*. New York: St. Martin's Press, 1997.

McNeill, John T. "Natural Law in the Thought of Luther," *Church History* 10 (1941), 211-227.

Menand, Louis. *The Metaphysical Club*. New York: Farrar, Straus, and Giroux, 2001.

Merten, Thomas. "Hegel's Homage to Kant's Perpetual Peace: an Analysis of Hegel's *Philosophy of Right* §§ 321-340," *The Review of Politics* 57, no. 4 (Fall, 1995): 665-691

Mickel, Howard. "Reinhold Niebuhr's Thought on War and Peace: An Analysis of the Development of His Views, 1916-1966." Unpublished PhD dissertation, Claremont Graduate School, 1969.

Milbank, John. *Theology and Social Theory: Beyond Secular* Reason. Cambridge, Mass.: Blackwell, 1991.

Miller, Richard B. *Interpretations of Conflict*. Chicago: University of Chicago Press, 1991.

Murray, John Courtney. *We Hold These Truths: Catholic Reflections on the American Proposition*. New York: Sheed and Ward, 1960.

Neuhaus, Richard John. *Speaking to the World: Four Protestant Perspectives*. Washington D.C.: Ethics and Public Policy Centre, 1983.

———. ed. *Reinhold Niebuhr Today*. Grand Rapids, Mich.: Wm. B. Eerdmans, 1989.

Niebuhr, H. Richard. *Radical Monotheism and Western Culture, With Supplementary Essays*. Louisville, Ky.: Westminster/John Knox Press, 1993.

———. *The Responsible Self: An Essay in Christian Moral Philosophy*. New York: Harper & Row, 1963.

Niebuhr, Reinhold. "America and the Asians," *The New Leader* 37, no. 22 (May 31, 1954): 3-4.

———. *Children of Light and Children of Darkness: A Vindication of Democracy and a Critique of its Traditional Defence*. New York: Charles Scribner's Sons, 1944.

———. "Christ and the Meaning of Our Existence," *Episcopal Churchnews*, 119, no. 24 (Nov. 28, 1954): 8.

———. "Christ vs. Socrates," *The Saturday Review* 37, no. 51 (December 18, 1954): 7-8, 37-39.

———. "Christ, The Hope of the World," *The Messenger* 19, no. 15 (August 10, 1954): 9.

———. "Christian Faith and Political Controversy," *Christianity and Crisis* 12, no. 13 (July 21, 1952): 87-98.
———. *Christian Realism and Political Problems*. London: Faber and Faber Limited, 1953.
———. "The Christian Witness in a Secular Age," *The Christian Century* 70, no. 29 (July 22, 1953): 840-843.
———. *Christianity and Power Politics*. New York: Charles. Scribner's Sons, 1940.
———. "The Climax of War," *Christianity and Crisis* 4, no. 9 (May 29, 1944):1-2.
———. "The Concept of Orders of Creation in Emil Brunner's Social Ethic," 265-271 in *The Theology of Emil Brunner*, ed. Charles W. Kegley. New York: Macmillan, 1962.
———. "The Developments in Indo-China," *Christianity and Society* 19, no. 4 (1954): 4.
———. "Editorials," *Christianity and Society* 16, no. 2 (Spring, 1951), 3-8.
———. *Essays in Applied Christianity*, ed. D.B. Robertson. New York: Meridian Books, 1959.
———. *The Essential Reinhold Niebuhr*, ed. Robert McAfee Brown. New Haven, Conn.: Yale University Press, 1986.
———. *Faith and History: A Comparison of Christian and Modern Views of History*. New York: Charles Scribner's Sons, 1949.
———. *Faith and Politics: A Commentary on Religious, Social and Political Thought in a Technological Age*, ed. Ronald Stone. New York: George Braziller, 1968.
———. "Frustration of American Power," *The New Leader* 37, no. 28 (November 29, 1954): 7-8.
———. *An Interpretation of Christian Ethics*. New York: Meridian Books, 1956.
———. "Is the Bombing Necessary," *Christianity and Crisis* 4, no. 5 (April 3, 1944): 1-2.
———. "The King's Chapel and the King's Court," *Christianity and Crisis* 29, no. 14 (August 4, 1969): 211-213.
———. "Kinsey and the Moral Problem of Man's Sexual Life," in *An Analysis of the Kinsey Reports on Sexual Behavior in the Human Male and Female*. New York: Dutton, 1954.
———. *Love and Justice: Selections from the Shorter Writings of Reinhold Niebuhr*, ed. D. B. Robertson. Philadelphia, Pa.: The Westminster Press, 1957.
———. *Man's Nature and His Communities: Essays on the Dynamics and Enigmas of Man's Personal and Social Existence*. New York: Charles Scribner's Sons, 1965.

———. *Moral Man and Immoral Society: A Study in Ethics and Politics*. Louisville, Ky.: Westminster John Knox Press, 2001
———. "Must We Do Nothing?" 422-425 in *From Christ to the World: Introductory Readings in Christian Ethics*. ed. W. Boulton, T. Kennedy, and A. Verhey. Grand Rapids, Mich.: W.B. Eerdmans Publishing Company, 1994.
———. "The Nation's Crime against the Individual," *The Atlantic Monthly* (November, 1916), 609-614.
———. "National Pride vs. the Church," *The Lutheran* 37, no. 6 (November 10, 1954): 12-13.
———. *The Nature and Destiny of Man*, 2 vols. New York: Charles Scribner's Sons, 1964.
———. "Our Responsibilities in 1942," *Christianity and Crisis* 1, no. 24 (January 12, 1942): 1-2.
———. "Piety and Politics," *Christianity and Society* 18, no. 3 (Summer, 1953): 3-4
———. "Politics in the Church," *The Lutheran* 31, no. 50 (September 14, 1949): 19.
———. "Prayer and a Global Civilization," *Christianity and Crisis* 4, no. 15 (September 18, 1944): 1-2.
———. "The Problem of a Protestant Social Ethic," *Union Seminary Quarterly Review* 15, no.1 (November, 1959): 1-11.
———. "The Quality of Our Lives," *The Christian Century* 77, no. 19 (May 11, 1960), 568-572.
———. "Religious Politics," *Christianity and Society* 16, no. 4 (February 14, 1951): 4-5.
———. "Soberness in Victory," *Christianity and Crisis* 5, no. 9 (May 28, 1945): 1-2.
———. *The Structure of Nations and Empires: A Study of the Recurring Patterns and Problems of the Political Order in Relation to the Unique Problems of the Nuclear Age*. New York: Charles Scribner's Sons, 1959.
———. "Ten Years that Shook My World," *The Christian Century* 56, no. 17 (April 26, 1939): 542-546.
———. "Vietnam and the Imperial Conflict," *The New Leader*, 49, no. 12 (June 6, 1966): 15-18.
———. "The Vietnam Elections," *Christianity and Crisis* 27, no. 15 (September 18, 1967): 199-200.
———. "Vietnam: The Tide begins to Turn," *Christianity and Crisis*, 16 (October 17, 1966): 221-223.
———. "Why They Dislike America," *The New Leader* 37, no. 15 (April 12, 1954), 3-5.
———. "Without Advice and Consent," *The New Leader* 50, no. 17 (August 28, 1967): 5-6.

Niebuhr, Reinhold, and Angus Dun, "God Wills Both Justice and Peace," *Christianity and Crisis* 15, no. 10 (June 13, 1955): 75-78.

Niebuhr, Reinhold and Paul Sigmund. *The Democratic Experience*. New York: Fredrick A. Prager, 1969.

Nussbaum, Martha. *The Fragility of Goodness: Luck and Ethics in Greek Tragedy and Philosophy*. New York: Cambridge University Press, 2001.

O'Donovan, Oliver. *The Just War Revisited.* New York: Cambridge University Press, 2003.

Odozor, Paulinus. "Proportionalists and the Principle of Double Effect: A Review Discussion," *Christian Bioethics* 3 (August, 1997): 115-131.

Outka, Gene. *Agape: An Ethical Analysis*. New Haven, Conn.: Yale University Press, 1972.

Pope, Stephen J., ed. *The Ethics of Aquinas*. Washington D.C.: Georgetown University Press, 2002.

Putnam, Hilary. *The Many Faces of Realism*. La Salle, Ill.: Open Court, 1987.

———. *Reason Truth and History*. New York: Cambridge University Press, 1981.

Putnam, Robert, *Bowling Alone: The collapse and revival of American community*. New York: Simon & Schuster, 2000.

Ramsey, Paul. *Basic Christian Ethics*. Louisville, Ky.: Westminster/John Knox Press, 1993.

———. "Beyond the Confusion of Tongues," *Theology Today* 3, no. 4 (January, 1947): 446-458.

———. "The Case of the Curious Exception," 67-135 in *Norm and Context in Christian Ethics*, ed. Gene Outka and Paul Ramsey. New York: Charles Scribner's Sons, 1968.

———. *Christian Ethics and the Sit-In*. New York: Association Press, 1961.

———. "The Church and the Magistrate," *Christianity and Crisis* 25, no. 11 (June 28, 1965): 136-140.

———. *Deeds and Rules in Christian Ethics*. New York: Charles Scribner's Sons, 1967.

———. "Does the Church Have Any Political Wisdom for the 70's?" *Perkins Journal* 26, no.1 (Fall, 1972): 29-40.

———. "Election Issues 1968," *Social Action* 35, no. 2 (September-October, 1968): 18-28.

———. "*Existenz* and the Existence of God: A Study of Kierkegaard and Hegel," *Journal of Religion* 28, no. 3 (July, 1948): 157-176.

———. "Faith Effective Through In-Principled Love," *Christianity and Crisis* 20 (May 30, 1960): 76-78.

———. "Force and Political Responsibility," 43-73 in *Ethics and World Politics,* ed. Ernest Lefever. Baltimore, Md.: Johns Hopkins Press, 1972.

———. "The Idealistic View of Moral Evil: Josiah Royce and Bernard Bosanquet," *Philosophy and Phenomenological Research* 6, no. 4 (June, 1946): 554-89.
———. "Is God Mute in the Goldwater Candidacy," *Christianity and Crisis* 24, no.15 (Spring, 1964), 175-178.
———. "The Just Revolution," *Worldview* 16, no. 10 (October, 1973): 37-40.
———. *The Just War: Force and Political Responsibility*. Lanham, Md.: Rowman & Littlefield, 2002.
———. "The Just War Theory on Trial," *Cross Currents* 13, n. 14 (Fall, 1963): 477-490.
———. "The Manger, Cross and the Resurrection," *Christianity and Crisis* 3, no. 6 (April 16, 1943): 2-5.
———. "Natural Law and the Nature of Man," *Christendom* 9, no. 3 (Summer, 1944): 369-381.
———. "The Nature of Man in the Philosophy of Josiah Royce and Bernard Bosanquet." Unpublished Ph.D. Dissertation, Yale University, 1943.
———. *Nine Modern Moralists*. Englewood Cliffs, N.J.: Prentice-Hall, Inc., 1962.
———. "Paul Ramsey Replies," *Christianity and Crisis* 27 (November 27, 1967): 280-282.
———. *The Patient as Person: Explorations in Medical Ethics*. New Haven, Conn.: Yale University Press, 2002.
———. "Political Repentance Now!" *Christianity and Crisis* 28, no. 18 (October 28, 1968): 247-252.
———. "Politics as Science, Not Prophecy," *Worldview* 11, no. 1 (January, 1968): 18-21.
———. "Right and Wrong Calculation," *Worldview* 2, no. 12 (December, 1959): 6-9.
———. "A Social Policy for Liberal Religion," *Religion in Life* 13, no. 4 (Autumn, 1944): 495-507.
———. "Some Rejoinders," *Journal of Religious Ethics* 4 (Fall 1976): 185-237.
———. *Speak up for Just War or Pacifism: A Critique of the United Methodist Bishops' Pastoral Letter 'In Defense of Creation.'* University Park, Pa.: Pennsylvania State University Press, 1988.
———. "The Theory of Democracy: Idealistic or Christian?" *Ethics* 56, no. 4 (July, 1946): 251-266.
———. "Two Extremes: Ramsey Replies to His Critics," *Dialogue* 6, no. 3 (Summer, 1967): 218-219.
———. "War and Peace as a Religious Issue," unpublished manuscript (1968?), Box 39, The Paul Ramsey Papers, Duke University Library.
———. *War and the Christian Conscience*. Durham, N.C.: Duke University Press, 1961.
———. *Who Speaks for the Church?* Nashville, Tenn.: Abingdon Press,1967.

Rauschenbusch, Walter. *Christianity and the Social Crisis*. New York: The Macmillan Company, 1916.

———. *A Theology for the Social Gospel*. Louisville, Ky.: Westminster/John Knox Press, 1997.

Rovere, Richard H. *The American Establishment and Other Reports, Opinions and Speculations*. New York: Harcourt, Brace & World, 1962.

Santurri, Edmund. "Christian Realism and the 'Law of Peoples.'" *Journal of Religious Ethics* 33, no. 4 (December 2005): 783-814.

———. *Perplexity in the Moral Life: Philosophical and Theological Considerations*. Charlottesville, Va.: University Press of Virginia, 1987.

Schneewind, J. B. *The Invention of Autonomy: A History of Modern Moral Philosophy*. New York: Cambridge University Press, 1998.

Simmons, J. Aaron and David Wood. *Kierkegaard and Levinas: Ethics, Politics, and Religion*. Bloomington, Ind.: Indiana University Press, 2008.

Stassen, Glen, ed. *Just Peacemaking: Ten Practices for Abolishing War*. Cleveland, Ohio: The Pilgrim Press, 1998.

Stone, Ronald. *Christian Realism and Peacemaking: Issues in U.S. Foreign Policy*. Nashville, Tenn.: Abingdon Press, 1988.

———. "An Interview with Reinhold Niebuhr," *Christianity and Crisis* 29 (March 17, 1969): 48-52.

———. *Professor Reinhold Niebuhr: A Mentor to the Twentieth Century*. Louisville, Ky.: Westminster/John Knox Press, 1992.

———. *Prophetic Realism: Beyond Militarism and Pacifism in an Age of Terror*. New York: T&T Clark, 2005.

———. *Reinhold Niebuhr: Prophet to Politicians*. Nashville, Tenn.: Abingdon Press, 1972.

Stout, Jeffrey. *Democracy and Tradition*. Princeton, N.J.: Princeton University Press, 2004.

Sweet, William. *Idealism and Rights: The Social Ontology of Human Rights in the Political Thought of Bernard Bosanquet*. New York: University Press of America, 1997.

———. "Was Bosanquet a Hegelian?" in *The Bulletin of the Hegel Society in Great Britain* 31 (1995): 39-60.

Taylor, Charles. *The Ethics of Authenticity*. Cambridge, Mass.: Harvard University Press, 1991.

———. *Hegel and Modern Society*. New York: Cambridge University Press, 1979.

Troeltsch, Ernst. *The Social Teachings of the Christian Churches*, trans. Olive Wyon. New York: The Macmillan Company, 1931.

Turner, Philip. "Social Advocacy as a Moral Issue in Itself," *The Journal of Religious Ethics* 19, no. 2 (Fall, 1991), 157-181.

———. "The Idea of Holy War in Ancient Israel," *Journal of Religious Ethics*, 20 (Fall, 1992): 215-228.

———. *Just and Unjust Wars: A Moral Argument with Historical Illustrations.* New York: Basic Books, 1992.

Weber, Max. *From Max Weber: Essays in Sociology*, ed. H.H. Gerth and C.W. Mills. New York: Oxford University Press, 1958.

Weigel, George. "Moral Clarity in a Time of War," *First Things: A Monthly Journal of Religion and Public Life* 129 (January, 2003): 20-28.

Werpehowski, William. "Christian Love and Covenant Faithfulness," *Journal of Religious Ethics* 19 (Fall, 1991), 103-132.

West, Cornel. *The Ethical Dimensions of Marxist Thought.* New York: Monthly Review Press, 1991.

Westphal, Merold. *Kierkegaard's Critique of Reason and Society.* University Park, Pa.: The Pennsylvania State University Press, 1991.

Williams, Rowan. "Politics and the Soul, A Reading of *The City of God*," *Milltown Studies* 19 (1987): 55-72.

Yoder, John Howard. *Christian Attitudes to War, Peace, and Revolution: A Companion to Bainton.* Elkhart, Ind.: Co-op Bookstore, 1983.

ARCHIVES

Consisting of recorded lectures, sermons, and addresses, The Reinhold Niebuhr Audio Collection is on Compact Disks distributed by Union Theological Seminary in Virginia.

The Paul Ramsey Papers are held by the Manuscript Department, William R. Perkins Library, Duke University, Durham, North Carolina.

Index

About the Author

Kevin Carnahan is Assistant Professor of Philosophy and Religion at Central Methodist University in Fayette, Missouri. In 2007 he was awarded his doctorate from Southern Methodist University. During his graduate work he was honored with a Dempster Graduate Fellowship from the United Methodist Church and The Schubert Ogden Fellowship for Academic Excellence in Theology from the Southern Methodist University Graduate Program in Religious Studies. Since graduating, he has held positions at Southwestern College in Kansas, Hendrix College in Arkansas and United Theological Seminary in Ohio. He is the author of articles that have appeared in *The Journal of Religious Ethics*, *The Journal of Law and Religion*, and *Political Theology*. He has also written for PBS's *Religion and Ethics Newsweekly*. He is a member of the American Academy of Religion and The Society of Christian Ethics, and is currently the Secretary and Treasurer for the Niebuhr Society.

Breinigsville, PA USA
03 October 2010
246551BV00004B/1/P

9 780739 144756